WITHDRAWN

PORTRAIT OF A STATESMAN

By the same author:

THE PRESS IN CHAINS
TRAINING FOR DEMOCRACY

Portrait of a Statesman

by
DENNIS BARDENS

PHILOSOPHICAL LIBRARY, INC.,
NEW YORK

PUBLISHED, 1956, BY PHILOSOPHICAL LIBRARY, INC.,
15, EAST 40th STREET, NEW YORK 16, N. Y.

All rights reserved

PRINTED IN GREAT BRITAIN FOR PHILOSOPHICAL LIBRARY BY
WYMAN AND SONS LTD.,
LONDON, READING AND FAKENHAM

(COPYRIGHT IN GREAT BRITAIN BY DENNIS BARDENS, 1955)

DA
566.9
E28
B3

LIST OF CONTENTS

Chapter		Page
I.	THE FAMILY TREE	11
II.	FATHER AND SON	22
III.	BOYHOOD AND ADOLESCENCE	33
IV.	INTO POLITICS	45
V.	A FOOT ON THE LADDER	56
VI.	IN SEARCH OF PROMOTION	66
VII.	PARLIAMENTARY APPRENTICE	79
VIII.	HIS MAJESTY'S OPPOSITION	90
IX.	CRAZY PEOPLE	105
X.	LORD PRIVY SEAL	111
XI.	ALL WORK AND NO PLAY	121
XII.	FOREIGN SECRETARY	143
XIII.	CONFLICT IN THE CABINET	160
XIV.	WAS IT A PLOT?	173
XV.	INTO THE WILDERNESS	194
XVI.	THE PATH TO WAR	203
XVII.	ON THE BRINK	212
XVIII.	INTO OFFICE	219
XIX.	MAN FRIDAY TO CHURCHILL	227
XX.	TRAVEL AND TALK	238
XXI.	ON TO VICTORY	247
XXII.	YALTA AND AFTER	255
XXIII.	OPPOSITION—AGAIN	265

LIST OF CONTENTS

Chapter		Page
XXIV.	PRIME MINISTER DESIGNATE	279
XXV.	HIS FIGHT FOR LIFE	293
XXVI.	TOP OF THE LADDER	306
XXVII.	EDEN THE MAN	312

LIST OF ILLUSTRATIONS

Sir Anthony Eden greets a voter during the General
    Election, 1955   *Frontispiece*

Facing page

Robert Anthony Eden at the age of three	32
Sir William Eden, father of Sir Anthony Eden	32
A photograph of the Eden family taken in 1911	32
Anthony Eden at Eton	33
After investiture with the Military Cross in 1917	33
Captain Anthony Eden and Miss Beatrice Beckett after their wedding	64
As Lord Privy Seal in 1935 with Sir John Simon and Hitler	65
Sybil, Lady Eden, mother of Sir Anthony Eden	96
Beau Brummel of 1938	96
Anthony Eden and Mrs. Beatrice Eden with their son, Nicholas	97
In Camp: Eden as Second-in-Command of the 2nd Rangers, King's Royal Rifle Corps	97
Touring the Middle East war zone, November, 1940	128
With Mr. Harriman and Mr. John Winant	128
Mr. Anthony Eden with his wife and his elder son, Simon	129
The Honorary Air Commodore of No. 500 Auxiliary Squadron of the R.A.F.	129
On Bondi Beach, Sydney	160
Father and son: Anthony Eden with Nicholas Eden	160
In thoughtful mood: at a United Nations Conference with Mr. Dean Acheson	161
With his son Nicholas at his coming-of-age party	161
Meeting with Tito	192
Sir Anthony Eden with Rita Hayworth	192
Off for the honeymoon: Mr. Anthony Eden with Miss Clarissa Spencer Churchill	193
The British Foreign Secretary kisses his wife good-bye	193
Lady Eden	224

LIST OF ILLUSTRATIONS

	Facing page
Mrs. Beatrice Eden in her New York flat	225
Mrs. Beatrice Eden and Nicholas Eden, 1954	225
Sir Anthony Eden greets Queen Soraya of Persia	256
With M. Mendes-France and Mr. John Foster Dulles	256
Sir Anthony Eden with Sir Winston Churchill	257
Where Britain's Prime Minister forgets his cares	257

INTRODUCTION

WRITING a biography of a living person presents certain problems to the author. Occasionally one sees "authorised" biographies of living people, the word implying that the subject has been allowed to comment upon and presumably censor the manuscript before it reached the printer. However great the goodwill between author and subject, it is the person written about and not the writer who really influences the form and content of the book. In this sense, such works portray their subject to some extent as he sees himself, and are therefore partly autobiographical. What a man thinks about himself is an autobiography and should be written by himself.

A biography is a quite different matter. "Here is a picture of a man as I see him," the author says, in effect. He is not claiming to be the mouthpiece or medium of somebody else, and his work cannot have integrity if he is. To be objective and frank he must have creative freedom—freedom to cull facts where he will, to decide for himself what sources of information are reliable or dubious, to assemble and interpret his material as he pleases—in accordance with his own ideas and standards and not somebody else's.

This book is a biography in that sense. It embodies nobody's views but my own, and I wish to make it clear that nothing in this book carries the express or implied approval of Sir Anthony Eden.

From some points of view Sir Anthony is a difficult subject for a biographer, and going back over time has been an onerous and at times discouraging task. The chapter on his first two election campaigns, for example, is condensed from 20,000 words of notes taken from contemporary accounts and interviews with people who played some part in them. Condensation is inevitable in a work of this kind, and is all the more a necessity because Sir Anthony's life is, to a great extent, an inherent part of the diplomatic history of Britain. For this reason I beg

INTRODUCTION

the indulgence of my readers for what may appear to be omissions.

I would like to thank my numerous informants, who have patiently answered my questions and assisted me in my researches. In particular I would like to record my gratitude to Dr. George Morey for much valuable assistance; to my secretary, Mrs. Pamela Cleaver; to Miss Doris Tindall, Librarian of the Reform Club, and her Assistant Mr. Slavoj Halman; to Mr. A. V. Hull, Chief Librarian of the British Museum Newspaper Library at Colindale; and to Captain Timpson, of the Old Comrades Association, King's Royal Rifle Corps, for permission to inspect their Regimental records.

I am well aware of the inadequacies of this book, and do not flatter myself that it will be the last to be written about Britain's Prime Minister; but I offer it as a sincere attempt to portray a man who holds the reins of government in his hands during one of the most critical periods in British history.

Reform Club, *Dennis Bardens*
*Pall Mall, S.W.*1.

ONE

The Family Tree

"WHO boasts of his descent praises what does not belong to him", an old saying goes. But Sir Anthony Eden has never boasted of his descent; " shooting a line " has never been a characteristic of his, but if he chose to probe into the archives of a family which has more than 400 years of continuity, he would find some very remarkable characters.

The forebears of Sir Anthony Eden include diplomats, a novelist, reformers, artists and sportsmen. The thread of continuity, which runs like a golden vein through the history of this remarkable family, is leadership. Robert Anthony Eden is a direct descendant of a landowning Durham family on which a baronetcy was conferred by Charles II in 1672 and which is linked, one way and another, with some of the oldest ruling houses in England.

His ancestors were a varied lot. So are their achievements: paintings; novels; *belles lettres*; the government of countries as large as India, or of colonies such as Maryland; penal reform; public service of all kinds. Aristocracy does not imply what it is taken to mean on the Continent. Aristocracy, to an Englishman, means the acceptance and transmission, from generation to generation, of an attitude to life; privilege and duty are inseparable. Achievement is emulated by those who follow; standards of patriotism and pride are kept bright.

It is undeniable that certain houses have produced an impressive succession of brilliant and able men. The saga of the Marlborough family continues with the incomparable Sir Winston Churchill. Yet even Churchill's family was once alleged to be new compared with Eden's, as one of Churchill's ancestors was once sharply reminded, in a heated debate in the House of Lords. The Earl of Arundel, fuming at some unacceptable comment from the first Lord Spencer, the first of Winston Churchill's ancestors to be ennobled, snapped at the upstart: "When these things were doing, your ancestors were keeping sheep!" The quibble is historically of no importance. It is true that the Eden family beat the Churchills to titled rank by a short head, but the Churchills did achieve a dukedom!

It is possible that Anthony Eden's ancestors kept sheep, too, but genealogically speaking it would be a tough job to prove it. Marriage connects the Edens with the most notable families in England, but although Charles II granted the first baronetcy to them, spectacular achievement becomes the keynote with the creation of the first Baron Auckland, William Eden. True, the Eden family had been distinguished before then, but in a leisurely sort of way. They led the lives of typical English country gentlemen, and while Sir Robert Eden, first Baronet of West Auckland, who died in 1721, was an M.P., like the second Baronet Sir John Eden, their visits to Parliament were more in the nature of a hobby than an onerous burden. The crowded legislation and long exhausting sessions which are commonplace today would have horrified them.

William Eden, the first Baron Auckland, was born in 1744 and was the third son of the third baronet. He was an intensely ambitious man who, like Anthony, was educated at Eton. He won high honours as a scholar at Christ Church, Oxford, studied law and was called to the Bar of Middle Temple in 1769. Three years later he created a sensation by publishing a pamphlet, *Principles of Penal Law*, whose disciplined passion makes one regret the passing of pamphleteering as a literary art and stratagem.

In it William Eden took the major categories of crimes in turn and examined with devastating effect the merits, follies and inconsistencies of the existing legal system in England. It is—judged as a product of the latter half of the eighteenth century—an enlightened work, and many of its suggested reforms were to gain general acceptance in the nineteenth century. In particular he opposed transportation for life, which, although ostensibly a punishment for theft and minor offences, was a convenient device for populating and developing the colonies. In an age in which flogging and hanging, drawing and quartering were standard punishments, it was a brave thing to publish such a work. In the same year he was appointed an Under Secretary of State. He represented the constituency of New Woodstock in the parliaments of 1774 and 1780, and Heytesbury in 1784 and 1790. In 1776 he was appointed a Commissioner on the Board of Trade and Plantations, and immediately he set to work to alleviate or prevent abuses and cruelties which were common, not simply in English Colonies, but in Colonies everywhere—in fact, England, as with the abolition of slavery, was well ahead of other countries in the evolution of a more human legal code in the colonies.

Two years later, William Eden turned his thoughts once again to the miseries of British prisoners, and carried an Act through Parliament which is a milestone in penal reform. He accompanied the Earl of Carlisle as a Commissioner to North America to sort out the dispute with the colonists—a mission, unfortunately, in which he failed dismally through no fault of his own.

Lord Auckland spent most of his life in high-ranking appointments. At one time he was Chief Secretary for Ireland: he advised an increase for the secret service fund, became Member for Dungannon in the Irish House of Commons, and became Ambassador to Spain. He had kept his ears open in Spain, and, being well aware of the threat to Britain from that country, returned in 1789, to be sent on a mission to Holland to represent British interests there, and to obtain the assistance of the Dutch fleet in 1790 against Spain. He was now a Baron in the Irish peerage.

Although his negotiations with North America were a notable failure, as a diplomat and go-between he proved himself energetic, far-seeing and astute. He married Eleanor, sister of the first Lord Minto, in 1776 and raised a large family, including Emily Eden, who was to distinguish herself as a novelist. Lady Auckland accompanied her husband, William Eden, on his travels in America, Ireland, France, Spain and Holland and had a child in every country to which they were sent—often in considerable discomfort. Altogether she had fourteen children.

Emily, who was to have literary gifts, was born in 1779. She was brought up on Eden Farm, Beckenham, Kent, and the ups and downs of rearing fourteen children are recorded in a diary kept by her mother, which chronicles faithfully all their tantrums, illnesses, problems and marriages. " Out of fourteen," wrote Lady Auckland, " I suckled thirteen. Eleven of the children had smallpox during their wandering, also cow-pox, whooping cough, measles and scarlet fever." Dragging round this enormous family did not seem to worry her husband who, writing from Paris, said in 1786: " Mrs. Eden is just returned from passing a week in the Circle and Society of the whole Court of Versailles without feeling a moment of discomposure. It is impossible to describe to you all the glorious attentions with which she is honoured by the Queen of France. . . ." He adds, in good humour, " . . . we now have as many nations in our Nursery as were assembled at the Tower of Babel." Mrs. Eden's nursery became the admiration of the Court and of the town, and she made domestic life " quite fashionable ". The " brattery " was the subject of jocular facetiousness in foreign courts to which her husband was accredited.

Lady Auckland was known later in life as Haughty Nell. William Pitt, Prime Minister of England, fell in love with her eldest daughter Eleanor, but Lord Auckland for various reasons was opposed to the match and in 1799 she married Lord Hobart. Lord Auckland died suddenly at Eden Farm in 1814. Six of his daughters married, but the remaining two, Emily and Fanny, lived with their elder brother George (later Earl of Auckland) and went with him to India.

In 1794, William Eden was awarded a pension of £2,300 a year (a prodigious sum for those days) and was created Baron Auckland of West Auckland, Durham, in the English peerage in 1793.

To some extent his career speaks for itself, but not altogether. A good scholar, an able administrator, a skilled negotiator, and a man of conscience who could interpret his ideals in terms of practical measures—such as his proposals for improving the prisons and ameliorating the lot of employees on the plantations. But, from contemporary comments about him, it is plain that he didn't register well with everyone. William Knox (1st June, 1799) observed darkly:

> "He had been called to the bar, but being a bad orator made no figure there ... he possessed a most insinuating, gentle manner which covered a deeply intriguing and ambitious spirit."

Not exactly a first-class reference. And Wraxall, in his *Memoirs*, reiterates the vague uneasiness some people felt about him:

> "In person he rose above the ordinary height, his figure was elegant, and wanted not grace. His countenance was thin and pale, his features regular and full of intelligence, his manner calm, polite and conciliatory. There existed in Eden's physiognomy, even in his manner and deportment, *something which did not convey the impression of plain dealing, or inspire confidence.*"

There seems to be general agreement that William Eden was, in private life, an agreeable companion and an amiable man. His reformist zeal suggests that he had more humanity than many men of his period. But one suspects that the extracts quoted give a truer estimate of the man than the laudatory and uncritical references to him in the *National Dictionary of Biography*. Amiable, conciliatory and accommodating, he achieved some success as a diplomat, but as a politician he had a not unmerited reputation for shiftiness. Beginning his career as a Tory, he was successively a Whig, a Tory and a Whig again!

Three of his brothers, incidentally, " registered " with some effect in other fields. Sir John was an M.P., Sir Robert Eden became the first Governor of Maryland, and Morton Eden, Lord Henley, was Minister to Copenhagen, Berlin and Vienna. It was, of course, a period in which rank and advancement went automatically together. Morton Eden, for example, was not a man of spectacular attainments, and even failed to take a degree at Christ Church, Oxford. But this did not prevent him, whilst still in his early twenties, from being sent as Ambassador to Copenhagen.

Just as the tradition of idealism persists in the Eden saga, so does the holding of high office. It is a sort of *Debrett* written as a serial story over the centuries, and if any man had the leisure, the money and the curiosity, the complete history of the family would provide an interesting study in the working of heredity. An ancestor with whom Sir Anthony would find much in common is Sir Frederick Morton Eden (1766–1809, son of Sir Robert, Governor of Maryland), who wrote *The State of the Poor*, a piece of economic sociology of the first importance and which is still widely quoted to-day. Even Karl Marx praised it, describing Sir Frederick in *Das Kapital* as " the only disciple of Adam Smith during the eighteenth century that produced any work of importance." It bears the imprint of extensive research, and, like his uncle's book on penal reform, did much to awaken the public conscience. There was a time when the homeless and dispossessed were " rogues and vagabonds " under the law, and although they were no longer whipped at the village cross, that symbol of Christian mercy, there was a distinct penal flavour about all legislation affecting them. The guilt of the poor was taken for granted, and it was this cruel assumption that Sir Frederick attacked so vigorously and with such success. Thus he and his uncle, whatever failings they may have had in other directions, made a distinct contribution to the progress of civilization.

It is fascinating, considering Sir Anthony Eden's career, to find qualities inherent in Sir Anthony Eden appearing and reappearing through generations of the Eden saga. The indignation of William at the state of our prisons, the sorrow of Frederick for the sufferings of the poor, the efforts to avoid war and maintain peace—how prophetic these prove to be! The trait of idealism, successful or not, is to be found in each generation, in one or more of its members.

Near contemporary with Sir Frederick Morton Eden was his cousin George Eden (1787–1849), who was called to the Bar in 1809 and in 1814, on the death of his father, he took his seat in the House of Lords as Baron Auckland. He supported the Reform party, and in 1830 was made President of the Board of Trade and Master of the Mint. He had a short spell as First Lord of the Admiralty and in 1835 he was appointed Governor-General of India, where he made a reputation as a painstaking, wise and humane legislator, doing much to improve industry and both increase and improve the native schools.

This reputation, however, was **to** be sullied by well-meaning but disastrous decisions in the military field. In 1838 Afghanistan was in a turmoil, a situation which alarmed the Home Government as much as it did the Anglo-Indian Government. Lord Auckland decided on war, and published a manifesto dethroning Dost Mahommed, despite the Duke of Wellington's warning that if the British crossed the Indus to impose a government on the Afghans against their will, they would have to remake the journey every year to enforce their decision. Because the early operations against Afghanistan were successful, Lord Auckland was made an Earl, but before long the British were to suffer a series of shattering reverses which entirely discredited his administration and led to his recall in favour of Lord Ellenborough. In 1846 he was made First Lord of the Admiralty and remained so until his death in 1849. It was while he was at the Admiralty for the first time in 1834 that he gave Captain Hobson command of the *Rattlesnake* after he had been for six years without an appointment. Captain Hobson became senior captain of the East India command in the same year that Lord Auckland was made Governor-General of India. Subsequently, Hobson was the first Governor-General of New Zealand, where his principal achievement was the founding of Auckland, which he named in commemoration of the patronage he had enjoyed from Lord Auckland. He named the county in which it lay Eden.

The Earl of Auckland had, it would seem, a considerable degree of philosophical detachment. His life was a mixture of success and failure, and he was to be remembered by many more for his failures than his successes. It was too easily forgotten, for example, that during the disastrous famine in the North-West Provinces in 1838 not only did Eden's energetic organisation of relief save hundreds of thousands of lives, but began a series of measures to provide against such disasters in the future.

The Earl of Auckland never married, and relied upon his two sisters, who accompanied him to India, to help him manage the immense household and act as hostesses. One was Emily Eden, who is shown in a painting by Sir William Napier as a remarkably pretty woman, with silky brown hair, deep, expressive eyes and a sort of impish pucker at the corner of her full lips.

Emily's letters show a love of adventure, an acute sense of observation, a matter-of-fact acceptance of wealth and station, a humorous tolerance of human nature and depths of affection which make one wonder why she never married. Perhaps she was too much of a romanticist, and, being the intelligent and perceptive woman she was, had no wish to substitute reality for illusion. She loved sketching, reading and gardening (the three greatest pleasures of Sir Anthony Eden's father), took a great interest in politics, and after her return to England in 1842, she published several works, including *Portraits of the People and Princes of India* (1844), *Up the Country* (1866), and two novels, *The Semi-Detached House* (1859), and *The Semi-Detached Couple* (1860).

During her stay in India, Emily enjoyed the colour, the privileges, the abundance of servants and the social round. She was also interested enough in ordinary people to regret the limitations imposed by her brother's position. " We could not get into any intimacies, even if we wished it," she told her friend Lady Campbell, writing from Government House, Calcutta, in 1836, " for in our *despotic* Government, where the patronage is in the hands of the Governor-General, the intimacy of any one person here would put the rest of society into a fume and it is too hot for any super-induced fuming. . . ."

But there were compensations: " . . . as a set-off to discomforts peculiar to the climate, we have every luxury that the wit of man can devise, and are gradually acquiring the Indian habit of denying ourselves nothing, which will be awkward." She gets up at eight, and with the assistance of " two black maids," has a bath. On her way to the breakfast room, she passes two Dacca embroiderers who are working a frame of flowers that look like paintings; Chance, her dog, being exercised by his own special servant; a *meter* with his broom to sweep the rooms, two bearers to pull the punkahs; a sentry to mind that none of these steal anything; a Jemardar (lieutenant) and four Hurkarus (postal runners)—all resplendent in red and gold turbans and sashes, like a Persian fairy-story come to life.

They salaam elaborately and Emily, with prim recollections of life on Eden Farm, gives a shy, distant smile of acknowledgment. She proceeds to breakfast in the immense marble hall, attended by two aides-de-camp, the doctor, the Private

Secretary and anybody who may be transacting business at the time. The day wears on, and the outside world seems far away. But " At six the whole house is opened, windows, shutters, etc., and carriages, horses, jogs, phætons, guards all come to the door, and we ride or drive just as we like, come home in time to dress for eight o'clock dinner, during which the band plays. We sit out on the veranda and play at chess or écarté for an hour, and at ten everyone goes to bed."

Emily watched with sorrow the coming of the industrial revolution. She was quick to perceive the new strains it would impose on society and how old standards and ideas would inevitably be swept away. In 1849 she suffered a double sorrow by the deaths of her brother, Lord Auckland, and her sister Fanny. For the next twenty years she divided her time between Eden Lodge, Kensington Gore, and a little cottage at Broadstairs, living with one of her nieces, Lena Eden. She died at the age of 72, and for the latter part of her life was an invalid.

The charm of Emily Eden's work lies in the picture it gives of periods that have gone for ever; of the leisurely, secure, perhaps even luxurious world which she knew. Three large volumes of her water-colours, sold at Christie's famous auction room in 1907, are now in the Victoria Memorial Hall, Calcutta.

Even towards the end of the nineteenth century the Edens were still in diplomacy and public service. We find Sir Ashley Eden (1831–1887), third son of the third Lord Auckland, entering the Indian Civil Service and quickly becoming an administrator, political agent and negotiator. He achieved distinction in 1855 as assistant to the Special Commissioner for the suppression of the Santal Rising, became Secretary of the Bengal government in 1860, negotiated a treaty with the Rajah of Sikkim a year later, and in 1863 was sent on a similar mission to Bhutan, which was restive under British rule. This time, unsupported by an armed force, he was received with insults: the result was war with Bhutan. In 1871, Sir Ashley became the first civilian Governor of British Burma and remained so until 1877, when he was made Lieutenant-Governor of Bengal. A statue of him in Calcutta attests the regard in which he was once held.

We come at last to William Eden, Sir Anthony Eden's grandfather, the fourth Baronet of Maryland and the sixth Baronet of West Auckland. His father, Sir Frederick Morton Eden, who had written *The State of the Poor*, had died when William was a baby. William had inherited the baronetcy in early youth owing to the death of his elder brother in action at the age of sixteen. He had studied the classics, learned a considerable number of foreign languages, travelled extensively and filled folio after folio with water-colours. He had been kept on the move all his life, visiting America, the Near East, the West Indies, besides France, Italy and Spain.

As a child, William had seen many historic sights, such as the remains of Louis XVI and Marie Antoinette being transferred to St. Denis's, a funeral which disappointed him, " it being nothing to compare to Lord Nelson's ". At Laxenburg, the country palace of the Emperor of Austria, he caught a glimpse of Napoleon Bonaparte's young son, " dressed in a black coat and waistcoat with white trousers. . . ." He later served with the British Navy, and once in an encounter had knocked out the brains of a Turkish pirate with an axe.

But the artist was strong in William. Wherever he went, whether to the Albanian mountains, the Prussian-blue waters of the Mediterranean or the shimmering olive groves of Italy, his nature responded to the sights, sounds and colours with peculiar sensitivity. He was also a good judge of art, and at least two of his discoveries—" An Instrument Dealer at his Booth in the Open Air," by Carel Fabricius, and the " Rokeby Venus " hang in the National Gallery.

William retired to Windlestone Hall, in Durham, at the age of forty-one, intending to raise a large family and conserve and increase his wealth for their benefit. He was glad to forsake his wandering and settle to the life of a country gentleman, with Divine Service on Sundays, a ride round his estate on horseback, and some painting and writing. But the years ahead brought little sunshine and fulfilment. One after another his children died—two sons, and four pretty little girls whose remains rest in a special chapel built for them in the grounds.

Towards the end of his life he became a woman-hater. He had always been frugal in his habits—the original idea being to leave as much as he could to his children—and was stern and often forbidding towards the end of his days. His wife was attractive, but narrow in vision and perhaps over-religious.

Which brings us to his eldest son, William, who was in the Army and was notorious for his ungovernable temper. He succeeded his father in 1873, and was the father of the man who is now Prime Minister of Britain. He was altogether a remarkable man, and cannot be tagged on to the Eden dynasty as a sort of anti-climax. He was not the end of a dynasty but the beginning of a new one.

TWO

Father and Son

ON a very hot day—the hottest of the year—in 1897, an unaccustomed silence had settled over Windlestone Hall, the ancestral home of the Eden family for 400 years, lying four miles south-east of Bishop Auckland. It was always peaceful *looking*, with its perfectly kept lawns, its trim flower-beds, and its detached air of timelessness; while the classic yellow stone house somehow contrived to look more ancient than it was (some old parts remained but much had been rebuilt about 1750). The spaciousness of the surrounding country added to the impression of peace.

But the impression of peace was often an illusion. The whole household revolved around the energetic, eccentric, unpredictable and often stormy personality of Sir William Eden, Bart., whose ruling passions were a love of art and sport, a contempt for humbug and an outspokenness odd in one who, in so many other respects, was conservative in outlook.

On this particular day, June 12th, 1897, Sir William was not in evidence. Perhaps he was out riding, hurling imprecations and contempt at some driver of a horseless carriage as it crossed his path at the suicidal speed of four miles an hour, puffing poisonous vapours as it went. Perhaps he was out with his paint-box and easel, committing to paper in delicate water-colours the countryside he loved so well. Whatever he was doing, we can be pretty sure that on this particular day he would be out of circulation until Anthony, the newcomer, had been born. It is true that Sir William, domineering though he undoubtedly was, felt affection for his lovely young wife Sybil, and his three children—Elfrida Marjorie, John and Timothy. But the company of children discomforted him; the effort of trying to bring himself down to their level of understanding, or to subordinate his egotism to theirs was always too great; so much so that Sir Timothy Eden, Sir Anthony Eden's brother, has put it on record that their father "fled from the house like a hunted deer" when the children were on holiday.

It was a strange home into which Anthony was born, but it was a secure one. Death duties had not reached their present confiscatory level. The huge mansion was adequately staffed with servants and a governess for the children; the staff included the efficient and deferential Woolger (Sir William's long-suffering valet) and the head gardener, who had once seen Sir William, in a fit of rage, sweep rows of flowerpots from the greenhouse shelves with his stick. Sir William was now the successor of a long line of Edens, and was surely the most tempestuous of them all. He delighted in rudeness, making not the slightest attempt to moderate his remarks. Egotistic himself, he hated egotism in others. He loved the privilege of his wealth and position, yet was constantly at loggerheads with the Conservatives of his period. But he hated "those damned Radicals" meaning, of course, the Liberals.

Sir William was a man of extraordinary energy, cultured tastes—he had travelled extensively throughout the world, including Egypt, India, China, Japan and America (which he professed to dislike). He loved good art, good architecture, good food, good shooting and good company. His great house was constantly alive with guests, from bishops to artists, from civil servants to cricketers. Windlestone Hall reflected a way of life that is now just a memory; of spacious stables filled with magnificent horses; of coachmen, grooms and servants in attendance and a whole range of elegant and comfortable carriages; of cricket and boxing and hunting and the sound of the hunter's horn in the crisp morning air.

In *The Tribulations of a Baronet*, a monograph which is a masterpiece of its kind, Sir Timothy Eden shows that although the overpowering, unreasonable personality of his father dominated everything at Windlestone, Sir William was a man loved by his servants, who knew that at heart he was generous, honourable and, above all, honest. Reared in what Sir Winston Churchill has described as the "august serenity" of the

Victorian era, he knew an England that had always been prosperous, secure from invasion, fruitful and fascinating. Or as Sir Timothy puts it: "There was an English summer, in fact, with the rough but sweet security of a bygone England, with laughter and oaths and loud voices and red faces, and a close companionship between master and man, and no thought of the dyspeptic morrow."

There is little doubt that Sir William was hypersensitive. The wrong colours, such as red, would induce the most startling explosions of bad temper in him. He saw nothing shameful in demonstrations of bad temper, though he would sometimes proffer a brusque apology afterwards. On one occasion, at least, he is said to have bitten the carpet in his rage, and on another, perceiving that the weatherglass said " FAIR " when, in fact, it was pouring with rain outside the house, he seized the offending instrument and threw it out into the garden with a resounding curse, inviting the rain to read what it said!

Throughout the North of England Sir William was known, and is still remembered by some, as an outstanding horseman. For six years he was Master of the South Durham Hounds, and Jack Bevans, in *Reminiscences of a Whipper-In*, gives a marvellous picture of Sir William, his companions and the hounds in hot pursuit of a fox over the Sedgefield country, and of Sir William's unprintable language when the fox, perhaps tired or bored with the chase, turned round and came towards them. The grass round there, said Mr. Graham of Morden, who "was attracted to the spot by Sir William's language," has never grown again!

But if Anthony Eden was born into a household where peace never reigned very long, he enjoyed very decided advantages which played a big part in moulding his character. He had spacious beauty of the surrounding countryside; the easy access to country pleasures and sports, coupled with a desire to emulate and please his father by at least being adequate in them; the companionship of his brothers and his beautiful mother, whose exotic beauty Sir William never tired of praising as he escorted her around the County. " There! " he would say as they arrived at a dinner or some public function—he would cock his head backwards and give her elegant and trim figure

a look of appraisal, as he might one of his water-colours—
" Isn't she beautiful? "

Lady Eden was not only beautiful, but full of wit and womanly understanding. Sir William was a romantic born out of his period. And there was an inherent conflict in his whole outlook on life, which may have accounted for his constant irritability and incipient rages. As an artist, he wanted freedom—freedom to think, to roam, to experiment and to paint or write. He had the freedom from worry that money brings, but he had also the ties of a home, the responsibility of rearing children, of managing an estate and of being a magistrate. There were times when these healthy and creditable ties were an irksome burden; they cramped the imagination. Besides, neither the Bohemians, who disdained formal society and felt that conformity to social custom was likely to make a creative worker toady to his social superiors to the detriment of his art, nor the aristocracy quite accepted him.

The Bohemians, as one may loosely describe the writers and artists and creative people with whom he loved to mix, might well wonder why an artist should bother with being a magistrate or managing an estate; the avoidance of overmuch conformity to social custom was, they thought, necessary to creative freedom, and some of them felt that Sir William, despite obvious talents, was too fond of his Tory landowning environment to develop intellectually. The aristocracy, on the other hand, did not like his manners or the near anarchy of some of his opinions, many of which ought not to be taken seriously. His ostentatious atheism, too, did not go down well with a people whose church-going was almost a symbol of respectability. Imagine him looking out on his parkland from his study window, getting more red in the face as the rain increases in intensity. With shaking hands, he opens the window to shout at the grey, unresponsive sky: " O God, O God! How like You! " Or imagine a party of guests (and there were always parties) threading their way down the drive on their way to a shoot. A guest asks politely: " Will it be all right to shoot hens? " " Yes! " thunders Sir William, " Shoot hens! Shoot everything! Shoot the Holy Ghost if he comes out! "

Lady Eden was the perfect foil for Sir William's temper. Nowhere is there a hint that he raised his voice to her or treated her with anything but the most studied and gallant respect. For Sir William loved beauty:

> "For Beauty he hunted and hungered, abroad and at home; for Beauty he battled, without hope, in letters to the press; and to Beauty he was constantly giving expression, daily, not only with his brush, but with his purse and his axe and his spade . . ."

The reference to his axe and spade is a reminder that Sir William was a brilliant landscape gardener with a hearty detestation of the "pretty-pretty" school which, in his day, would fill a garden with flowers of every colour in the rainbow. As an artist he sought harmony, and chose borders, shrubs and flowers with the most painstaking care. He planted contrasting shrubs and trees as he might add a deft touch of brilliance with his brush to a water-colour.

No boy, probably, had greater opportunities for outdoor sport and exercises than young Anthony. But despite a fierce pride that showed itself early, and a complete willingness to stand on his own feet and give blow for blow in a fight, he was by nature shy. He would rather be quiet with a book in the nursery than ride one of the ponies in the open air. He was intensively imaginative but—probably from a feeling that he was overshadowed by his father (like everyone else at Windlestone)—he was inclined to keep his thoughts to himself.

This sensitivity wouldn't commend itself to Sir William. He himself was sensitive, quick to take offence at criticism, swift to condemn trivial errors or oversights; but he was certainly no company for children, and his occasional, awkward attempts to find common ground with them embarrassed them as much as it did him. Sometimes, gruffly, he would inform them, through a servant, that they were coming out riding with him. That meant that for an unstated number of hours they must mind their p's and q's. A word misinterpreted, an instruction misunderstood and all hell was let loose.

Lady Eden, wisely, did not encourage her husband to accompany the children too much. They had pleasures enough—hide and seek in the park, "exploring" the countryside, riding on ponies and horses, or going out with their governess in one of the numerous carriages.

Sometimes, on the greensward, Anthony would play at

soldiers with Nicholas, in tragic mimicry of a more grim battle that lay in wait for them, a few years ahead. In their games their father played no part, and although he was admired from a distance (for the children could sense the awe that waited on his coming), he was too puzzling a character for even adults to understand.

Yet, imperceptibly, Anthony Eden was learning a greal deal from his parents and his environment. From his mother he learned elegance, patience and charm; not consciously, of course. From his father he learned something that was constantly dinned into all of them—courage and honesty. Anthony was not an especially good horseman, but those who grumbled that he would never equal his father in this were stating the obvious; Sir William was one of the best and most fearless horsemen in the county. As for honesty: " There is only one thing in life worth living for," he told his sons, " and that is to run straight. Don't for God's sake, ever play a double game or give people away who trust you." Years later Anthony was to refuse to play a double game, or to betray people who looked to the League of Nations and collective security to protect them from aggression.

Anthony was an attentive but not an outstanding pupil. He received, as his brothers and sister did, a good grounding in most subjects, but he shone at none of them. Reading and listening to conversations between adults on all manner of advanced subjects were his favourite pastimes. His mother would be talking of the latest fashions, or George Moore, the famous Irish novelist, might be appraising one of Sir William's latest water-colours. Moore, as it happens, was an admirer of Sir William's art: he once said : " Sir William is an amateur; we use the word in its original sense and can, therefore, conceive no higher epithet of commendation. A glance at the pictures show that he is a painter who travels rather than a traveller who paints."

Or, horror of horrors, there might be one of those interminable musical sessions his mother liked so much. Anthony was not tone deaf, but he had a frank dislike of music. He hadn't the slightest interest in clothes, which might have been a reaction to the sentimental habit of photographing infant children in clothes that dissembled their sex. A photograph of

Anthony taken at the age of three might as easily be that of a girl; nobody, without being warned, would guess that it was that of a boy. The cupid's bow lips, the full, feminine cheeks, the wide, innocent and sensitive eyes, the long gossamer-fine hair carefully brushed and trained in a fringe over his forehead; the feminine dress, with its lace collar patterned like leaves unburgeoning around a flower; the elaborate needlework and the carelessly flowing ribbon. I doubt if Sir William admitted to liking the picture when he first saw it, and may even have had it in mind when, indignant at Lady Eden's understandable desire to protect their children against his worst rages, he had stormed " petticoat rule will be the ruin of them! "

But Sir William was a man who was frightened to profess or exhibit affection. He would have considered that feminine, but none the less, in his heart, he had the warmest affection for all his children, all of whom were given the best education, the finest clothes, and the best meals that money could buy. He took a greater pride in their achievements than he ever admitted, even if his letters sometimes took their hero-worship for granted. " Buck up, you tiny little man," he once wrote to Timothy, " I wish you Many Happy Returns, with an increase of wisdom and stature in proportion to your years *and in imitation of your papa.*"

But " Papa " was a human being, and it is possible to love an imperfect man when he is as human as Sir William—as Timothy's sensitive and moving monograph on his father shows so well. When a man has faults as blatant as rudeness, inconsistency, and occasional violence, it says much that all those faults cannot diminish love. And the professed atheist once wrote to Anthony when he was unhappy to say " Be not downcast, oh my soul! Hope thou in the Lord! You are not a waster, thank God. You may yet be as great and good a man as
                Your affectionate
                    Daddie."

An odd letter from one who pretended to abhor children, and who with resounding curses and in purple rages had been known to dismiss religion as a lot of nonsense, and defy all the hierarchy of heaven. The truth is, that Sir William was never an atheist. He loathed humbug, and, intense in his mental curiosity as with his love of beauty, he suspected many neighbours and friends of subscribing to the Christian faith as a social convention, because it was easier to go with the herd than against it. By what coincidence did he so often choose as subjects for his paintings, the interiors of churches and cathedrals? At St. Paul's Cathedral, or Westminster Cathedral, or Durham, he was a familiar figure to the vergers, who would often suffer his presence even when a service was in progress. Sometimes they would go through the motions of asking him to leave, but as he never did, nobody cared to assert themselves.

Odd, surely, that an atheist should be so moved and inspired by the play of light through a stained glass window, or the play and counter-play of light and shadow around the crucifix above the altar. Stranger still that despite vehement protestations of atheism he so often wanted to paint whilst a church service was actually in progress, perhaps the chanting of the Epistle and Gospel at High Mass at Durham. One can almost hear him saying, " A damned lot of nonsense—but it makes a good picture ".

Sir William, undoubtedly, was a character, although it was a mischance that made him a public figure. That was his dispute with the artist Whistler, whom he commissioned to paint Lady Eden. She had been painted by many other artists —by Herkomer, for instance, as a lovely creature in a yellow evening dress silhouetted against a somewhat depressing landscape, and by Blanche, Swan and Sergeant.

In this particular quarrel Sir William was certainly not to blame. On the contrary, he was rather ill-used by an artist who proved rude, unreasonable and impossibly egotistic. Sir William had mentioned a fee of between a hundred and a hundred and fifty pounds. The picture was adequate though not exceptional, and on taking delivery of it Sir William handed the artist a cheque for 100 guineas. The picture was a small panel in oils (whereas Sir William had asked for a sketch portrait in water-colours). Whistler cashed the cheque, exhibited the picture, and refused to deliver it. Sir William sued him in the Paris courts, with the result that Whistler had to return the money with interest and costs, and pay £40 damages. He was allowed to keep the portrait—which would scarcely have been of any use to Sir William or posterity, as in a fit of anger and petty spite, Whistler had scraped out Lady Eden's face and substituted another!

Throughout this controversy Sir William kept his temper and behaved with remarkable dignity. But many had observed that triviality taxed him more than trial. As a local magistrate, for example, he was known for his fairness and forthright contempt of privilege. " Mr. Seven-and-sixpence," as the locals called him, was so popular as a magistrate that everyone hoped he would be on the bench when they found themselves in trouble.

From an emotional point of view, the family background was not ideal, though probably no family background ever is. But the constant tension inherent in living under one roof with Sir William couldn't have been the best atmosphere in which to develop self-reliance. As a matter of fact, in some respects Anthony lacked it; his introspection, dislike of noise (including music, at which so often he would protest: STOP THAT DIN!) and his diffidence at games and sports, hinted at a desire to retreat from it all. Much as Sir William might sneer " Petticoat rule will be the ruin of you! " it was a good thing sometimes that Lady Eden's ample skirts were there at all. Not that Anthony was nervous in any obvious way. And Timothy, his elder brother, felt protectively about him, and was later to be at his side at Eton, where bullying was almost a convention.

In appearance, Sir William was bound to dominate almost any gathering. He was over six feet tall, carried himself as straight as a ramrod, and was inordinately proud of his figure. Rhapsodising about his build, he wrote to a friend: " Ask Beauchamp if he knows anyone at 60 who has better measurements than: Chest 44, Waist 36, Weight 13 stone and Height 6 feet." His cheeks were full-blooded, his eyes " blue and choleric," his moustache and short beard of a reddish-brown, his eyebrows tufted and imperious and his nose " tilted aggressively forward like a weapon of offence." His cap, usually pulled down over his forehead, concealed hair as fine as silk. His clothes revealed the dandy; sometimes a grey velvet knickerbocker suit, or a specially-woven brown check, which he liked to wear with spats, plain brown stockings, a deep mauve tie and a vivid red carnation.

Anthony Eden has many happy memories of childhood; of lessons with the governess; the games children invent for themselves; browsing over history books; rowing and boxing, swimming and riding, watching the pageantry of Victorian society as it came and went at Windlestone. Tours with Wilson the gardener, who would describe the enormous variety of flowers and shrubs and trees; chats with the long-suffering Woolger, who had once complained that what Sir William really needed was a keeper, but who on another occasion had felt constrained to say: " Ho, Lord, Sir William, you 'ave the 'eart of an helephant! "

In other ways, those days at Windlestone were, for Anthony, a preparation for stormy days ahead. When he was born, Britain was in its hey-day. Queen Victoria had just finished her sixtieth year of reign, and ten days after Anthony's birth Britain was crowded with rulers and potentates come to do her honour. Confidence in British omnipotence was so great that it was possible for a reporter to write, on the occasion of Queen Victoria's Jubilee procession: "At the very moment when the head of the Queen's procession came through the archway into the courtyard of Buckingham Palace the sun, which until then had been waiting its opportunity behind the clouds, tried an experimental shine." How obliging of the sun, and how good to be born into a world in which values, right or wrong, were at least definite.

During, therefore, the most formative years of his life, in other words, until he reached the age of nine, Anthony Eden lived in an environment in which sport and culture were part of his daily diet, where the requirements of physical health could hardly have been bettered. What a wealth of memories must come flooding back to the Prime Minister as he thinks of those days. Of his father, white and shaking, waving his walking-stick at that monstrosity, the Albert Memorial; of Lady Eden, swirling out of the library with a flurry of satin skirts as she observed her husband colour with anger at something which had suddenly taken his disapproval; of solitary rides through the lovely beech avenue of the estate on Tom Tit, his favourite pony; of the long, painful hours he was forced to pose in his absurd silks and laces, *à la* Little Lord Fauntleroy, whilst his father, after looking up at him now and again with fierce gimlet eyes, would mix a colour on his palette and take what seemed like an interminable time to apply it to his picture. Perhaps Anthony would fidget or stretch his muscles, to be recalled to duty with a command that came like the fire of a machine-gun: " Keep still, boy! You're not a ballet dancer—thank God! "

And perhaps Anthony Eden remembers the day when, riding down a country lane on his estate, he saw a man with a cart, mercilessly belabouring the docile horse with a whip. In a flash he had dismounted, jumped on the cart, snatched the whip from the astonished man's hand and lashed at him until his young arms were too tired to do more. It was not the first time that he was to be aroused to passionate fury by the sight of cruelty and injustice.

Photo: Picture Post   *Photo: Picture Post*

Robert Anthony Eden at the age of three.   Sir William Eden, father of Sir Anthony Eden, painting a picture.

A rare photograph of the Eden family taken in 1911. *Left to right:* Timothy Eden (now Sir Timothy); Lady Brooke, Anthony Eden's sister (later Countess of Warwick); Sybil Lady Eden; John Eden (standing); Nicholas Eden (seated); Sir William Eden; Anthony Eden. John and Nicholas were both killed during the First World War.

Photo: Mirrorpic

Photo: Picture Post

Anthony Eden at Eton. All his brothers went there, and both his sons.

Photo: Picture Post

Leaving Buckingham Palace after investiture with the Military Cross in 1917.

THREE

Boyhood and Adolescence

BY the age of nine Anthony Eden had developed into an intelligent, thinnish, somewhat introspective boy whose dreamy moods were interspersed with sharp flashes of temper. There was nothing exceptional about him; he liked collecting postage stamps, as most boys do, and had learned riding and cricket, boxing and football. He did not enthuse over any of these sports, which drew him simply because his brothers were doing the same thing and that otherwise he would have been the odd man out.

Early photographs give an odd impression of frailty despite the fact that he had no physical disability. There is not the slightest touch of fugitive humour in any of his pictures; his eyes are thoughtful and sometimes even a little sad. One feels that the environment of Windlestone, despite its obvious advantages, had taken considerable emotional toll of him at a time when he should have been free of care. He had been moulded into the accepted English pattern too quickly and too rigidly; there had been too little mischief in his life, too much apprehension as to how his temperamental, bullying omniprescient father would react. Sybil Lady Eden has described him as a " sure, slow and steady boy ". He was also a dreamy lad. Often he would be looking for his hat when it was in his hand. Once he was heard reciting his prayers as he was on a swing in the grounds; asked why, he replied that he was going to bed! And apart from a precocious interest in politics (which did not, of course, go very deep) some might think that his religious education was perhaps a trifle overdone. Lady Eden was a devout—though by no means self-conscious or bigoted—Anglican, and in that faith Anthony was raised. He enjoyed reading the Bible, and he sometimes went into the chapel at Windlestone with no prompting from anyone.

In 1906, at the age of nine, Anthony was sent to Sandroy School, near Cobham, in Surrey, which, educationally speaking, is a sort of half-way house to Eton (where he went in 1911) and Christ Church, Oxford.

At Eton Anthony Eden was definitely unhappy. Highly strung, sensitive and in certain respects lonely, carrying the burdens of maturity before he was ready for them, it was a difficult period for him. His one desire was to efface himself, to conform, to give no offence, to disobey no rules, to learn all he could. His brother Timothy protected him against much of the bullying that would certainly have come his way. He did not have to " run the gauntlet "—a sort of initiation which was in fact no more than mass bullying of a newcomer. " Oh, he's Timothy Eden's brother," they would say, and leave him alone. His unhappiness was reflected in his letters to his mother, who must have interceded on his behalf with Sir William, whose letters to Anthony at that time show the flickerings of tenderness towards the boy. His note " Be not downcast, oh my soul! Hope thou in the Lord!" was an attempt to cheer the lad and to sustain him by reference to a God whose existence Sir William, as a professing atheist, had disowned. Sir William knew that Anthony was deeply religious and that this reference would strike a responsive chord.

There is absolutely nothing about Anthony Eden's career at Eton that would have encouraged anyone to predict that he would ever be a leader of men, or make a mark. He was lucky to be placed in the house of Ernest Lee Churchill ("Jelly" to the boys at Eton), a splendid athlete and stroke and a great advocate of physical training. " Jelly " had an uncanny way of instilling self-reliance into young lads of totally different temperaments, and, recognising in Anthony a youngster who had courage and application but was simply quiet by temperament, Churchill did not force the pace. Anthony did reasonably well at rowing and athletics, but did not shine. Churchill has described him as " neither taciturn nor gay—just a pleasant and typical example of the best type of English public school boy ". Anthony played football, belonged to the cricket eleven of his house, but liked rowing best.

During his years at Eton, Anthony Eden continued his study of the Bible with renewed zeal. He loved its glowing prose, the majestic sweep of its vision and its message of hope. His letters to his mother reveal a deep-rooted faith and the mere fact that his father echoed his phrases in writing to him proves that Anthony's transparent sincerity had touched even him. Perhaps he envied the lad's faith in a God whose strength and peace he himself would like to have shared—could he but believe.

It is probable that the elegance one associates with Anthony Eden was acquired at Eton. Until then he had not cared a fig about clothes. But self-discipline, the keynote of English education, makes a point of appearance without making it the only thing that matters. Amongst the stiff white collars, the black coats and waistcoats—and on the glorious Fourth of June (which for eleven hundred Etonians is a day of celebrations, with special ties and collars and, as a decorative touch, slate-grey waistcoats) Anthony looked as dapper as any of them, strutting with peacock pride beside his lovely and affectionate mother.

On these annual days Anthony would wait for his mother in a fever of excitement. After breakfast he would hurry down to Barns Pool to buy a buttonhole for his dark tail coat. Some boys worried lest their mothers should appear in tasteless, flamboyant or cheap clothes—as some occasionally did—and put them to shame with their schoolmates, but that was the least of Anthony's worries, for Lady Eden always arrived composed and looking like a Degas painting. They would watch cricket, or sit and stroll under the shade of the chestnuts and beeches. There would be lunch, far more elegant than the usual joint and pudding—usually cold lobster followed by strawberries and cream. Then would follow the hilarious procession of boats, with the *Monarch*, a ten-oared boat, leading the way and not infrequently being the only boat in which anybody knew how to row properly.

There would be supper, a brass band playing and a firework display, ending with a large set-piece showing the Eton shield; frenzied cheers—and then—a kiss from Lady Eden, a gruff " Good-bye, my lad, and work hard," from Sir William, and Anthony was back again with Latin verbs, with his history books and his theological studies. The latter were to bear strange fruit, for he was awarded the Brinckman Divinity Prize, a piece of news which his atheistic father received with gruff incredulity. Clearly Sir William's constant exhortations that Anthony should emulate his father had not borne fruit in this instance.

But Lady Eden was overjoyed at the news. His school reports showed him to be a steady, dependable, plodding worker, capable of application. She knew him to be absolutely honest and straightforward, devoid of any mean instinct and full of courage. His self-confidence had been shaken by his upbringing, but he was determined to stand on his own feet. His letters to his mother show, too, how early and precocious was his interest in politics; this one, for instance, written at sixteen:

" Dear Mummie—thank you very much for your letter. Only three more weeks on Friday. I am looking forward to being home again. I have done very badly in the history thing, I am afraid. The French exam. is on Tuesday; there is one boy who is rather good, but I think I can manage to beat the rest.

On Thursday, St. Andrew's Day, we stop compulsory football. I will write to you again on Thursday because I think a good many things are going to happen on Thursday. Good-bye for the present, with much love from your very loving son, Anthony.

" *P.S.* These bye-elections are simply splendid. They show how people hate the Insurance Bill, and I think we may have some chance of winning the next General Election, unless the Government tell the country too many lies."

That is an illuminating document, when one considers that its writer was only sixteen years old. It says so much between the lines; his longing to be home again, the seriousness with which he tackled his studies and worried about his progress; the fact that football was no longer compulsory was, apparently, a piece of news worth passing on, and implies that he is not sorry about it; but the postscript is by far the most revealing touch. I imagine that few boys of sixteen are absorbed, as he obviously was, in a forthcoming General Election, and his interest in domestic politics is decidedly precocious.

Soon Europe was to be embroiled in the bloodiest struggle in its history, and before long, as a mere boy, Anthony Eden was to walk with death and danger and come to terms with them, with himself, and with the world. Just as certain of the joys of childhood had passed him by, so now his disciplined nature was to be tested in war; he was to be glad—and so were other people—of that emotional reserve and thoughtfulness which were part of his make-up. He was to prove that, contrary to his father's prediction, petticoats had not been the ruin of him, and that the shy smile and reserved demeanour did not imply timidity.

In September, 1915, young Anthony Eden, a pink-cheeked, boyish-looking youth, volunteered for the Army straight from school. He was gazetted as a temporary Lieutenant to the 21st Battalion, King's Royal Rifle Corps, and within a matter of months was made Adjutant—the youngest in the British Army. The Earl of Feversham, a Yorkshire landowner, was the Commanding Officer, and the staff of battalion headquarters were mostly men from his estate.

The reaction of the men to Eden's appointment was not altogether favourable. They respected the youth and his authority (the latter they would have had to do anyway), but many of his subordinates considered him to be young for the job, and felt that, but for his family connections, his path to promotion would have been longer and more difficult. The Eden and Feversham families were, in fact, connected, and there is not the slightest doubt that in youth and early manhood, Eden's family background and his family's connection with influential circles were of the greatest use in getting him launched on a particular level of responsibility. Later Feversham was to be killed in action, and his widow, daughter of the fifth Earl of Warwick, married Sir Gervase Beckett, who later became Eden's father-in-law.

But leadership was sorely needed at that time—and Feversham was to prove a good judge. Eden at eighteen had physical courage a-plenty, and must have blessed his stern father's insistence, so early in life, that he should have his full share of tumbles and knocks, and should learn through football and cricket, riding and swimming, to pit his body against the elements and against other men. He was by no means intimidated by seniority, and was reputed to be a little fond of telling them how he would do things in their position. He was impeccable in turn-out, his buttons gleaming like burnished, gold, his belt polished like a mirror, his finger-nails scrubbed, his hair trained with precision. But these were only the outward marks of an inner discipline of which he was to give impressive proof in the field.

I have before me a photograph of Anthony Eden with the officers and N.C.O.'s of his Company, taken in 1916; it is easy to see why he earned the friendly nickname of "the Boy". It is also obvious that he was a boy with mettle, exuding keenness and alertness with his whole demeanour and expression.

Eden's family had already suffered the loss of Anthony's elder brother; and of his classmates at Eton, twenty-six volunteered and nine of them were killed.

In the early spring of 1916 Anthony Eden was on the Western Front. He had no enthusiasm for war, and his letters home echo the fond desire of most soldiers: "I do wish this beastly war would end". His mother, Lady Eden, was managing a war hospital, and she knew as much as he what war involved; yet in all his letters, except of course for the understandable wish to see an end to the war itself, he makes light of his own troubles and ignores the dangers of which, anyway, his mother was well aware. For two years he was in constant action on the Front, calm, pink-faced and impeccable in the muddy and bloody holocaust of Ypres and, later, the Somme, where, separated by no great distance, he was fighting a man whom, by a supreme irony of fate, he was to meet later on in life—Private Schickelgruber, alias Adolf Hitler, whose burning sense of inferiority was to make him hate himself, project his hatred on the world, and spread renewed misery in another generation. A well-aimed bullet then would have altered history.

Those who served with Eden remember with pride his quiet leadership and complete fearlessness—and especially the detachment which enabled him to do his duty to his country without losing his innate humanity. The heady jingoism of the sort expressed in the popular recruiting posters, the music-hall songs of the period and by patriots often far from the line had no effect on him, and in his heart he felt as much for the killed and wounded of any nation as for those who fell around him. In this he was in agreement with his father, Sir William, who now moped around Windlestone Hall watching his world fall to pieces. The artist in Sir William couldn't accept the black-and-white assessment of opposing nations: "We hear of nothing but those gallant Belgians!" he exclaimed irritably, "but what of those poor devils of Germans mown down in thousands as they advance!" But Sir William's humanitarianism was kept within due bounds. "Don't you go giving your money to those damned refugees," he warned the people on his estate, "we shall need every penny of it for ourselves."

But Anthony Eden's attitude to war was different from his father's. The savagery, the senselessness, the wastefulness of it all appalled him. The death in action in France of his eldest brother, John, after he himself had been in the Army only three months, had touched him deeply. It had also touched Sir William, now fast becoming an invalid and suffering all the agonies of an active man condemned to near idleness. He had stormed against John, ranted and raved, denigrated and discouraged him, sworn that he was spoiled and inadequate and selfish, belittled his achievements in polo and hunting; a boy who had been so popular with all his friends, respected at college, a boy upright, brave and cheerful. But Sir William had always been terrified of displaying sentimentality or parading his innermost emotions; " suppressed emotion is more noble than hysterical gush! " he liked to say, and although he carried this lack of tenderness to absurd and selfish limits, one must not mistake emotional reticence for heartlessness. He was sitting by the fireside at Windlestone when the news was broken to him that his eldest son had been killed in action. No flicker of emotion passed over his face. He continued to stare at the dancing flames, and murmured "A fine death". That was all.

Anthony, grieved as he was, wrote these words of comfort to his mother:

"Poor little mummie. You are having a fearfully trying time. But we must all do our share and the greater the share the greater the honour if it is nobly borne. And we must all die some day, why not now by the most honourable way possible, the way that opens the gates of paradise—the soldier's death? "

It was Anthony's fine organising talent that had led to his rapid promotion in the Army. He has never "shot a line" about his active service, and, speaking about it on one occasion —it was during a debate on disarmament—he underplayed his rôle during the crucial years of the First World War:

". . . those who have seen war are least likely to want to see its repetition. . . . I remember one evening in the very last weeks of our advance, when we had stopped for the night at

Brigade Headquarters in some farmhouse. The night was quiet and there was no shell-fire, as was usual at the end of the war, but quite suddenly it began literally to rain bombs for anything from ten minutes to a quarter of an hour. I do not know how many bombs fell in that time, but something between thirty and forty, I suppose. It seemed to us to be hundreds. I do not know what the explanation was, but perhaps it was the enemy aeroplanes had failed to find their objective and were emptying out their bombs before crossing the line on their way back. Whatever the explanation, what rests in my mind is not only my own personal terror, which was quite inexpressible, because bombing is more demoralising in its effects than the worst shell-fire, but comment made when it was over by somebody who said: ' There now, you have had your first taste of the next war! ' "

Anthony's fellow-soldiers have put it on record that when, during some bitter trench warfare, the news was broken to him that his sixteen-year-old brother Nicholas, a mere boy, had been killed at Jutland, he leapt over the parapet and led a charge like a man demented, charging and fighting with the strength of ten men.

On August 14th, 1916, young Eden, after displaying coolness, leadership and resource under the gruelling conditions of constant trench warfare, was to prove how wrong his father had been in thinking him a mother's boy. So far, individual acts of gallantry were not easy to achieve for the good reason that most actions involved the deployment of huge masses of men —it was a vast, impersonal game of chess, with nobody able to see the board as a whole. But on this particular night " the Boy " was to mark " sterling " indelibly on his character.

Eden's battalion was entrenched at Ploegsteert, and his orders were to take out a platoon for a surprise raid on the enemy trenches.

As zero hour drew near and Anthony stood in his trench, as spick and span as if he were about to go on parade, the second-in-command of the battalion, Major Foljambe, called to one of Eden's party—Sergeant W. H. Harrop.

" Lieutenant Eden is the sort of man the army can't spare, but there's nobody better to do this job to-night. But listen, Harrop; at all costs look after that young officer. That boy has a wonderful career in front of him."

It is interesting, in retrospect, that the Major could look at a boy of nineteen and make such a prediction. But on this night, while shells whined and bullets splashed into the mud almost every second, the Major's plans were to work in reverse; it was to be Eden who was to protect and succour Harrop.

Zero hour arrived. Eden and his men smeared their faces with black, filled their pockets with Mills bombs and, in a momentary lull, crept forward until they reached the barbed wire entanglements when a burst of machine-gun fire showed that they had been seen. Under a hail of bullets they turned and made for their own trenches, and in the darkness it seemed that the troop was complete. Nobody had been seen to fall or heard to cry out.

Back in their trenches, Eden counted his men. One man was missing—the man who had been detailed to protect him. Not that Eden knew it. "Harrop has been hit. We must go back," he said immediately, and, selecting two men, went back to face an enemy already expecting them. Totally ignoring the fire, but keeping as low as possible, Eden found Sergeant Harrop terribly injured, his thigh shattered by a dum-dum bullet. Amidst machine-gun fire he fixed a tourniquet to Harrop to save him bleeding to death, and managed to get him back to the lines. His action saved Harrop from certain death. Even as it was, he was so badly wounded that it took thirty-five operations before he could get back to normal life.

The following day Eden wrote to his mother, concealing the fact of his own heroism:

"Another bit of bad luck. My new Platoon Sergeant has been badly hit in the thigh. He was very brave about it, poor man, but I'm afraid he suffered terribly. . . . I asked you to send me a pair of STOCKINGS, not socks. Please send them soon."

Ever afterwards Sergeant Harrop has never tired of telling how the lean, pink-cheeked youth, whose polite ways and clipped language had caused many a joke in the ranks, had saved his life. They have been in correspondence with each other ever since.

The exploit brought Eden the award of the Military Cross, which was gazetted on June 5th, 1917, when he was also given the rank of Captain (he was barely twenty years old) and promoted to Lord Plumer's staff. By the time the war ended and he had reached twenty-one, he was a Brigade-Major.

When the First World War ended, Anthony Eden had achieved manhood. He returned home to find a changed world. Windlestone was there, its yellow stone glowing in the soft sunlight, although parts of the beautiful gardens were given over to growing cabbages and his mother, instead of moving through the great rooms with a rustle of silk, now looked brisker and more modern in a Red Cross outfit. Sir William had died in 1915 and Timothy—who had been an internee at Ruhleben in Germany for two years and later saw active service as a Lieutenant in the Yorkshire Light Infantry on the Western Front from 1917–1919—had succeeded to the title.

Now Anthony had more verve, more assurance and definite ideas of what he wanted to be. He still wanted to be a politician. He had seen the turmoil and tragedy of international affairs mismanaged, and wanted, with the passionate intolerance of youth, to get it all reformed as quickly as possible. He longed for peace, as only a soldier can.

A temporary setback awaited him, however. He had forgotten that the war had interrupted his education. He had left Eton at eighteen. The years and energy he might have spent at University had been dissipated in battle. Sybil Lady Eden insisted firmly that he must recommence his studies where he left off. Anthony's first answer was, " What! Go back to school, Mummy? " It seemed an odd anti-climax to years of dash and daring and responsibility. But there it was. Lady Eden was adamant, and she was right.

But Anthony could not have found the venture as attractive as he would have done, say, on leaving Eton. The war had left a mark on him; even as a boy he had been quiet and serious-minded. Now he was almost solemn, or earnest to the point of gravity. In a certain sense of the word, he had missed his youth; he had seen misery at an age when one is most disposed to gaiety, had been disciplined during those years when a young man feels the need for an increasing measure of purely personal initiative, taste and adventure. He had enjoyed the comradeship of men and acquitted himself well as a man; but the war had fixed that trait of seriousness as one fixes a photograph with hypophosphite.

And so, at Christ Church, Oxford, established by King Henry VIII in the sixteenth century, Anthony Eden found himself completing his education. Once he had accepted his mother's advice he threw himself into his studies with energetic purpose. But somehow those missing years cut him off from the levity and light-heartedness of some of the younger men, whilst the hiatus in his own studies put him at a disadvantage with men older than himself. The discussions in the Oxford clubs, the social activities and the Debating Society interested him very little. That he should have been uninterested in the Oxford Union Debating Society is strange, considering his determination to enter politics; it is a good opportunity to master the elements of rhetoric, of crisp and convincing exposition, and, come to that, of confidence.

Eden was a good scholar, though not an outstanding one. He mixed very little with the undergraduates, though there were plenty of others contemporary with him whose conversation was stimulating or amusing, and who were to make their mark in later life—Lord Scarbrough, for example, now Lord Chamberlain to Queen Elizabeth II; Louis Golding; Beverley Nichols; Beverley Baxter. But Anthony did a certain amount of entertaining in his lodgings, and Lord Scarbrough remembers that as a host Eden was punctilious in detail; nothing but the very best wines would do—there was no question of buying a bottle of cheap anonymous sherry, as a poorer undergraduate or one without taste might do. The Eden charm was at work already. When he relaxed, it is said, and once he had accepted you on terms of personal friendship, there was no more charming or dependable person in the world. But for most undergraduates he was a remote figure; somebody wearing a suit of invisible armour.

While studying the conventional subjects, Anthony Eden also showed a growing interest in art; it was safe enough now to approve Rimbaud as a poet and Cézanne as a painter. A little earlier such advocacy would have earned him the reputation of intellectual daring; but by now both had been accepted by the world. But he had inherited from his father a distinct interest in art; often he would inspect a picture in the museum or art gallery for ten minutes or more at a time, making no comment, his features showing no animation. It is interesting to look back on a lecture which he gave, as an undergraduate, on Cézanne:

> " To live entirely for his art, to renounce all else—that was the example Cézanne gave us—a hatred of worldly things, whether practical or scheming; a hatred of prejudice; a hatred of honours and flattery; a hatred of commerce and hypocrisy—Cézanne embodies all that."

Eden read the newspapers avidly, kept up-to-date on political affairs, and studied two Oriental languages, Persian and Arabic, due to the fact that, having accompanied Sir Mark Sykes on a mission to Mesopotamia during the war, he had become interested in Near East affairs. Some thought the choice of languages a peculiar one, but Eden tackled both with intense concentration.

Eden's tutor, Professor R. Paget Dewhurst, is reputed to have been impressed with the young man's quiet application. He is also said to have prophesied that one day Anthony Eden would be Foreign Minister—a remarkable piece of intuition.

Not that he neglected French, a language of which he was very fond, and which he had learned to some extent during the years of fighting in France. To improve his knowledge of this language and stop his forgetting the accent, Eden used to spend his holidays with a Protestant French pastor who lived near La Rochelle.

All these languages were to prove of inestimable value to him in later life. And so, until the age of twenty-five, by which time he had taken his Finals and won First Class Honours in Oriental languages, Anthony Eden was virtually cut off from the world, except for brief visits home and holidays abroad. Now, added to the inner discipline which had always been part of his temperament and which had been developed still further in the Army, he could add academic status.

What future lay ahead of Anthony Eden now? He had health, good looks, energy, a capacity for concentration, an easy grace, influential connections, means of his own, experience of administration, courage and education. How would these serve in politics, and how could he start? He was soon to find out.

FOUR

Into Politics

TWENTY-ONE is an early age at which to decide upon politics as a career, but that had been Anthony Eden's decision. His mother's remark, made when he was eleven, that if he knew all the names of the local M.P.'s by heart (as he did) he was obviously born to be a politician, was nearer the mark than she could have guessed.

If Sir Anthony Eden could put the clock back, and appear in any election now as he did then, he would have faint hope of success, so far as personality went. The sight of this tall, handsome ex-officer, with his bowler hat, stiff white collar and a white handkerchief sticking from his top pocket with geometric precision, trying to get on mammocking terms with two babies in a pram is, in retrospect, slightly absurd. But it was—and I suppose still is—good election strategy.

In his first election campaign, as Conservative candidate for the Spennymoor Division of Durham in 1922, he was a failure from the start. It was a mining area, and Captain Eden's assumption (or, more probably, that of the Conservative Central Office) that to have the Marquess of Londonderry as a sponsor was an asset was, to put it mildly, optimistic. The Marquess was a coal-owner, whereas John Batey, the Labour candidate, was a miner well known and liked locally. Mr. Eden's other opponent was Tom Wing, a Liberal. Anthony had been an officer in the First World War and a gallant one, but he seemed too stamped with class distinction to commend himself to the rough-and-ready miners. It must be admitted that his speeches to Spennymoor were a potpourri of platitudes which would have served the purpose of any comic playwright who wanted to parody an election. But to be fair to Eden, one must remember that he had seen little of life, had not mixed very much with ordinary people and had gone straight from school into the Army, where he admittedly showed not only verve and gallantry but a decided flair for organisation and the management of men. In managing men, however, he had had the War Office behind him, and on this occasion he hadn't. His sincere but colourless advocacy of Conservatism, his championship of Mr. Bonar Law and vague references to the necessity to revive trade were no foil for the human and forthright utterances of the popular Mr. Batey, who secured more votes at the poll than Captain Eden and the Liberal opponent put together—13,766 votes to be precise, or 6,000 more than Captain Eden.

The experience was valuable, however, in teaching him the mechanics of an election; the role of canvassers, the organisation of constituencies, the procedure for the nomination of candidates, the role of an election agent and the whole conduct of a campaign. It was better to start with a small failure than a big one, and it was not to be long before Captain Eden was to prove that he had learned from his first failure. Within a year he was pitchforked into an election in which anything might happen and a lot of things did.

In 1923 Captain Eden was chosen by the Conservatives as a candidate for the Warwick and Leamington constituency; he was a second best, for he was a stranger to the town and was only accepted because their original choice, a local man, had dropped out. It was a traditionally Conservative constituency which the former Conservative M.P., Sir Ernest Pollock, had held for five years—indeed, at the 1922 election he was returned unopposed and even at his first election only a quarter of the inhabitants bothered to vote.

Aristocracy was still a passport in 1923, but its privileges were no longer unquestioned and it could no longer, of itself, win elections. A distinguished line of ancestors, education at Eton, wealth and an honourable record of Army service were certainly an advantage in this rural stronghold, and especially in " the chintzy-chintzy cheeriness of Leamington Spa," to quote John Betjeman. But the *Leamington Chronicle* certainly spoke the truth when it forecast to its readers that the electors were in for " a rare exciting time ".

The election had many unusual features. Sir Ernest, the previous Conservative M.P., had retired because he had been made Master of the Rolls, but since 1918 the electorate had nearly doubled. Women now had voting rights—and nobody could guess which way their 19,000 votes would be cast.

Never before had a Labour candidate dared to show his face in this haven of pump rooms, baths and pleasant gardens—and certainly never a woman candidate. As it was, Eden's main opponent was the Labour candidate, the Countess of Warwick, a determined old aristocrat who had embraced Socialism rather late in life. The apparent anachronism of her living in one of Britain's stateliest of stately homes, Warwick Castle, and throwing herself into the ding-dong of an election campaign, fulminating against privilege and the lowly state of the poor before she took herself off to the Castle that dominates Warwick from the top of the hill, created some amusement in both camps.

In fact, the Countess was quite sincere, and she deserved more credit for her courage than she received. She had been a famous Victorian and Edwardian hostess, and in the great dining-room, where Queen Elizabeth had once been entertained in state, she loved to give lavish parties, some of which cost thousands of pounds.

It was inevitable that as the popular press came into its own, these parties should attract attention, be written about. In the eighties she was so talked of as a beauty that Disraeli had planned to marry her to Queen Victoria's youngest son, Prince Leopold. Instead, she fell in love with his Aide-de-Camp, Lord Brooke, later Earl of Warwick. Living in the grand manner was something she took for granted, but the industrial revolution and the rise of popular education had produced a more literate and more critical—or, at any rate, a more articulate—working class.

After the Countess had given a spectacularly expensive banquet costing thousands of pounds, Robert Blatchford, the Socialist writer, launched a bitter attack on her in his paper, *The Clarion*, denouncing her party as extravagant, vulgar and in poor taste, having regard to the widespread poverty.

With a frantic tug of the bell-pull the Countess, who had read the paper with shaking hands, summoned her carriage and drove post-haste to London, where she bearded Blatchford in his humble office. " You—you dared to write this? " she asked. " Yes, madam," replied Blatchford; " you dare to justify that which I have criticised? " For hours the two argued, and at the end of it all Frances emerged a convinced Socialist. She worked quite hard on social and educational work, and if her methods were unorthodox, there was no arguing her sincerity.

An aristocrat fighting the Labour cause was novelty enough —but there was another unusual aspect. How would the women react? Would they support one of their own number because she was a woman? Would they vote for a personality or a policy?

To make this historic election stranger still, Lady Warwick was a relative of Anthony Eden. Her son and heir had married Elfrida Marjorie, Anthony Eden's sister, so that the Labour candidate was the mother-in-law of the Conservative candidate's sister. But Lady Warwick was also a relative of Anthony Eden's fiancée, Beatrice Beckett, whom he actually married during the election, taking time off from the campaign for the purpose. Beatrice, who was eighteen, was a handsome, dark girl and a daughter, by his first marriage, of Sir Gervase Beckett, proprietor of the famous Conservative newspaper, the *Yorkshire Post*. They had met before in family circles, but the election campaign brought them constantly together until the handsome ex-officer allowed it to be known, to the delight of the women voters, that he was to get married during the campaign itself. And on November 5th, at the fashionable church of St. Margaret's, Westminster (which, because of its close proximity with the Abbey, is sometimes mistaken by strangers for part of the Abbey itself), and before a congregation representing the cream of Britain's landed gentry, the couple were joined in matrimony by the Archbishop of York, assisted by the Bishop of Wakefield. Major the Hon. Evelyn Eden, M.C., acted as best man.

The election campaign was one of the longest on record, lasting six weeks because of the dissolution of Parliament and the supervening of a general election. It was a large and awkward territory in which to campaign, but Captain Eden did all the right things, even to patting the heads of strange babies and answering questions from apprehensive or militant pressure groups. Three meetings a day was a minimum, and in all Eden made eighty speeches. There were long motor drives through country lanes, meetings in village schoolrooms lighted with oil-lamps, and *ad hoc* meetings, often in the chill late November air, at odd street corners and market places.

Eden's election address was more adequate than historic. " Our primary need is for more markets, and I most wholeheartedly support the Government's endeavour to find those markets within the British Empire. It is essential that our Imperial resources should be developed to the uttermost. That way, and that way only, lies a permanent cure for unemployment. In this connection I welcome the Government's action in assembling the Imperial Conference now meeting in London. . . ." He went on to bemoan our luke-warm exploitation of " Imperial resources " and talked of trade protection as a possible solution of unemployment " to protect our industries from unfair foreign competition ".

It wasn't brilliant stuff. To say, " our primary need is for more markets," when he meant that we would have more money if we sold more goods was not only to state the obvious but to do so in a tedious way. But this verbal orthodoxy was backed, at least, by youth, charm and manifest sincerity. To be young, handsome, rash, brave and gallant may not guarantee the soundness of your policies, but they help a lot when 19,000 women are wondering what to do with their votes.

The Countess, for Labour, opened her campaign at the Town Hall, Leamington. The Assembly Rooms were crowded and a star turn for the audience was Mr. Percy Cole, solicitor to the Iron and Steel Trades Confederation. It might be, he said, that Lady Warwick would not be at the top of the poll, but he was sure most people were against the Government policy.

Mr. Cole talked at interminable length about tinplates. When he had finished the Countess discounted rumours that she was not a *bona fide* candidate. " I am here," she said, amidst cheers, her long bead necklaces swinging like pendulums as she moved from side to side in emphasis, " and I am going to stay until the polling has taken place ". She attacked protection, demanded a vigorous handling of the unemployment problem (as did all the candidates) and advanced a theory rather novel for one of the richest women in Britain:

" . . . the upper classes were the people who worked by hand and brain, and to her mind the ' lower ' classes were the idlers."

From a human point of view, of putting herself over, she was certainly more effective than Eden. Eden represented a policy and a way of life: the Countess represented herself and spoke as a human being:

" . . . it is twenty-five years since I joined the Labour movement. This transference of my political allegiance was taken in no spirit of levity, for it meant social ostracism by old friends, the severance of many old ties, and the denial of class privileges which I had been taught to accept without question or reserve, but I was irresistibly attracted to the Labour movement by its new and broader conceptions of human rights and human values. My heart instinctively responded to the lofty social message which this movement had for the people, its appeal to the social conscience of the nation rang with deep and passionate sincerity. . . ."

Otherwise, her strategy was *maladroit* and often attracted ridicule. The knowledge that she and Anthony would be bound to be having cocktails together at Warwick Castle within a mere matter of time somehow took the edge off her criticisms.

Anthony Eden's decision to get married during the campaign was not well received by his opponents. It seemed too much like a ruse to get sentimental backing where logic and reason might not appeal. The *Yorkshire Post's* references somehow encouraged this suspicion, more especially since it was a daughter of that newspaper's proprietor that Anthony was marrying. " Romance is to play its part in the election contest in the Warwick and Leamington Division," a correspondent reports, coyly. His marriage is " a happy omen of his success in the electoral contest "—logic which is hard to follow. " Anyway," he adds, as though uncertain whether he has made his point, " they are all, and *particularly the ladies*, working strenuously to make him the most acceptable of wedding presents—the title of M.P." No doubt the marriage was played up as election propaganda. But Anthony was young, and he wanted to succeed.

Meanwhile, Eden was getting moral support from the son

of his Socialist opponent, Lord Brooke. He had taken only one day away in Sussex for a honeymoon, had been greeted by a party of well-wishers at Leamington railway station as he returned with his bride, who was presented with a bouquet of yellow chrysanthemums as the press cameras clicked. Nor, to Lady Warwick's intense annoyance and intense amusement of *The Times*, was he the only near relative of hers to champion her opponent. Lord Warwick's brother, the Hon. Louis Greville, sent Eden best wishes for the Conservative cause on behalf of himself and his brothers. Lord Warwick himself, who was ill at the time, kept aloof from it all, which is not to say that he did not admire his wife's pluck in contesting the election.

The Liberal candidate was probably the most colourful of the three candidates. George Nicholls lacked the showmanship of Lady Warwick and made his main appeal to the agricultural workers. He was a farm labourer who, in his early years, had been down and out and forced to tramp in search of work. Eventually he acquired a smallholding of a single acre and hawked his own produce. He had hoped to become a Nonconformist minister, and passing through a Methodist Training College he became Pastor of churches at Chatteris, Silverdale and Chesterton. But the paucity of his smallholding had made him enthusiastic for land reform.

His political career, on inspection, proved to be somewhat chequered. As a Radical (a word as opprobrious then as Communist is to-day) he had represented North Hants in Parliament from 1906 to 1910. Defeated then, he stood again in the second election of the same year and was beaten once more. From 1914 to 1918 he had been Mayor of Peterborough and in 1918 stood for the mining constituency of Camborne in Cornwall, as a Labour candidate. He was unsuccessful, and now came to Warwick and Leamington asking to be returned as a Liberal.

Eden had been given a safe Conservative seat to contest, but there were many imponderables about this election which made him decide that nothing could be taken for granted. What he lacked in sparkle he made up in industry. There was not much fun to be got from listening to him, but he was smart, debonair and smiling, and somehow his promises to protect the labourer and stop the wicked foreigner stealing his just rewards seemed more convincing than Lady Warwick's sallies about privilege, nepotism and the hardships of the working class.

An unfortunate piece of electioneering propaganda put out by Lady Warwick's own committee rooms destroyed whatever chance she had of being taken seriously. She would, it had been announced, tour the constituency in a carriage drawn by four milk-white steeds. The very idea of Labour's champion touring a rural constituency in semi-state gladdened the hearts of everyone and gave the correspondent of the *Yorkshire Post*, whose perceptive sallies and dry humour make delightful reading even to-day, a great deal of scope. Lady Warwick's handling of the press had from the start been unfortunate; she had herself invited the press to a conference and then gone away without bothering to tell them; she decided to take a week's holiday as soon as her nomination had been announced; she had accused the press of pestering her, when in fact she and her committee-room helpers were doing their best to get her noticed; and had declared that she would not be interviewed by anyone except the *Daily Herald*.

As one observer wrote at the time:

> "It is somewhat surprising that a lady who insists on being considered as a serious politician only, who has thrown herself into a state of fury by the publication of the remarks about herself instead of her views 'on unemployment, women's interests, economics and internationalism' and who, on her own confession, loathes publicity, should seek this method of shrouding herself from the public gaze. Cunning, worldly-wise organisers of circuses know that this method of the milk-white steeds and the four-in-hand is absolutely the worst way of passing unnoticed. . . ."

The only way she could secure such anonymity, one correspondent observed, would be to pass in a crowd; round up all the horses and let all the Labour people ride them; let Ramsay MacDonald be seen gallantly reining in his champing coal-black stallion beside the Countess; Mr. Sidney Webb pricking daintily behind on his barb; Mr. Clynes, in a dinner jacket, mastering an Arab charger and the Glasgow squad bringing up the rear in fours on their palfreys. Thus, and thus only, could Lady Warwick attain her ideal of the inconspicuous.

Anthony Eden refrained from any facetiousness or jokes at the expense of the other candidates. To Lady Warwick, in particular, he referred always in terms of the most scrupulous courtesy; a high-spirited youth would have enjoyed the situation, one feels, rather more than he did, but in any event his restraint and good manners, if they made him rather less stimulating than the other two candidates, conveyed a sense of responsibility and purpose. In fact, it was a weakness for which he can scarcely be blamed that he spoke and behaved as though he had carried the cares of the world on his elegant shoulders. But his not-too-happy home, his strict discipline at Eton and the bloodshed and battles he had been through so recently in the First World War—and of course, the conventions of his social circle—were hardly calculated to develop a sense of humour.

Mrs. Eden, meanwhile, was a loyal and energetic helpmate, enjoying the contest hugely and driving Anthony from one meeting to another, rallying every friend she could under his banner.

In a single day Eden addressed three village meetings, at Stoneleigh, Westwood and Cubbington. It was easy for him to give a pat answer to something called the National Workmen's Council, which interrogated all three candidates on their attitude towards field sports and prohibition. Captain Eden declared: " I will, of course, do my utmost to protect racing and all other field sports, which are the birthright of every Britisher. I am strongly opposed to prohibition." Questioned as to his views on divorce, he replied, " I think it is rather hard you should ask me about that already," and continued that as a Churchman he was naturally opposed to any weakening of the marriage law, and did not want to see our divorce law modelled on American practice. Furthermore, if elected, he would be all in favour of upholding religious instruction in schools, especially remembering the undermining influence of the Communist Sunday Schools.

Clearly Warwick and Leamington would still hear the hunters in frenzied chase over the fields, and the villagers would not be robbed of their cool, sustaining beer—then 4d. a pint.

Lady Warwick was less accommodating on this issue. She

liked open-air pursuits, she declared, and loved racing, but was opposed to blood sports. Her ponies continued to be a source of amusement, but Lady Warwick's plan to drive around the constituency in a carriage drawn by four ponies misfired badly. To cheers from nine press photographers, four casual loungers and a greengrocer's boy, she drove her ponies to the committee rooms. But they were not four white ponies, as had been promised, but a couple of cobs, one bay and one chestnut.

This initial disappointment, however, didn't matter. A happy chance made her entry to the town more theatrical and impressive than it would otherwise have been. A play, " The Garden of Allah," was being performed in Leamington that week, and was being advertised by a procession of animals. These happened to be passing as Lady Warwick's phaeton drew out of the livery stables. Her carriage got mixed up with the general procession, which included two camels, a pair of milk-white mules, a small donkey and a foal, and many onlookers took it for granted that she was part of the show. Did she figure in the play as the unhappy prisoner of a wicked sheikh? Somehow she didn't look cast for the rôle. Meanwhile her Ladyship fretted and fumed and tried, vainly, to extricate herself from the procession. " The roads are *awful*! " she informed an unsympathetic gathering as she arrived at last at the committee rooms, " absolutely awful. The ponies are slipping all over the show." And with that sally she went inside to discuss plans for unseating the ruling class.

Eden's meetings and activities, by contrast, were good English stuff. Words like Imperialism, Patriotism, and Empire could safely be used in those days as a spur to enthusiasm; a meeting at the Town Hall in Leamington on the night of November 9th, 1923, was filled to overflowing and there was a flutter in hundreds of female bosoms as the handsome young Captain, supported by Major Boyd Carpenter and Lord Willoughby de Broke, the chairman, came on to the platform. There were resounding cheers as Lord Willoughby described Baldwin as a " good, sound, honest, English, patriotic Tory ". Captain Eden devoted most of his speech to a defence of Protection, an attack on the evil of unemployment, which, he claimed, could be cured by reforming our fiscal system.

On the eve of the election on polling day, Captain Eden

issued his final appeal to the electors. His statements were plain and unequivocal: "I am a Conservative, and a supporter of the Prime Minister. I stand for the protection of British industries. It is also the only country with a vast army of unemployed."

Polling day showed a resounding victory for Eden. He was returned by the electorate by 16,337 votes against 11,134 for the Liberal candidate and 4,015 for the Labour candidate, Lady Warwick. Lady Warwick never contested another election. Anthony Eden has represented this constituency ever since.

FIVE

A Foot on the Ladder

NOW Anthony Eden was a Member of Parliament and a husband. He took a pleasant little house at 1, Mulberry Walk, in Chelsea, whose atmosphere of refined Bohemianism and environment of small, individual cafés and artists' studios suited both his disposition and that of his wife. The house was tastefully decorated and they soon became known as quiet and pleasant neighbours; some may have felt that Mrs. Eden, so warm and vital, teeming with love of life, intensely gregarious, relaxed, and interested in people irrespective of their social backgrounds, was an odd match for the rather solemn and ultra-political Anthony. But at this stage at least they appeared to be an ideally happy couple. Mrs. Eden, in countless ways, was helping her husband to get a firmer foothold on the political ladder; through her he was able to get a platform for himself in her father's paper, *The Yorkshire Post*, his art criticisms and political commentaries appearing under a pseudonym. He had, of course, a very influential connection in his own right; but his marriage was of immense importance to him in his career. At this stage, if the truth be told, Eden's temperament and demeanour encouraged respect rather than friendliness. His wife's easy-going and natural approach to living made them socially more interesting as a pair than he would have been singly.

The period in which Anthony Eden began his career as a Member of Parliament was one of acute industrial unrest, disillusionment and political instability. One dispute followed another in swift succession. Workers used to high wages during the war could not reconcile themselves to the lean post-war years. The trades unions had become conscious of their strength; the Labour Party, which on the outbreak of war had scarcely more than two million members, had swollen its numbers to about four and a half million by 1923 and was growing still. Liberalism was on the wane. In the Parliament of which Anthony Eden was a member, the Socialists had gained 191 seats in Parliament, compared with the Liberals with their 159 seats.

Anthony Eden must have understood the root cause of this growing unrest. The whole social life of the country had been revolutionized. Women, who during the war years did the work of men and learned to be wage-earners, had been given the right to vote. The cruelty of war had shocked almost everybody, and established traditions and ideas were now examined with critical and often hostile eyes. The normal outlets of trade had been lost with the war, and now began the difficult task of developing industry again and finding fresh markets abroad.

Plans for improving education and agriculture, formulated during the years of the First World War, had had to be scrapped because of the trade slump that had set in during 1921. So, too, had an ambitious plan for rehousing the workers. Britain was never far from revolution during the early twenties. There was a tendency to force up wages even when trade was getting worse and the efficiency of particular industries could only be impaired by further economic strains. The miners were restive, agitating for State control and threatening to strike if this were not granted. Railwaymen were equally aggrieved, maintaining that the railways should never have been restored to private control (during the war years they were, of course, controlled by the State). Transport workers were in sympathy with both these classes of workers, apart from making demands of their own. If these three groups of workers were to join forces and strike together, the life of the nation would have been paralysed. The miners carried out their threat to strike, and the general stoppage caused distress and inconvenience in all the related industries.

But underlying it all was the general feeling that capitalism had failed, that a way of life which had produced a war so destructive and protracted must never return.

When Anthony Eden took his seat for the first time in the House of Commons, the political situation could hardly have been less promising. Theoretically it was a Conservative government, but though backed by the largest single party, it could not pass any legislation against the combined forces of Liberal and Labour.

The British public, at this time, were more preoccupied with domestic matters than with foreign affairs. The sort of topic that interested Eden most, they liked least. A new generation was, for good or ill, creating its own standards and rebelling against time-honoured conventions. There was a drift from the churches, although Gipsy Smith, a colourful evangelist whose meetings at the Albert Hall were full to overflowing, had been successful with his simple and non-sectarian appeal.

At Oxford and Cambridge floppy, wide-bottomed trousers became fashionable and were christened " Oxford bags ". Somebody had invented the new craze of crosswords and fortunes were made by those who knew how to compile them. Fancy dress parties, some thought to be quite daring but which would be considered fairly dull nowadays, were the rage amongst groups called " bright young things ". And the development of the rayon industry meant that women of modest means could afford expensive-looking clothes and that the distinction between them and " ladies " could not be drawn as arbitrarily as it could have been, say, before the war. Short hair had become fashionable. For those with money to burn, " bottle-parties " (night clubs describing themselves as " parties " for the sake of legality), had sprung up all over the place.

A few days before the General Election a minor event had taken place which interested nobody very much. A man calling himself Hitler was tried and imprisoned for treason. In July the Union of Soviet Socialist Republics had been formally constituted.

The situation abroad reflected the tensions and turmoil which the war had created. The Franco-Belgian occupation of the Ruhr; a revolt in the Spanish army followed by a military dictatorship; an inflation in Germany which had reached astronomical proportions—one Rentemark was worth one billion of the depreciated paper marks.

Anthony Eden took to his job as an M.P. with a calculated enthusiasm. Everyone in his constituency who came to see him at the House of Commons commented on his unfailing courtesy, his transparent honesty and quick grasp of essentials.

The Eden charm had begun to develop. It was integrity plus friendliness. He made frequent visits to his constituency, and sat through almost every debate in the House, including many which he must have found dull or over his head.

Stanley Baldwin had, however, misjudged the temper of the electorate when he had forsaken Free Trade and made Protection his main platform. Because of this, he had no real majority in the House, and six weeks after forming his government a unique constitutional situation arose. Baldwin had counted on Liberal support, but did not get it. On an amendment to the King's Speech the Liberals, under Asquith, supported Labour, and the Conservatives found themselves out of office on a vote of no confidence.

It is not surprising that Captain Eden, an unknown back-bencher, should not have been heard of yet; the Government was trying to get established, and in the confused and abnormal situation, had failed.

Meanwhile King George V invited J. Ramsay MacDonald, as leader of the second largest party in the House, to form a government. On January 22nd, 1924, Britain had its first Labour Government, and Captain Eden, M.C., was not only a back-bencher but a member of His Majesty's Opposition.

The new Labour Government was as weak as the government it had ousted. Like the Conservatives, the Labour members were outnumbered and could only depend, like their predecessors, on Liberal support. A full-blooded programme of Socialism was something which Ramsay MacDonald's government could not hope to implement. At one moment measures to increase the Navy were supported by the Conservatives; an increase in subsidies for building working-class homes was supported by the Liberals. They had little to propose regarding the curse of unemployment, but some useful work was done in securing the adoption of the Dawes Report on German reparations, which produced a slight improvement in relations with Germany which was to last for a few years.

Eden's maiden speech in the House of Commons was made on February 19th, 1924. He spoke in support of a resolution proposed by Sir Samuel Hoare pressing for an Air Force adequate to resist attack " by the strongest Air Force within striking distance of her shores ".

The Conservatives could not hope to dissuade the Labour Party members from their pacifism, which had a strong emotional appeal to the electorate after so many years of bloodshed, which had left hardly a family in Britain unscathed. The cry was for Disarmament at any cost. Mr. Leach, Labour Under-Secretary of State for Air, insisted that preparedness for war only made it more inevitable, and that those who prepared most suffered most.

In this atmosphere Sir Samuel Hoare pointed out that when he became Air Minister in 1923, at a time when war looked like breaking out again, Britain had a first line air force of only twenty-four planes. He moved a resolution by which the House " whilst earnestly desiring the further limitation of armaments so far as is consistent with the safety and integrity of the Empire, affirms the principle laid down by the late Government and accepted by the Imperial Conference that Britain must maintain a Home Defence Air Force of sufficient strength to give adequate protection against air attack by the strongest air force within striking distance of her shores ".

Anthony Eden, in support of this resolution, rose to his feet with a prepared speech. It was short, modest and unimpassioned, yet unstimulating though it is to read now, one must admit the clear foresight of Anthony Eden as regards the implications of aerial warfare and the urgent need to prepare defences in time.

" In the first place," Captain Eden warned the House, " it is not in the nature of things possible to provide hastily and at a moment's notice for air defence; and, in the second place, the heart of the country, the City of London, is especially vulnerable to attack from the air. For these reasons I hope that the Government will not be tempted too much by sentiment . . . and will, as a matter of insurance, protect the country from the danger of attacks from the air."

This reasonable warning elicited from the Under-Secretary a reiteration of his belief in pacifism and the effectiveness of being unprepared. To this Captain Eden replied that, on the contrary, attack was the best form of defence; he added, hastily, what he meant by this: that Britain must be able to meet attack with attack. He reproached those members who adopted " the attitude of that very useful animal, the terrier, and roll on their backs and wave their paws in the air with a pathetic expression," but that was not the line on which we could hope to insure the country against air attack, " the greatest peril of modern war ".

Within seventeen years Eden's words were to come true, and high explosive bombs, oil bombs, land mines and incendiary bombs were to come screaming down upon the " vulnerable " City of London, killing four hundred people in a single night and injuring thousands. Captain Eden's maiden speech might be pedestrian and its attempt at humour laboured, but it was sincere and to the point. He had seen enough action to know what war implied; he could not labour under the delusion that the nations of the world had abolished war as an instrument of policy—there was nothing in the international situation to indicate that they had. He was to be one of the hardest workers for international security; he was to preach peace with a fervency that brooked no question; but even in his twenties he was a realist. He had learned, very young, to recognise facts for what they were and not deliberately to evade them.

A few weeks later—on April 1st, 1924—Captain Eden was to show that an obscure back-bencher could be well informed on foreign affairs. This time he was concerned with Britain's relations with Turkey, a country of which most British people were ignorant; we knew little, and that little was unpleasant —that the Turks had fought against us during the war; that they had shown great savagery in their sacking of Smyrna; that they had unseated a monarchy. Carlyle's phrase, " the unspeakable Turk," had been quoted with great effect by newspapers and magazines.

Eden, however, realized that the Ottoman regime had been finally discarded and discredited: the modernisation of Turkey —however ruthlessly Mustapha Kemal pursued it—was an event of enormous importance in the Middle East. In speaking during a debate on the Second Reading of the Treaty of Peace (Turkey) Bill, which was to implement some of the clauses in the yet unratified Treaty of Lausanne, which had been signed in July, 1923, Captain Eden had a decided advantage. He had actually visited the country under discussion and could speak with authority.

Not every politician's speeches may be read in retrospect and proved sound in their judgment. Nobody could tell for certain which way Turkey was going. Yet Eden felt in his bones that the disagreement between Turkey and Britain must be temporary, and that friendship between the two countries was worth trying for. At other Conferences, he reminded the House, Britain could talk as a victor to the vanquished, and could feel supported by the other Allies. The case of Turkey was different. Flushed with her triumphs against the Greeks, resentful of British sympathy with the Greeks and well aware that the Allies at Lausanne were disunited, Turkey had dug her toes in.

We were fortunate, said Eden, to reach any agreement at all in our weak bargaining position. I doubt if his reference to the Turkish army, " fresh from a great victory, proud, *and justly proud* of the achievements of their armies," went down very well with the Greeks. Nor am I greatly enthused with his sophistry on the question of how Christian minorities could expect to be treated by the Turks. It was being urged that they were insufficiently protected by the Treaty; such guarantees had been sought, but were not forthcoming and, in any case, we were unsupported by others. " What has been the history," he asked, " in these matters of minorities? Have we not over and over again obtained in treaties Turkish guarantees for the protection of Christian minorities, guarantees which were then deemed adequate, and has there ever been an occasion on which those guarantees have been of the slightest use in defending those minorities? Better, then, to achieve protection for such people by friendly negotation than by insistence on clauses ".

Eden was sure of one thing: that the causes of the revolution that had overtaken Turkey went very deep, and that the new State would be a power in the Middle East and one with which we should cultivate friendly relations. At the end of the war Turkey felt paralysing holds upon its future as a nation. " Is is to be wondered," he asked, " that they made a supreme national effort to free themselves and, that effort having been successful, is it to be wondered at that nationalism reigns in Turkey at this hour? It was nationalism that saved Turkey; it is nationalism that rules Turkey to-day." Eden's plea becomes almost eloquent. He believed, he said, in " the promise of great and increased happiness to come " and in increasingly friendly relations between Britain and Turkey.

Eden's belief that " as time goes on other influences will prevail, and that a spirit of toleration will make itself felt " was to prove true. Like his maiden speech a few weeks earlier, it can be read in 1955 without diffidence by the man who delivered it.

Ramsay MacDonald's prestige was undoubtedly enhanced by his successful handling of the Dawes Plan: so far discussions about German reparations were based on passion rather than reality; "squeeze her until the pips squeak" had been the popular feeling. Now a committee of informed experts had examined the whole question, and an American, General Dawes, was elected chairman. Their long and complicated report recommended, in effect, the formation of an International Transfer Committee to which reparations should be paid. The Committee were to decide, on the basis of their specialised knowledge, what Germany could and could not pay; to act as collector, and to see that reparation payments were made in the currency of the creditor states.

Mr. MacDonald convened a conference in London of all the interested parties, brought his persuasive eloquence to bear on the touchy and suspicious M. Herriot of France, and as a result the Conference worked out a plan by which America would lend Germany £40,000,000 as an essential preliminary to economic recovery—without which, of course, Germany could not pay her reparations. German representatives were then invited to London, the plan was accepted and France undertook to evacuate the industrial Ruhr within a year.

Anthony Eden had little to say about all this. But he followed with the keenest interest the Anglo-Russian Treaty negotiated by Ramsay MacDonald. It was a Treaty bitterly opposed by Eden's party, for MacDonald had reversed Lord Curzon's policy and shown almost precipitate haste to recognise the Bolshevik government. He had sent a note recognising the Union of Socialist Soviet Republics as *de jure* rulers of Russia, and had invited it to send delegates to London to discuss the question of Russian debts to Britain and the wider question of friendly relations.

MacDonald's feelings towards the Russian revolutionaries was, of course, nothing new. There had been an abortive rising in 1906, and when, two years later, King Edward VII paid a visit to the Czar, MacDonald had protested at his " hobnobbing with a bloodstained creature ".

Now feelings ran high, and the end of the first Labour administration was in sight. MacDonald, in accordance with his constitutional rights, had initialled the Treaty although requested by the Conservative opposition not to do so until authorised by Parliament. In defiance of this request, MacDonald did as he pleased: as Prime Minister he could act for the Crown and argue on the merits of his action afterwards in the House of Commons. Yet although he had promised that he would not offer the Russian Government a loan, it transpired that the Treaty did in fact provide for a loan to Russia. There was a further loss of face to the Labour Government due to the withdrawal of a prosecution for sedition instituted against a Communist journalist.

Anthony Eden was as indignant as his Party at the way in which Britain had been committed to relations with Russia without Parliament being consulted sufficiently. He was especially concerned at the inclusion of Maxim Litvinoff on the Anglo-Russian Commission. " Does the Government know that Mr. Litvinoff was expelled from Sweden and Denmark in 1919? " he asked. Some years later Eden himself was a guest in Moscow and had many dealings with him in connection with the League of Nations.

Most of Eden's speeches during the short lifetime of the Labour Government might be described as sound, though dull. He had some criticism to make of the fees charged for secondary education, and of the Government's wish to prevent art treasures leaving the country by an " appeal to private enterprise ". Private enterprise, snapped Captain Eden, would be immune to such an appeal; we should follow the example of Italy and prohibit the export of art treasures altogether. Furthermore, he hoped children would be encouraged to see good art and be allowed time enough to understand it. He quoted, as an example of the unimaginative presentation of priceless art treasures, his own experience in a famous Italian art gallery. " This," said the guide, " is the famous Titian room. This is

Photo: Picture Post

Captain Anthony Eden and Miss Beatrice Beckett after their wedding at the fashionable St. Margaret's Church, Westminster, in November, 1923.

Photo: Picture Po

As Lord Privy Seal in 1935, Anthony Eden accompanied Sir John Simon, then British Foreign Minister, to Berlin. This picture with Hitler was taken at his Chancellery in Berlin.

the famous picture of Venus, and the lady was seventeen years of age when she was painted. Now we will pass on to the next room "!

The dissolution of the Labour Government was due to an accumulation of critical circumstances. In October, 1924, another General Election was held, which was important from several points of view. The public was understandably sick of all these vaccillations. The Liberals were discredited on one hand for helping the Labour Party and on the other with sustaining the Conservatives, so that they earned the distrust of both left and right; and the middle classes were thoroughly alarmed at the kid-glove policy towards Russia, a revolutionary state that openly talked of overthrowing capitalism in other countries.

Anthony Eden, of course, contested his old seat at Warwick and Leamington, this time without the opposition of the colourful but disillusioned Countess of Warwick. It was a straight fight with the Liberal candidate who had stood at the last election.

The Election resulted in an overwhelming victory for the Conservatives. The Conservative Party returned with 413 seats in the House of Commons against Labour's 151 (a drop of 40 seats on the previous election) and the Liberal Party's pathetic 40 (a drop of 119 seats). Thus Labour had lost nearly a third of their seats, the Liberals had gone into a decline from which they were never to recover—as a Party they were virtually annihilated—whilst the Conservatives now had a working majority which could, and perhaps did, make them complacent.

Anthony Eden was returned, this time with a greatly increased majority, in circumstances infinitely more favourable to his political advancement than a year ago. For one thing, although Captain Eden attracted scarcely any attention in the press, and was so little known to the public that *The Times* did not even print a photograph of his wedding in 1923, Stanley Baldwin was watching Eden's progress. In the real sense of the word, Captain Eden had now begun to climb the political ladder.

SIX

In Search of Promotion

THE new Conservative Party was now back in office with an overwhelming majority. Baldwin was Premier for the second time, Mr. Austen Chamberlain became Foreign Secretary, Birkenhead was made Secretary of State for India, Sir William Joynson Hicks Home Secretary and Lord Curzon President of the Council.

The Conservative Party now boasted a greater measure of unity than it had enjoyed for some time. It also welcomed back to the fold the voluble and irrepressible Winston Churchill, who had walked out of the Conservative Party twenty years before in disagreement over tariff policy, and had rejoined on the eve of the November, 1924 General Election. For a time Churchill had been wandering and experiencing some curious reverses. In the election of 1922 he had been defeated at Dundee by a teetotaller Socialist, and early in 1924, standing as an Independent Anti-Socialist, he had been defeated by a Conservative candidate in a contest for the St. George's Division of Westminster.

The Government's first job was to attempt a revival of trade, and Mr. Churchill, now Chancellor of the Exchequer, restored the gold standard so that other countries would feel more confidence in the pound once it had a definite and unchangeable value in gold. Unluckily, the pre-war gold standard which was restored, proved to be too high, so that the pound had been raised 10 per cent. in relation to other currencies. Foreign buyers of British goods found that they had to pay 10 per cent. more for them: the result was a fall in British exports and practically to extinguish profits in a number of trades. This caused, in turn, a decline in coal exports, a crisis in the coal-mining industry and, as a climax to it, the General Strike of 1926. A scheme of partial protection of industry had been introduced, but it was in the coal industry that industrial depression was at its worst. The price of coal fell, and the mine-owners, to cut the cost of production, asked the miners to accept reduced wages and an increase in working hours—a proposition which no wage-earner could be expected to welcome. The miners refused to accept a cut, the operators retaliated by letting the wage agreement terminate on July 31st, 1925, as they were entitled to do, and Mr. Baldwin, to prevent a coal strike, agreed reluctantly to subsidise the industry until May 1st, 1926. Before that date a Royal Commission under Sir Herbert Samuel was asked to report on the conditions of the industry.

There were, at the beginning of Baldwin's government, over a million unemployed, and their plight was not met by talk of tariffs and exports and imports. Britain was never nearer revolution than in the early twenties, and although Russia was blamed for sending agitators to make a bad job worse, grave industrial unrest was inevitable without the sinister backing alleged by some of the more excitable of the popular newspapers.

British foreign policy abroad was in some respects simplified and in other respects complicated by the change of Governments. The Russians were informed that the treaty negotiated with them by Mr. Ramsay MacDonald would not be ratified, and a certain negative satisfaction could be derived from that. On the other hand, Mr. MacDonald had achieved some success in Franco-German reconciliation. Now that short-lived diminution of mutual suspicion between France and Germany was to end. The League of Nations, launched with so many protestations of altruism, was weakened by the absence of the United States, and it looked as though Britain, impoverished by the First World War, would be saddled with naval and military obligations with no corresponding guarantee that other nations would live up to theirs. A " Protocol for the Pacific Settlement of International Disputes " was accepted provisionally by the Assembly of the League, but as one commentator put it: " It has never been any part of British policy to sign a blank cheque." In October, 1925, came the Locarno Pact, by which France, Germany, Belgium, Poland and Czechoslovakia undertook in no circumstances to go to war with each other, but to settle any disputes by arbitration; Great

Britain and Italy undertook to see that this principle was applied in Western Europe, and France promised to see the Pact carried out in Eastern Europe—including Czechoslovakia, which she was later to desert in her greatest hour of danger.

The Locarno Pact was hailed as the end of war in Europe. It was, declared *Round Table*, " the definite termination of the war era ".

The Conservative Government was in a strong position numerically, but it was not strong in other senses. Unemployment did not decrease and large-scale programmes of public works, such as were being adopted in France and Italy, were rejected as impossible. Economy had been an election promise —especially economy in public expenditure. In fact, although Mr. Winston Churchill had promised a reduction of expenditure by £10,000,000, Government expenditure increased.

However, the Baldwin Government of 1924-29 did give Anthony Eden his first real chance in politics. He was made Parliamentary Private Secretary to Commander Godfrey Locker-Lampson at the Home Office. The Home Secretary was Sir William Joynson Hicks, known popularly as " Jix ". Now Eden's organising talents had plenty of scope.

Neither Anthony nor his wife was well-to-do, although both had come from extremely wealthy families. Their house in Mulberry Walk, Chelsea, was tastefully furnished and decorated and enlivened with examples of modern art—including, of course, Cezanne—but their standard of living was quite modest.

Quite early in his marriage Anthony had thrown most of his energies into politics. The administrative detail of his job, coupled with all the duties of a Member of Parliament— correspondence with constituents, visits to the constituency to keep the seat warm for the next election, question-time in the House of Commons, and debates claimed the bulk of his time.

In the early days of the Parliament Eden spoke on unemployment. His speeches were full of good intentions, though verbosity often cloaked his faulty logic. The Dominions and Colonies must be economically more closely-knit with the Mother Country; Britain must stop the drift from the land and encourage agriculture more; so, on one hand, he was advocating an increase in agricultural production at home and an increase of imports from such countries as Australia and New Zealand, whose products were mostly agricultural. How these two conflicting policies were to be reconciled was not explained. In saying of Britain that " we are too much industrialised and too little agricultural for the size of the country," he was stating not only a fact, but a dangerous fact—that Britain was an overcrowded island whose agricultural resources could only feed about half her population.

In the meantime, Anthony Eden had become a father. His eldest son, Simon Gascoign, was born shortly after the election, and had been christened at Chelsea Old Church on February 28th, 1925. Despite the work of running a house and raising a small boy, Beatrice helped her husband with his tasks as an M.P., pasting up his speeches in a cuttings book, reading the newspapers before he received them and forewarning him of any item she knew he was waiting for. At this time, she took a lively interest in his political work, but it was a more relaxed, take-it-or-leave-it attitude than his. She never did have his over-weening seriousness. Anthony was wedded to the habit of thinking before he spoke; this made for caution but not for spontaneity. Beatrice, on the other hand, kept up her dancing —she was very fond of jazz—and her painting (like Anthony, she was interested in art and no mean artist herself). She was never too tired for a party, and was a frequent visitor to the cinema, a pleasure which Anthony shared with her. But in general Captain Eden was absorbed with political thoughts. He would arrive back late from the House of Commons, his brief-case crammed to overflowing with order papers, notes and memoranda. He would often peruse them during dinner. Perhaps the conversation, when they had guests, would drift to lighter things: Alan Cobham's record-breaking flight from Croydon to Zurich in 13 hours 49 minutes, or the controversy over Epstein's *Rima* memorial in Hyde Park. But not so often.

In July, 1925, Anthony Eden had the most exciting and pleasant assignment of his career thus far. The Imperial Press Conference was to be held in Melbourne in September, and Eden was commissioned by the *Yorkshire Post* to attend it on their behalf. It was a decision which scarcely pleased the *Yorkshire Post* staff: qualified journalists with more experience and with a greater flair for writing in an interesting and intelligible way were being ignored in favour of somebody more influential and a friend of the proprietor. His journalistic work so far had not impressed the sub-editors. His parliamentary causerie was based largely on notes supplied to him by the *Post's* Lobby Correspondent; his copy needed a good deal of rewriting and words were often misspelled. The Lobby Correspondent, it seems, was known as The Voice that Breathed O'er Eden.

Geoffrey Grigson, the poet and critic who was at one time a sub-editor on the *Post*, has written of him: " Once a week a back-bencher's articles arrived from the House in his unformed hand on House of Commons notepaper . . . we had always to correct the spelling and insert, I remember, an extra ' g ' in ' exagerate ' ".

An examination of Eden's articles, based on his travels through Canada, New Zealand and Australia, with brief periods in such places as Honolulu and Fiji, amply confirm Grigson's judgment. He thinks almost like a bluebook. Canada is dismissed with a few cursory descriptions of the scenery, of the sort one might find in guide books. He has inherited his father's feeling for nature, but lacks his father's human and candid response to situations. He draws freely on painting for his analogies. Canada " is a country of painter's skies. A vast stretch of cloud overhead, cloudbanks grey and white, puffs of white cloud tinged with gold ". Enough, in fact, " to make a painter's palette itch." Somehow his immature poetic feelings never find expression. The desire to feel is clearly there, but one senses that he does not feel enough. He travelled thousands of miles, yet in not one of his articles is there an effective portrait of a human being as such; there are no snatches of dialogue that ring true, no belly-laughs, no exploration of forbidden or unexpected highways. Suddenly he will stop a piece of descriptive writing before he has become airborne; the style changes to that of a year book. He stops describing the clouds over Canada, which behave in a manner extraordinarily like that of clouds anywhere else, and digresses on the subject of immigration.

As he travelled, one vivid scene would replace another—but not in print. His comment on Waikiki is almost unbelievably banal: " On Waikiki beach rolls the surf. Let those ride it who can; it is a graceful art." But soon we are out of Waikiki, where the surf, for want of any other place, rolls on the beach, and we find that Fiji could export " cotton bananas, rice and cacao." In New Zealand Eden watched Parliament at work (here his powers of description are at their best, probably because he is asked to comprehend institutions rather than people; and what he sees is near enough to Parliament at home to be intelligible). He visited Auckland, which was so named by its founder, Captain Hobson, in gratitude to Anthony Eden's ancestors. In Australia he switches from a quasi-poetical description of the Blue Mountains to a description of a canning factory. Queensland's Labour Government prompted the remark that no portion of the British Empire " has had so many legislative experiments." Legislation evidently is an experiment when enacted by your political rivals, and can only be described as government when your own party is in power.

We see in these articles, which were reproduced in a book *Places in the Sun*, (now mercifully out of print), that Eden is usually at his worst when he tries to be humorous. He can smile, but it is not in his nature to laugh or make others laugh. Take this on the nationalisation of Queensland's railways:

" The State owns and controls the railways (some might add, subject to the railwaymen's control of the State, reminiscent of the mutual swallowing of two cobras; we begin by the tail) ".

One gets the impression that all his visits were too hurried, and that the literary predicament of a would-be artist who became an M.P. and then tried to be a journalist proved too much for him. The book had no impact, in spite of an introduction by Stanley Baldwin.

A good deal had happened during Eden's absence. The League of Nations had asked Britain to extend its connection with Iraq to 25 years or until Iraq joined the League; the historic Locarno Treaty had been signed, which some took to be an alliance that would prevent war in Europe, whilst others felt that even at this early stage in its life the League of Nations had been let down on its policy of collective security. Several leading Communists had been arrested in Great Britain on a charge of inciting to mutiny and later sentenced to prison.

Unemployment was as rife as ever, and the morale amongst miners deteriorated steadily. The Royal Commission on the coal industry had commenced its work. For Anthony Eden, 1925 had been a transition, a settling-in process during which he was taking much in but giving little out. He had crammed an immense amount of work into his year; his terrific application proved his ambition. " Softly, softly, catchee monkey " might well have been Eden's motto. It was his very unobtrusiveness which was enabling him to go far without being noticed. That, and his transparent honesty.

Anthony Eden showed during 1926 that his loyalty could be relied upon if a principle were at stake: he never was a fairweather friend. When the powerful *Daily Express*, owned by Lord Beaverbrook, and the *Daily Mail*, owned by Lord Rothermere, were attacking Baldwin for seeking friendship with Turkey (and on dozens of other counts, too) Anthony Eden sprang to his chief's defence. But his speeches were always carefully considered, factual, and usually dispassionate. He had none of the gifts of a demagogue—nor any of his more obvious faults. The quick, easy way to publicity and fame never appealed to him.

But 1926 saw Eden becoming more vocal, and speaking with authority on subjects about which he was informed, but not known to be informed. Such speeches were thorough and often packed with specialised knowledge. We find him, on February 19th, 1926, demonstrating his insight into Middle Eastern affairs, in which he had always been interested. During the debate on the Anglo-Iraq Treaty he pleaded for a loan to Iraq so that she could become self-supporting as quickly as possible. At the same time he ridiculed the Government for having a representative in Constantinople instead of Angora, the real Turkish centre. It was as futile, he said, amidst laughter, as it would be for a foreign power to station their Ambassador in Glasgow.

At the same time, Anthony Eden was writing political commentaries, art criticisms and snippets or featurettes for newspapers and magazines, especially the *Yorkshire Post*, his father-in-law's newspaper. The *Yorkshire Post* concealed his identity under a *nom de plume* which, even to-day, they will not reveal, whether from etiquette or a suspicion that the present Prime Minister has little to gain from a retrospect of his literary output I am not altogether clear. His journalistic talent was not marked, and but for the backing of his wife's father, he would have had difficulty in getting his work published. His writing lacked verve and zest; there was no humour in it; pervading everything he wrote was an awful earnestness, an implication that nobody had ever had such thoughts before. To quote just this extract from his article on " Conservatism To-day " in the *Saturday Review* of February 20th, 1926:

> " The complaint has been made in the past that the Conservative Party has lacked imagination, that in its meticulous devotion to form and detail, to precedent and to tradition, it has lacked the vision of true statesmanship; the genius of a Disraeli has been required to infuse vitality. Whatever modicum of truth that complaint may once have held, it would hardly be brought forward as serious criticism to-day. Rather the complaint might be that in the practice of excessive latitudinarianism essential principles had lost their strength . . ."

In that extract, from a much longer piece, one sees Eden at his worst: turgid and self-conscious, proud of platitudes, using words as though he is determined to impress the fourth form master. Yet, if one can bring oneself to accept his particular way of expressing himself—which can be hard going—one finds a consistency of attitude and integrity which compensate for a manifest lack of human warmth. Even in this same article, which I picked at random from scores of others, one gets a clue to his personality.

" The practice has to be reimposed *that, once elected, a Government should, in pursuit of its just ends, forgo popular favour and sometimes even court unpopularity.*" (A government should do what it believes right, whether people like it or not.) " There must," he said, " be no weakness born of blandishment. *The tendency to wait on popular favour is not only wrong; it will not prove successful.*"

That could almost be a presage of his stand over the appeasement of Italy, in disapproval of which he resigned as Foreign Minister. Quite a few of Eden's prognostications stand inspection. His warning that England was no longer an appendage to Europe but part of a scattered Empire makes sense to-day. " Singapore is not one whit less important than Portsmouth, Vancouver than Hull."

Eden's interventions on foreign affairs had not passed unnoticed. On July 28th, 1926, it was announced that Captain Anthony Eden, M.P., had been appointed Parliamentary Private Secretary to the Foreign Secretary, Sir Austen Chamberlain. His chief was heavily under fire for having returned from a meeting of the League of Nations at Geneva with little progress to report. Germany's admission to the League had been delayed. The Geneva Protocol outlawing war had been rejected but the Locarno Treaty would be made to work, however, even though Germany was not a League member. Both Ramsay MacDonald and Lloyd George tore this argument to shreds, and Eden, who was later to be the League of Nations' most consistent and militant supporter, found himself in the odd position of defending what amounted to a neglect of League principles. The Locarno Treaty was an agreement between a number of states to protect each other against war; but on a larger scale, this was the League's job, and the inference could only be drawn that the countries trusted each other but did not trust the League of Nations.

In a debate on the League he showed almost too great an ability to justify a bad case. The League of Nations had been started with high hopes, and war-weary people prayed that at last nations might agree between themselves and formulate plans for mutual protection against aggressor nations. But Eden's words could hardly have cheered the League's supporters then, for in effect he said much and said nothing:

" For my part I never expected in its earliest years the League would be called upon to give heaven-sent judgments, to formulate impeccable decisions. That is to ask too much. What I had hoped of the League, and do hope still, is that its greatest benefit will be the opportunities it will create for statesmen of different nations to meet and exchange those opinions."

That extract illustrates Eden's truly marvellous capacity for saying a lot without committing himself to anything. In effect he was justifying inaction. Why should decisions have to be " impeccable "—what reproach is the word intended to imply? In matters of life and death, as agreements on war surely are, isn't a certain definiteness to be sought? Was the League conceived simply as a talking shop? It was not, although, tragically, it became one. As to the Locarno Agreement, which he described as " a real and true agreement arising from a desire of the nations to make that agreement real," he cannot perhaps be blamed for not foreseeing the chaos it was to cause; many others failed to see it, too. But for the moment Captain Eden was somewhat in the position of a lawyer defending his client; his job was to take what favourable features he could find and defend the Government's policies as best he could. For the moment Eden was a die-hard Tory, though he was not to remain so, and had the Liberal Party not died he would probably have been happier in it.

A less attractive feature of Eden, revealed by a close analysis of all he said and did, is his genius for keeping out of controversy. It seems impossible that great events, such as the General Strike, which was a by-product of the disastrous Coal Strike, which began on May 1st, 1926, and continued for five months, should have provided Anthony Eden with no scope for comment or suggestions.

It is easy to see that at this period in his career, perhaps by conscious design, Eden was registering slowly but surely as a sound and informed observer of foreign affairs. There were innumerable domestic issues not simply of imminent but potential seriousness. The distress in the mining areas had been and still was intense, with some areas derelict; the burden of alleviating poverty from the rates in areas where hardly anybody worked was so great that the small nucleus of solvent or prosperous people had no choice but to decamp for some area where living was not so expensive. Unemployment continued to rise.

One marvels at the reticence of Eden over the General Strike. London was without transport of any kind, power plants had been taken over by the Government, newspapers ceased publication (though there were improvisations, such as the *Daily Mail* being flown from Paris, and an official broadsheet, *The British Gazette*, run by Mr. Winston Churchill). It had looked at times as though Britain were on the verge of revolution, and the hysteria of the *Daily Mail* lent colour to it: " Dissolve the T.U.C." and " Clear out the Soviets " were typical head-lines. In fact, the General Strike, in a general way, did a good deal of good, for both industry and labour were distressed at the consequences, and as a result the National Industrial Council, a joint standing committee of important trades unions and industrial bodies, was formed; it was to prove the keystone of the whole edifice of union-employer relations.

From his own point of view, however, Eden may have thought it wise to keep out of the controversies that raged around the strike. His interventions in 1926 were on subjects that most citizens found remote or dull; the debt settlement with France, for example, negotiated by Mr. Churchill. In effect we had agreed to wipe off France's indebtedness to Britain to the tune of £600 millions, without seeking from other nations—the U.S.A., for example—any modifications of our indebtedness to them. There were others who saw in this piecemeal handling of international questions a threat to the success of the League of Nations; could not war debts have been decided on principles that applied to everyone? Or was this gesture of Britain's just a by-product of the Locarno Treaty, a lubricant to make smooth military co-operation between the two countries?

Eden had no difficulty in defending the settlement. The settlement was a real benefit, he declared, though it was unfortunate that it should coincide with the fall of the Herriot Government, or, as he put it, " while France is undergoing another of her political crises." That France lacked stable government did not, it seems, make the debt settlement an investment that could produce no dividends. It was not, as he explained, a purely financial question. " I do not suppose that there is any member of this committee who has travelled in France in recent years who has not frequently noticed that France's indebtedness to us is a subject of anxious comment and conversation " (a long-winded way of saying " France wishes she didn't owe us anything, and doesn't know how to pay us ") and—an aphorism which debtors should engrave in golden letters over the doorways of their insolvent households—" Indebtedness creates friction."

On this supposition nobody ought to give credit or demand it; but the neutral, conciliatory tone in which these things were said made them sound convincing. And behind it all there was the comforting thought that here was a young man who would like to pull contestants apart and get them to co-operate, if he could.

Now Eden had his foot on the bottom of the particular ladder he wished to climb; now he was in foreign affairs, able to see the workings of Britain's complex foreign service. There is no doubt that Eden had always been intensely ambitious; his sustained application, the degree of concentration which underlay everything he did, the virtual subordination of his home life and his serious approach to things—indeed, his automatic preference for heavy and serious topics and causes as opposed to light-hearted ones—all point to a man who knows where he is going and is determined to get there. He had learned, for example, to cultivate people older than himself and to wear down their prejudice against youth; Baldwin was certainly no admirer of young men in Government, but he had taken to Eden on sight. Eden in fact gave the impression of compliance to his elders—an impression not altogether justified. Self-assertion and a critical attitude to his own Party and its policies developed in simple proportion to his own advancement. As an old soldier, he knew that consolidation is sometimes a good idea before attack.

Locker-Lampson, whose advice Sir Austen Chamberlain had sought in seeking a new P.P.S., was reluctant to let Eden go, but did so for the sake of the young man's career. He had enjoyed working with Eden and admired his ability in debate. Now, at twenty-nine years of age, Eden had gate-crashed that Holy of Holies, the British Foreign Office. The year closed with Eden making, very belatedly, a heated attack upon the Socialists for their attitude to strikes. Both strikes and lock-outs, he declared roundly, were "the scalping knife of the twentieth century, abhorrent alike to reason and truth, and yet it it still used." He pleaded for some instrument of arbitration, some objective and outside body to which these grievous disputes could be referred; the parties in the House should between them form some body which could speak with a united voice when the prosperity and stability of the country were at stake. But the suggestion was too vague and unspecific; in the existing climate of political partisanship there was no hope of it achieving any results. Eden's intervention in industrial matters was not a happy one, for he had little inside knowledge of the workings of industry; and although he was correct in supposing that the Communists had a vested interest in industrial unrest and were doing their best to promote it, he knew little of the emotional factors involved—the inevitable restlessness that men feel after a war, the very real suffering involved in widespread unemployment, the feeling of drift and disillusion. Nor did he realise that there was a feeling amongst industrial workers that the Bolshevik bogey was invoked whenever they attempted to better their conditions or query the validity of Tory legislation. But Eden, one feels, had clear ideas about what he sought: a position of importance in the Tory Party, and a career in foreign affairs.

SEVEN

Parliamentary Apprentice

THE ordinary day-to-day work of a Parliamentary Private Secretary left Anthony Eden little time to shine in debate—and, as I have noted, the subjects on which he chose to speak were usually those on which people at home did not feel enthusiastically either for or against him.

The general atmosphere was more relaxed. But it was an industrial peace not of goodwill but of exhaustion. J. H. Thomas, the leader of the National Union of Railwaymen, echoed the feelings of most workers when he declared that 1926 was a year to which most would gladly bid adieu. The upheaval had had a disastrous effect on the prosperity of Britain. Imports had dropped by over £77 million, whilst our export trade had dropped by over £150 million. Amongst employees and employers there was a general feeling of " enough's enough ". The need for a new spirit in industry was much talked about.

But some class warfare was still in the air. Speakers who had been to Moscow were active amongst the miners, describing the state as a new Utopia. There were still a million unemployed. It was not so much on these issues, however, that the rival parties crossed swords in the House of Commons. In China anti-British feeling flared up, and on January 4th a Chinese mob stormed the British and other concessions, causing the bulk of the British population to flee for safety to Shanghai, and for British settlements to leave the Yangtze Valley.

These disturbances in China were used by the Government as a justification for a hardening of attitude towards Russia, whose agents were suspected of having fomented hatred against the British. Anthony Eden, on March 8th, justified the sending of British forces and described the contestants in China as " prodding each other with a rather leisurely bayonet." I do not know how leisurely a prod with a bayonet can be: perhaps it depends upon who is the prodder and who the prodded. He did, however, insist on proper protection for the British in China, whose danger was under-estimated or ignored by the Socialist opposition.

On March 23rd, 1927, Captain Eden showed that as an ambitious Parliamentary strategist he could give some older members lessons. His Empire tour had not achieved very much, at least in his original role of special correspondent to a newspaper; but he had seen a good deal of the Empire's problems at first-hand. Now he had another opportunity to assert himself in that quiet, unobtrusive way which was to prove so effective as the years went by; to register with the House, in an indirect fashion, that he was much-travelled, well-informed and forward-looking. He moved a resolution concerned with Empire settlement. In effect, it was an appeal for increased migration from Great Britain to the Dominions.

The language of the motion is a little tedious—" very widely drawn " was how Eden described it. But his speech was excellent. Much thought and research had gone into it. He wanted migration to be " smoother, and even a little more rapid, than it is to-day." He was dissatisfied with the post-war figures for settlement overseas compared with pre-war years. Presumably, during his journeying through Australia and New Zealand, he had heard criticisms of unsuitable types which had arrived expecting an easy life and returned aggrieved to the more compact life of England. "One failure may have more influence than ten successes," he declared, and added the sensible suggestion that the failures, rather than the successes, should be investigated so that Britain might have sound criteria by which to speed emigration. In a roundabout way he implied that the picture of life in the Dominions was not accurately or convincingly conveyed by Dominion offices in Britain to intending settlers, and that those who left Britain to settle overseas often did so under the illusion that life would be easier. He pleaded for better public relations on the whole question—although the phrase was unknown then—and finished with a plea for stepping up trade with the Dominions, failing which we could not expect them to absorb newcomers.

The debate that followed was a long one in which, in compliance with Eden's plea that the issue might be regarded as a non-party one, tribute was paid to Eden's skill of advocacy. The question was put, and carried.

Until the autumn Captain Eden was not much in evidence in Parliament. The duties of a Parliamentary Private Secretary involve a good deal of day-to-day routine work, not excluding the responsibility for assembling facts and arguments for the Minister's use in the House of Commons. In a sense a P.P.S. is a sort of ghost; he must assemble the facts on almost anything at short notice, but he is also responsible for their accuracy. The least inaccuracy in a reply puts a Minister at the mercy of his political opponents in the House, who will immediately cast doubt on everything else he has said. But, like his late chief, Commander Locker-Lampson, Sir Austen Chamberlain had the highest regard for Eden's cool efficiency. He had the reputation amongst his superiors of being dependable, hard-working and always agreeable. The first two qualities could hardly be questioned, but the latter is more dubious. Not all who have worked with Eden are agreed on his charm; indeed, he would be a remarkable man if he could be as even-tempered as his calm exterior suggests. He was capable of hot flashes of temper, so much so that one colleague remarked, " Eden lives in a no-man's-land inhabited entirely by superiors and inferiors. He acknowledges no equals." An interesting comment.

Eden was able to keep aloof from such vexed questions as the Trade Disputes Act, which was a sort of legislative afterthought to the General Strike; its main purpose was to prevent the use of trade unions for subversive or illegal purposes, and especially to make another General Strike illegal. It aimed also to prevent men being intimidated into joining a union, or being forced to pay a political levy against their will.

For Anthony Eden, acting behind the scenes, it was quite a busy year. Frantic efforts were being made to woo France, and even the phrase *Entente Cordiale* was revived. There was a state visit from Doumergue of France, accompanied by much pomp and ceremony and the usual quota of obligatory gluttony. The break with Russia after the Arcos raid, meant much extra work, and constant briefing of Sir Austen Chamberlain, who was persistently badgered in the Commons about British foreign policy. The War Committee of the Egyptian Government was planning to transfer control of the Egyptian Army from a British officer to an Egyptian, and as token of Britain's astonished indignation, and to " exercise a restraining influence " three British warships were despatched to Egyptian waters.

In this year the question of disarmament, which was to absorb Anthony Eden later in his career, was making little progress, and in the eyes of some people Britain was the obstacle. A conference on Naval Disarmament was convened at Geneva between Britain, the United States of America and Japan, with Italy and France holding watching briefs. America and Britain could not, or would not, agree between themselves on who should have particular types of warships. Lord Cecil, a member of the British delegation, resigned in disgust and, in a moving statement, declared that for his part disarmament was an ideal he must seek without the Government's help. It was a trifle pathetic, perhaps, that two democracies who insisted that neither had any animosity against the other should care overmuch which had superiority in arms. By " security " Britain meant enough tonnage to protect her trade routes; by " parity " America meant the same tonnage, but distributed in cruisers of whatever size and armament she pleased.

" Inside the Cabinet," said Lord Cecil, " it seemed to me that I could do no more in the cause of disarmament." Lord Cecil had resigned for a principle, just as, at a future date, Anthony Eden was to claim to do. Cecil's altruism was unquestionable, his record of public service long and worthy, his attainments impressive. Resignation was a big sacrifice for him to make, a sacrifice which Eden belittled. He made Lord Cecil's firm stand in the cause of peace sound like exhibitionist petulance: " I believe the Noble Lord, Viscount Cecil, went there (Geneva) with the ecstasy of a martyr on his way to the stake. The stake in his case was quite unnecessary and entirely self-imposed, but it does not in any way affect the genuineness of his martyrdom." In other words, Cecil was a crank who need not be taken too seriously; no point of principle was involved, only difficulties of Cecil's own making. These " reasonable " words and their pedestrian humour show an interesting lack of charity; the great thing was to defend the

Government, whose delegation had not acquitted itself with much brilliance at Geneva. Progress was slight and slow. . . .

Ah, said Eden, "did anyone expect that progress would be other than slow?" Nobody should think that "you can bang and bustle the world into peace. That has been tried before: we saw it tried. We saw the attempt to drive the world into peace by leaps and bounds, and the result was a Celtic somersault." A little more credit, one feels, might have been accorded to Lord Cecil, who was simply an honest man who, however naïvely, insisted that nations should do something about disarmament instead of talking about it, and that some nation, sometime, must set a moral example. On many occasions in his life Anthony Eden has called for action. When political expediency has dictated, he has been as eloquent in the defence of inaction. Is progress slow? Well, you'll do more harm if you try to hurry.

If I linger here on long-forgotten events, or what may seem like irrelevant detail to a later generation, it is to spotlight an inconsistency. Later in life, Eden was to be one of the most vocal champions of collective security. In the interest of accuracy, however, it needs to be noted that at this stage in his career loyalty to his party was uppermost in his mind. For, in 1927, Eden attacked those who wished to see the Geneva Protocol become a reality.

Like most important measures, the title of the Geneva Protocol gave not the slightest indication of its immense importance to human beings. The first World War had made it as plain as a pikestaff that the accumulation of armaments creates an atmosphere of suspicion, a mounting arms race and an ultimate clash between nations as the tension becomes intolerable and suspicion gives way to fear. Therefore, at the Paris Peace Conference the statesmen present declared that "the maintenance of peace requires the reduction of armaments to the lowest point consistent with national safety and the enforcement of common action of international obligations."

There was to be a measure of compulsory disarmament of Germany, Austria, Hungary and Bulgaria, as a first step towards a more general reduction of armaments amongst the nations comprising the League of Nations.

But if nations were to disarm, they would need, as an

insurance against any single warmongering nation, a system of collective security. Singly, they might have too little to defend themselves; united, they could cope with the odd aggressor. That was the theory. After much debate, discussion and legal argument, the Geneva Protocol was formulated, providing for the peaceful settlement of all disputes. War was outlawed, and any nation guilty of it became an aggressor, against which " sanctions " could be imposed under Article 16. It was, however, rejected—a fatal blow from which the League never recovered.

No nation had renounced force as an instrument of policy, and for this of course Anthony Eden was not to blame. But his playing down of the League's initial failure, his soft-pedalling on what was a major international tragedy with immense implications for the future, shows how advocacy for its own sake sometimes sweeps him away. Instead of regretting the failure of the Protocol he actually attacked it. He reproached the Opposition for their " deep sympathy and love for it." He spoke with misgivings of " the extension of our commitments and greater responsibilities " that the acceptance of the Protocol would have brought. As for the application of sanctions against an aggressor, he put it this way:

> "The Protocol means that we have to undertake increased obligations if we are to join in applying sanctions to any *recalcitrant* members of the League." (My italics.)

My dictionary defines " recalcitrance " as meaning to refuse compliance, to be refractory. The hypothetical offending nation is made to sound almost innocent, as though the issue might be mere disagreement with other member nations. " Recalcitrant " does not evoke mental images of thundering tanks, screaming aeroplanes, the whine of shells and the agonised groans of injured men. Eden, a brave soldier, knew what war meant, and as a young Parliamentary Private Secretary he also knew that " recalcitrant " was a mild word indeed to apply to a potential aggressor. As to the smaller nations, he understood their enthusiasm for the Geneva Protocol, because " the smaller nations get all the advantages and this country has to bear the greater share of the burdens." On the whole, nobody could have made the whole business of collective security between nations sound less attractive. In another respect, however, he showed foresight and was justified in attacking the Opposition. On one hand, they clamoured for the acceptance by Britain of the Geneva Protocol and the unpredictable military commitments which it could involve in restraining an aggressor; on the other hand, they pressed for disarmament.

The fact is that in this debate, as in many others, Eden was primarily an echo of the Government's policy. Baldwin and his Cabinet pinned their faith in the Locarno Treaty, which seemed to them a more manageable scheme of local insurance. " For my part," Eden declared, " I believe that in the Locarno Agreement we have gone as far as we are entitled to go. I do not believe the Empire as a whole . . . is prepared to pledge its future to any further extent."

Later, in the course of Mr. Baldwin's Bill for giving " flappers " a vote, Eden had some curious things to say about government:

> " We have not got democratic government in this country to-day. We never had it, and I venture to suggest to the Hon. Members opposite that we shall never have it. What we have done in all the progress of reform and evolution of politics is to broaden the basis of our oligarchy."

Slowly and surely, Eden was becoming a name: a name one could associate with nothing in particular. But in Government circles, as distinct from the public, which had hardly heard of him, he had been identified as a hard working man, a harmless man and a loyal party supporter. In some senses, most decidedly, he was a very shy man; he has always had a knack of advertising his more trivial qualities and hiding his best gifts. He had a tremendous appetite for work. He never shirked the drudgery involved in coping with masses of documents. His personal life was often subordinated to his government work, which, in its nature, could not be confined to ordinary office hours. Although later his wife, Beatrice Eden, was to declare that politics bored her, and she couldn't face a future so crammed with treaties, documents, memoranda and minutes, and that their marriage was shipwrecked on the rock of politics, she took a lively interest in his work, often spoke at meetings with him, and acted hostess to a growing coterie of politicians and diplomats who came as guests to Mulberry Walk. Often she would watch the House of Commons in session when her husband was speaking. She would paste into a book press cuttings mentioning him, or articles written by him, most of them in the *Yorkshire Post*. But inevitably many of her pleasures could not be shared because her husband could not be with her to share them.

In 1928 Captain Anthony Eden devoted himself largely to administrative work in the Foreign Office. His chief, Sir Austen Chamberlain, was now 65, and was glad to have the assistance of a P.P.S. so many years younger and so attuned to his own way of thinking. Sir Austen had worked long and loyally in the public service, and could remember the day when England's naval supremacy was unchallenged, and when our foreign policy was based upon a series of alliances. A new complication arose from the world's preoccupation with international security and longing for peace. The League of Nations Covenant entitled a country to go to war after nine months if its opponent had refused to accept the unanimous decision of the League Council. Of course, nine months of passive resistance in face of a determined onslaught might well knock all the will to resist out of a nation; but there the ruling was, and in theory at least the possibility of war as a just weapon was presupposed. Similarly, the Locarno Treaty obliged the contracting nations to go to war if one of them should be attacked by Germany. War, therefore, was not outlawed, but simply prohibited as a means of imperialistic expansion, exploitation, coercion or malice.

Now, Mr. Kellogg, the United States Secretary of State, proposed the outlawing of war altogether, and badgered the European nations with such persistance that, almost to keep him quiet, the Kellogg Pact was signed in Paris. But it contained qualifications which would provide an easy get-out for any militaristically-minded nation. Nothing in the Pact " restricted or impaired in any way the right of self defence " —and what is or is not self-defence is often a matter of opinion. " Every nation is free at all times," said Mr. Kellogg, " and regardless of treaty provisions, to defend its territories from attack or invasion, and *it alone is competent to decide whether circumstances require resource to war in self-defence.*" It is hardly surprising that the nations whose plenipotentiaries signed this Pact (sometimes called the Pact of Paris) at the Quai d'Orsay on August 27th, 1928, did so without any feeling of heavy commitment. A country determined on aggression invariably makes accusations against and provokes incidents with its intended victim beforehand; there cannot be much peace—there certainly cannot be collective peace—if any nation can decide for itself what constitutes self-defence. But the dismal story of conflicting nationalisms in Europe made everyone reluctant to forego the right of action in an emergency; the feeling that one's national security might depend on whether or not a committee sat quickly enough, deliberated wisely enough and could translate its decisions into effective action quickly enough was pretty discouraging. The choice lay between old-fashioned military alliances disguised as non-aggression pacts, and wordy, amorphous " internationalism " of the sort so popular with Bloomsbury Socialists at the time.

Meanwhile, the Kellogg Pact was hardly signed before Eden's chief committed a major indiscretion in France. Britain and France, after much bickering over disarmament, had reached a compromise: we agreed, reluctantly, to accept France's contention that " reservists " should not be counted in with military forces—an absurd contention, since a reservist can slip into a uniform in ten minutes; France agreed, with equal reluctance, to accept Britain's claim that countries ought not to be permitted to use their shipping tonnage as they pleased, but should be restricted as to the *type* of cruiser they could build, especially the larger ones.

From this exchange grew something called the Anglo-French Convention. Chamberlain was pleased with his work, although his statement, during one of his visits to Paris, that he " loved France as one loves a woman, for her defects as well as for her qualities," did not go down too well. In any case, Germany, Italy and America were mortally offended. Germany saw in the " reservist " business a distinct threat to herself: a reserve simply means an army in reserve. To imply that it is something of which no account need be taken is manifest nonsense. France's fear of Germany and her desire to have a sufficient number of trained men on hand to cope with any future attack was—so recently after the long and terrible first World War—understandable. But Germany's reaction can be imagined. Germany needed no lessons in the military interpretation of harmless phrases.

All these negotiations kept Anthony Eden hard at work in his office within a stone's throw of Big Ben. Those who worked with him mentally pigeon-holed him as the born administrator and politician. The strange world in which, if you speak to the man in the office next door you must send him a written minute, (" We spoke, 14/2/28; yours of the 12th refers; we agreed no action") appealed to his meticulous and detail-loving mind. And to do him justice, in dealing with matters of moment, such detail is necessary; public affairs cannot be run on a basis of guess-work and memory. If no note is made of a telephone conversation at the time, either party can later interpret the conversation as they please.

The year 1928 is summarised in *Round Table* as " the eighth lean year ". Britain's post-war convalescence was pallid and protracted. Unemployment was widespread still in the coal, steel and textile industries, and in the winter of 1928/29 unemployment had risen again to a million and a half.

Now the long-drawn tragedy of the mining areas was reaching its climax. There were towns where the only places of activity were the Labour " Exchange '—where relief was handed out, not work—and the police station. So grave was the situation that a conference of Lord Mayors and Mayors of England and Wales was held at Mansion House. The situation of the mining areas, declared Mr. Neville Chamberlain, then Minister of Health, was the worst in living memory. A fund was launched by the Lord Mayor of London for the relief of miners' families, and Mr. Baldwin, not very willingly, agreed to give pound for pound.

It was a flat year, a mixed year, but one not without a gathering impetus in certain fields. The grandiose new Underground station had been opened in Piccadilly Circus. Now franchise had been extended to all over 21 by the Women's Franchise Act, whose course through the House had been assisted by some rather laboured humour from Anthony Eden. Suffragettes were now old-fashioned, and in the vanguard of feminism were women aviators, such as Lady Heath, who was the first woman to pilot a plane from Cape Town to London, and Amelia Earheart, who, with Wilmer Stultz, flew the Atlantic from Newfoundland to South Wales. Mrs. Anthony Eden, adopting with enthusiasm all the advances which the brave new world brought with it, took to flying herself, and liked it; at the time it was unusual for British women to fly very much. She took, with equal enthusiasm, to jazz, and both at home and at social parties she typified the bolder, less inhibited and more forward-looking attitude of a new generation of women. The tension that Fascism was to bring to Europe had not yet made itself felt. There was a gay set in London whose optimism and merriment were not, like gaiety in wartime, an escape from gloom, but a genuine faith in the future, a feeling that the first World War, with its ugly memories, was receding, that prosperity was returning. Her glowing vitality contrasted with the quiet preoccupation of her husband. She liked company for its own sake: Anthony sedulously fostered relationships that were likely to be influential. She might be content to dance into the early hours to the tune of " My Blue Heaven " or " Ramona "; Anthony, with an amused tolerance, would settle down in his study to read *Parliamentary Reports*, or Blunden's *Undertones of War*.

But all who knew them then felt that they complemented each other perfectly. Beatrice admired Eden's ambitions and application and did everything she possibly could to help him advance, often engaging in conversation at home with politicians and others whom she privately thought the most shattering bores. Anthony must have found her light-heartedness a refreshing change after the Gothic stuffiness of the debating chamber or his Whitehall office. The marriage barometer seemed to be set fair.

EIGHT

His Majesty's Opposition

STANLEY BALDWIN'S second Government, after four and a half years of rule, ended its days in an atmosphere of disillusionment. The complacency of Conservative spokesmen could not disguise the deep-rooted distress in industry—especially in coal, textiles, shipbuilding and the iron and steel trades. South Wales was desolate. Farmers were discontented at the dumping of foreign wheat in Britain, a move which forced them to reduce their prices. The Prince of Wales, as President of the Lord Mayor's Relief Fund, toured the distressed areas in the Northumberland and Durham coalfields. He was shocked at what he saw—the desert of slag-heaps, the rows of back-to-back houses, with their listless and pallid families standing and staring, the pathetic attempts of the miners to bolster their morale and fill their time by hymn-singing, football and such few handicrafts as demanded neither money, materials nor tools. " Something must be done," he said, a little unwisely for anyone with no political power. His real function on that occasion was to lend his moral support to the efforts being made by the Mansion House to raise money for relief.

The General Election of May 30th, 1929, was unremarkable except for the fact that it was the first in which everyone of 21 years and over, both men and women, was entitled to vote. Baldwin had hoped that his vote to the " flappers "—a term for young women in the early twenties—would induce them, out of gratitude, to vote Conservative at the following election. He also used a fatal electioneering phrase, " Safety First! " Safety for whom? And in what? In home affairs? Foreign affairs? The middle classes had liked and supported Baldwin, the cheery, John Bullish, pipe-smoking family man, the sort of man who knew about farming, who could be trusted, who thought before he acted. But the working classes were not sold on "Safety First!" The persistent unemployment might or might not have been the aftermath of war, but whatever the merits of that, the Conservatives had been unable to cure it. This was also the first General Election in which political broadcasts, as we now know them, were a feature.

It was an election without excitement, but from Anthony Eden's point of view, an easy one. His status in Warwick and Leamington was by now very high. His articles in the *Yorkshire Post*, if they had not stimulated, had at least not gone unnoticed and had kept his name before the electorate. *The Times* had become accustomed to reporting Captain Eden's statements in the House of Commons with increasing frequency. He had gained a reputation as a sort of benevolent Imperialist; and to be fair, his Imperialism had been less narrow than the pre-war variety. He conceived the Empire as a co-operative unit and a force for peace within a general fabric of collective security. His method of expressing himself has never been too happy, often lacking directness, warmth, humour, or any real contact with people; but he was developing a very effective sense of strategy and timing. He knew when to speak and when to be quiet. He knew, one feels, that as a young M.P. with a career ahead of him, the first essential was to be useful to others, to be wanted and needed by the Party of which he was a member. His rising status in the Conservative Party had been indicated by the fact that he was chosen at its last Conference in Yarmouth to move, on behalf of the Party and its representatives in the House, a resolution on the Reform of the House of Lords.

The result of the election was a victory for the Labour Party, whose seats were increased from 151 to 287. The Conservatives were out of office, with 260 seats as against their previous 413. The Liberal Party rallied very slightly, increasing their numbers from 40 to 60. The Labour vote had been split, many of its members disliking the extremism of A. J. Cook, whose pro-Soviet views had received wide publicity, and others who felt that Ramsay MacDonald had ceased to be the Socialist leader he once was, had veered too sharply to the right. Eden fought a three-cornered fight: and the increase in women voters since the last General Election was a factor most certainly in his favour: there were now more than 60,000 women voters on the electoral register of Warwick and Leamington compared with 40,000 previously. The debonair aristocrat with the imprint of youth still fresh on his features won easily. He was well-born, physically upstanding, beautifully dressed, exuding in his manner a way of life ordered, safe, uncontroversial and gallant—and in an area traditionally Conservative we may assume that the Flapper Vote helped him a good deal. It was Stanley Baldwin himself who once remarked, in cynical mood, that because of Eden's good looks " Anthony is good for 2,500 extra votes for the Conservatives in any constituency he visits."

How did Anthony Eden like being a member of His Majesty's Opposition in the House of Commons? The records of Hansard testify in a dusty way to his prodigious energy and insatiable appetite for the things that are purely political, statistical, blue-bookish and dull. Sir (then Mr.) Winston Churchill threw himself into the task of opposition with verve and zest, and the chamber reverberated to his glowing prose and salty sallies. He would stand up to Maxton (a highly individualistic Socialist whose barbed tongue belied a warm heart) with strength and glee, and everyone would enjoy and perhaps profit by the verbal ding-dong.

Anthony, by contrast, chose subjects that were solid and important and calculated further to impress the world with the fact that, though he might have youthful shoulders, the burdens of the world rested heavily upon them. He spoke hundreds of thousands of words in the course of the Labour administration: on Conversion Loans, Egypt, Housing, India, the League of Nations (a subject in which he was making a corner of his own), troubles in Palestine, Extra Territorial Privileges, Diplomatic Relations with Russia. True, he did not altogether disdain subjects of a more homely or human nature: he had acid questions to ask on the refusal to grant Leamington power as Supervising Authority under the Midwives' Act; he was worried about an outbreak of parrot disease in Warwickshire; and he defended that fine old British institution, capital punishment.

The more I look at Eden's career, the more I am amazed at the legend of infallibility which has gathered round his name.

For such gifts as he has his friends, Party and country can be grateful; but the popular conception of a drawing-room diplomat whose smooth exterior hides the steel beneath is not the whole story. As for clear thinking, throughout his parliamentary career Eden has uttered platitudes without number. Sometimes the head reels and reason departs at the mere contemplation of them; in some speeches he says everything and says nothing. Nothing is clean-cut, brief, direct.

But if his speeches lacked humanity, wit, pace and lucidity —as I feel they did, and usually still do—full marks are due to him for his energy. The study of the numerous subjects on which he spoke from 1929 to 1931 shows that he could have had very little leisure, despite the fact that he no longer had the duties of a Parliamentary Private Secretary to contend with. And, of course, he was by no means the only M.P. whose oratory was of indifferent standard. There were times when Ramsay MacDonald got lost in his own verbosity, whilst the clichés of the famous Socialist leader, J. H. Thomas, whose dropping of aitches were as much a symbol of his individuality as are Sir Winston Churchill's cigars, were unbearably repetitive. Margaret Bondfield had been charged with the unenviable task of reducing unemployment under the new Socialist administration. The Tories had been under fire for not doing so, but now the Socialists wished heartily that somebody else had the worry. For unemployment increased until there were over two million workless.

During this period of Socialism, Eden was in good heart and sound health. He worked hard, paid frequent visits to his constituency, kept abreast of Party policy and never lost an opportunity to score a point against his political opponents. Not that the Government which had just been ousted could boast a high measure of success in any of its achievements. The financial policies of Mr. Winston Churchill had not come up to expectations; Sir Austen Chamberlain, former Foreign Secretary and Eden's old boss, had antagonised America, Germany and Italy by giving in too easily to France's demands over her right to train reservists.

A Government report on finance and industry, known as the MacMillan Report, forecast a budget deficit of £120,000,000. With her budget unbalanced, the unemployment insurance fund bankrupt and foreign trade shrinking constantly, Philip Snowden had to admit in the House of Commons, when challenged by Mr. Neville Chamberlain on behalf of the Conservative opposition, that the national position was very grave. It was strange for a Socialist to have to produce a Labour Budget whose main recommendations were cuts in the salaries of teachers and reductions in unemployment benefit. But on August 13th, 1931, a Cabinet committee said flatly that the crisis could only be met by " equality of sacrifice "—half the Budget deficit to be found by fresh taxation, the other half to be found by economies in public expenditure. Eleven days later Ramsay MacDonald declared that he intended asking King George V to accept the resignation of the Labour Government. Most people expected that a Conservative Government would be formed, but instead it was announced that Ramsay MacDonald was to continue as Prime Minister of a " National " Government, an emergency affair made up of four Labour men, four Conservatives and two Liberals. Mr. Stanley Baldwin was made Lord President of Council, Philip Snowden Chancellor of the Exchequer, Sir Herbert Samuel Home Secretary, and Mr. Neville Chamberlain Minister of Health.

It was a curious development in British politics, giving rise to a feeling of political apathy and confusion from which only one party—Oswald Mosley's Fascist Party—could hope to profit. But to propound a policy acceptable to Conservatives, Liberals and Socialists was not too easy. For a few weeks this hotch-potch of a Government remained in office and on October 27th, one of the strangest General Elections in history was held. What was to be the rallying cry of such an election? Here was no clash of obviously opposed policies, and as both the major parties had failed dismally to make any impact on unemployment, such arguments would seem to be academic. It was decided to make a broad—and vague—appeal to the electorate; to ask for " a free hand "; to say, in effect, " the country's in a mess; you've *got* to give us power to do as we like."

But there was a dangerous mood about. A National Hunger March of 2,500 people bearing a petition signed by a million unemployed, demanded an abolition of the Means Test—a device by which unemployment benefit was made more difficult to get. The Means Test was quite simply an economy measure, a deliberate attempt to cut down expenditure on unemployment relief. The unemployed, especially the miners of Wales, were furious with Ramsay MacDonald; they felt they had been betrayed by the very people who should be protecting their interests. There were demonstrations in Parliament Square and police charges had to be made.

The General Election resulted in 554 seats for the National Government candidates and 61 for the Labour Opposition. The Government M.P.'s included 471 Conservatives, 35 National Liberals, 33 Liberals and 13 National Labour. Had the Conservatives chosen to fight the election on an ordinary Conservative programme, it is fairly certain that they would have won easily.

Eden's appeal to the electorate was brief and to the point: the country was in a mess and national unity was essential for recovery. On this appeal he was returned with the huge majority of 29,000—an index of his enviable status in the public eye. Still in his thirties, he had held down jobs of the highest responsibility, applied himself to complex and often thankless problems, studied all manner of dull but vitally important subjects and built up a reputation for unhurried efficiency which was to carry him on to greater honours still. As it was, the " National " election was a turning-point in his career. This time he was made Under Secretary of State for Foreign Affairs. As an Opposition speaker he had been by far the most energetic and informed of the speakers on foreign affairs. James Johnston, in his book, *A Hundred Commoners*, gives this impression of Anthony Eden as he was then:

> " He is highly polished, has the bearing and manner of an aristocrat that gives him distinction in a House where the aristocrat is so much rarer than in Parliaments of the past . . . he is intensely interested in politics, take his parliamentary duties most seriously, devotes much study to political questions and spares no labour to make himself efficient. . . . He has done what only a few politicians take the trouble to do—he has trained his mind, and then set himself to master the subject he has desired to discuss. . . . He thinks for himself and has a measure of intellectual independence."

The National Government was to remain in power until May, 1940, giving that continuity to Eden's career which enabled him to consolidate his position, add to his experience, enlarge his contacts and generally to build up on a foundation of work, influence and knowledge; there was, of course, to be his widely-publicised resignation in 1938. But the point I am making is that he was irrevocably associated in outlook and loyalty with a party that was to remain in power for a very long time. By the age of 34 he had become a Junior Minister in one of the most important government ministries, the Foreign Office. To the public he was still a shadowy figure; and if at times his logic wandered, or he addressed people somewhat like a schoolmaster who expects nothing from his class, there were times—especially when speaking of disarmament—when his speeches showed not only skill in assembly but a prophetic insight as well. This was no better illustrated than by his contribution to the debate on disarmament on June 29th, 1931 —a few months before his appointment as Junior Minister. He warned the House that the League of Nations had been weakened. To the sentimentalists who would have seen Britain stripped of the last vestiges of armament, he pointed out that at the end of the war we had scrapped seven-eighths of our Air Force, and " it was the finest Air Force at the time in any part of the world, and we are the most vulnerable nation to air attack in Europe." And while Britain had reduced her arms, France had increased hers by 140 per cent., Italy by 40 per cent. and the United States by 160 per cent. " The seeds of war psychology," Eden declared, " still exist in Europe." There was not yet that instinct to refer disputes to the League of Nations. And in certain countries (which Eden did not specify) children were being brought up along militaristic lines. Ten years later bombs were to rain on Britain in confirmation of his words; but in 1931 it was not everyone who saw, as Eden did, that the revival of nationalisms in Europe demanded that Britain should not leave herself defenceless.

The return of the National Government proved that for the public, recovery mattered more than politics. There was a real hunger for firm and wise leadership and a general realisation that Britain was faced with a serious crisis. One interesting example of that was the Government's appeal to people to pay their income tax fully and promptly; it really worked. Without

Photo: Topical Press

Sybil, Lady Eden, mother of Sir Anthony Eden, dressed as Catherine of Braganza for an historical pageant. This photograph was taken in 1936.

Beau Brummel of 1938. Eden's sartorial splendour had become a byword throughout the world.

Photo: Mirrorpic

Photo: Kemsley Picture Service

Anthony Eden and the first Mrs. Eden saying good-bye to their son Nicholas on leaving for the United States in 1938.

In Camp at Beaulieu, Hants., in August, 1939. Mr. Anthony Eden was second-in-command of the 2nd Rangers, King's Royal Rifle Corps, the regiment with which he served in the First World War.

Photo: Keystone

proper receipts from income tax there was but a forlorn hope of balancing the budget. The unemployment figure stood at two and a half million.

Eden's appointment in Ramsay MacDonald's first and short-lived National Government was due to Lord Reading, who was Foreign Minister from August 25th to November 5th, 1931. When the country sent back the National Government with a huge majority, Lord Reading asked to be excused the appointment, and Sir John Simon, a Liberal whose views could scarcely be distinguished from those of the younger Tories, was put in as Foreign Minister. Simon was a cautious man not over-fond of making decisions, and one may assume that the choice of the young, active and sometimes sharp-tempered Captain Eden was Baldwin's rather than his own.

Simon had a long and distinguished career behind him, but his gifts were of the highly disciplined and organised kind; his legalistic mind tended to see so many sides to a case that you were left wondering, sometimes, what the resolution of it all was. As a lawyer, and as a worker on the Committee that considered the future of India, he had shown tremendous acumen. Concentration, a capacity for immense detail, perception—he had all these. Warmth, wit and executive energy did not come easily to him. And, above all, his job demanded elasticity of mind and sense of action. Those who knew Anthony Eden wondered how the two would get along, but Eden always did have a special gift for getting on with his elders.

During the recent election a war had started. It was not called a war, of course. On September 18th, 1931 Japanese troops seized a Chinese army barracks at Petaying following the destruction by Chinese of a portion of railway track in Southern Manchuria. The Japanese also seized the aerodrome and arsenal at Mukden. There were questions in the House of Commons, which Eden answered as fully as the incoming despatches permitted. This hint of resurgent Asian militarism seemed scarcely to register with Members of Parliament; but the problem was still a real one when Eden took up his post under Sir John Simon.

However, the matter, on being referred to the League Council, was for a very short while resolved—so far as the rest of the world was concerned—by the Japanese claim to have no territorial ambitions in Manchuria.

Nobody bothered about Manchuria during the election, and when Eden found himself back at the Foreign Office the country was absorbed with three main topics—recovery, reparations and disarmament. A Disarmament Conference was due to be held in Geneva on February 2nd, 1932 (the First International Conference on Limitation and Reduction of Armaments), and on January 14th the Lord Mayor of London convened a meeting of Lord Mayors and Mayors of England and Wales and Provosts of Scottish burghs in connection with it. His object was to impress upon them the importance of the conference, presumably that their citizens might better understand the issues involved.

Sir John Simon did not attend this gathering, but in a letter warned it that too much hope should not be entertained of a settlement. Mr. Eden, addressing the meeting, said that the British Delegation would be able to attend the Conference with a clear conscience because British Governments, irrespective of party, had since the war set an example in disarmament. Britain was the only great power not to increase her armaments during the last five years. The Army was little more than a police force; the Navy had been whittled down; and we were fifth amongst the air powers. We could go no farther than this (" unilateral disarmament " was the miserable term coined by officialdom to describe Britain's rather perilous altruism) and now other countries, too, must set an example.

Eden, as an expert on League of Nations matters, followed the Disarmament Conference at Geneva with anxious interest. He had, during Baldwin's administration, defended Great Britain's rejection of the Geneva Protocol, because Britain's obligations would have been too vaguely defined; there appeared to be no potential limit to our military obligations under it. But the dropping of the Protocol in favour of the Locarno Treaty, a localised military alliance, or mutual insurance scheme, was no substitute for it.

But the Disarmament Conference, which had taken years to convene and which was attended in Geneva by representatives of sixty nations, including the United States of America and the Soviet Union, soon got lost in matters of detail. Fine words could not camouflage the atmosphere of mutual distrust; diplomats who for the best part of a lifetime had used politeness and pleasant words as mere weapons of expediency could not convince themselves that their counterparts from other countries could be actuated by sincerity. As we are, so we judge. And so an issue on which the lives of millions depended was befogged with tedious arguments about the calibre of guns, the tonnage of cruisers and the definition of a soldier (some would include reservists and some would not). France wanted a centralised armed force to be at the disposal of the League in case sanctions had to be applied against an aggressor nation. Germany insisted that trained reserves should be included in a country's strength. Russia wanted a sustained and accelerated reduction of armaments, culminating in their abolition; but countries doubted her good faith and realised that facilities for an international body to ensure that any promises Russia made were also kept would never be forthcoming.

And so argument followed argument, committee spawned committee until the deliberations were so protracted, scattered, detailed and unco-ordinated that nothing tangible or effective could emerge from it all. It was a tragedy and a precursor of greater tragedies. Even whilst these academic discussions were going on the Japanese were consolidating their hold on Manchuria and installing a boy-Emperor, Pu Yi, as dictator under their direction. Fighting between Chinese and Japanese had broken out and the Japanese bombardment of Shanghai was the most severe artillery barrage since the first World War. The primary object of those who created the League of Nations had been to prevent war, but in this instance, as in so many others, the League had no effective means of preventing it.

Whatever else could be claimed about Britain's efforts at the Disarmament Conference, it had to be admitted that the delegation was impressive. It was headed by the Prime Minister, J. Ramsay MacDonald; Sir John Simon, Secretary of State for Foreign Affairs; " Jimmy " Thomas, then Secretary of State for the Dominions (later to resign in disgrace following an enquiry into a leakage of information before the declaration of the Budget); Viscount Hailsham, War Minister; the Air Minister; the First Lord of the Admiralty; and Mrs. Corbett Ashby. They were helped in their abstruse deliberations by one secretary-general, 30 experts and other officials, 19 clerks and typists and five messengers.

In February Mr. Eden, asked by Mr. Morgan Jones in the House of Commons whether as an answer to Japanese aggression in China, sanctions would be applied against her under Article 16 of the League Covenant, was able to give the short answer: No.

A good deal has been said about Anthony Eden's thoroughness. His duties at the Foreign Office, even in 1932, quite often exceeded ten or twelve hours a day, whilst question-time in the House of Commons made further inroads upon his time; as Under-Secretary he was constantly under fire on matters of policy. Between February 2nd and February 9th, for example, he had to speak in the House on twenty different subjects, ranging from defaulted shares held by British subjects in the Anglo-Argentine Tramways Company, to the Disarmament Conference; from loans to Japan to unemployment insurance in Switzerland. Even at this stage in his life, Eden was inclined to overwork in the public service. It is a good fault, though in later years it was to play havoc with his health and bring him dangerously near to physical collapse.

In Europe the shadows gathered. France was obsessed with the need to be strongly armed; Germany was coming more and more under the hypnotic sway of Adolf Hitler; in Italy Benito Mussolini was saying such things as " Better to live like a lion for a day than a lamb for a thousand years "—and little boys as young as eight or ten were joining the *Balila* and learning to train with real bayonets. In Spain the grinding poverty of the agricultural workers had led to seething unrest and to bloody riots at Castilblanco, and risings of Communists and anarcho-syndicalists coupled with strikes all over the country.

An odd time to talk of peace, but Anthony Eden, in his sincere and plodding way, did so often. In a speech to the Rhodes Trust dinner on June 17th, 1932, Eden talked of peace and of his own conception of British Imperialism. It is not one of his best speeches; it is in his " ten-words-do-the-work-of-one " style. In a wordy way, he disabused his listeners of any hope of being isolationist:

> "There is in this country a school of thought whose conception of British Imperialism is that we should concentrate upon the problems that are especially our own and that we should ignore and even repress every inclination to take our part in the troubles of others. However attractive at first sight, such a conception is not wise politics. There can be nothing exclusive in modern British Imperialism. There is no room in this world for isolationists."

He attacked "excessive indulgence" in tariffs. He pleaded that every country had its part to play in international affairs. He admitted something that was, to most people, painfully obvious that—" the improvement in European relations . . . that we hoped to see after Locarno has not fructified." The endless wrangling at the League of Nations must have disheartened him, as it did the rest of the world, for he said:

> "While one-half of Europe has been dominated by apprehention and the other by impatience there has been the tendency to pay too much attention to the mechanics of peace and too little to its fundamentals. There is no real substitute for understanding, and when nations drift apart it is of little use to construct elaborate machinery for which there is no immediate call."

The post-war generation must concentrate its thoughts on "the essentials of peace"—but, alas, he had not introduced any essentials which were in any way new. Understanding is indeed essential—but how to go about it? However, one can't put everything into a short speech, and it was well meant.

In his Rhodes Trust speech Anthony Eden had referred to Germany. With elaborate euphemism and genteel chiding he spoke indirectly of sinister happenings there. "We have all of us been glad to read in recent weeks the repeated declarations of the German Chancellor . . . of the peaceful intention of the Government of the Reich . . . yet I should be less than frank if I did not add that there are disturbing evidences, the removal of which would do more to reassure us than any number of the most pacific speeches."

Those mild words could hardly convey the immensity of the drama then being enacted in Germany. After the first World

War Stresemann and Bruning had tried to rally their people to a policy of international co-operation and modern democracy. Circumstances beyond both had worked against them. An inflation had wiped out the savings of the nation. Germany had no international credit, and for fifty years was committed to paying huge reparations; yet the money for these reparations could scarcely be found, since, cut off for years from raw materials, she must now import them in return for her manufactured goods instead of receiving gold or foreign currency for them. To make matters worse, industrialists and others with stocks of money sent it out of the country, fearing that it might be seized to pay reparations. Wages and salaries dropped. There were six million unemployed. They were surrounded by armed neighbours, whose talk of disarmament had led to no action whatever. Where people have nothing to lose they will try anything, and in this atmosphere of despair both Fascism and Communism grew and flourished.

Several times Eden attended the meetings of the moribund Disarmament Conference as a substituted delegate, and each time, in his own mind, he must have seen the hopes of peace receding. Another man might have said so, flatly and defiantly. But the traditions of the Foreign Office do not encourage plain speaking, and it is a serious responsibility to touch off an explosive situation. Militarism was now firmly established in Italy and in Germany, which was known to be arming rapidly in defiance of the Treaty of Versailles. Russia was interfering in British affairs and exploiting every opportunity, through the Communist Party, to foment discontent or exploit genuine discontents for her own advantage—a breakdown of law and order being, in Communist theory, an essential preliminary to a " workers' " revolution. The Means Test, for example, introduced to effect economies in the dispensation of unemployment benefit, led to serious riots in Birkenhead. They were found to have been organised by the National Unemployed Workers' Movement, a Communist body taking its propaganda cue from Moscow.

War in China; Fascism in Italy and Germany; intrigue from Russia—no, it was not the sort of post-war world that Captain Eden had dreamed about when he was a soldier and had written to his mother that he hoped " this beastly war " would soon be over. Now, the emotional restraint which might be said to make Eden a somewhat flat personality, was to be an enormous asset. Patience, industry and coolness were sorely needed. The truth was that disarmament had failed; no nation would make any sacrifices for peace, although war itself demands sacrifice without limits.

During these years an interesting metamorphosis was being achieved so far as Eden was concerned. There is no denying that as a boy he was sensitive, given to flashes of temper and long periods of introspection, and in some senses not too sure of himself. His kindly, understanding brother, Timothy, knew what he was about when he contrived that his younger brother should fag for him and so escape the bullying which could have delayed the development of that self-reliance of which Anthony was to give such spectacular evidence in the first World War. Even so, there were times in the House of Commons when Eden's dogmatisms smacked more of fear of failure than certainty of success. He was a young man determined to show that he could do things; a slightly different matter to being quite certain that he could. He liked to have reassurance. " How do you think I did? " he would ask a friend, or " I hope I didn't overdo it; but I did feel very strongly about it." Similarly, he was one of the few M.P.'s who would go up to the Reporters' Gallery in the House to check with the shorthand writers on what he had said.

But in the early thirties his growing confidence in himself became very marked. He began to discard some of his more irritating oratorical tricks, such as classical allusions mugged up at the last moment from a dictionary of quotations, and used as an illustrative anecdote. The truth is that in demanding so much of himself, he found increasingly that he could give it. The experience of being constantly on his feet in the House had put a certain polish on his speeches, though of course they still reflected his temperament, with its mixture of idealism and caution. The idealist in him longed for peace; his caution told him that Britain had gone as far as she could with gestures and sacrifices, and that in a world seething with nationalism and discontent a certain amount of realism was essential for survival. Significantly, he at no time counselled despair, despite the fact that the League of Nations had not stopped the production of a single bullet, destroyed a single gun or scrapped a single battleship. Italy was an armed camp. The Weimar Republic in Germany was in its last death throes. Russia was busy decimating her middle classes by bloody " purges "—a political euphemism for massacre.

But on the credit side, Britain had begun slowly to recover her lost trade. Unemployment was still widespread, of course, but its increase had been halted and the country was being lifted out of bankruptcy. Britain had abandoned the gold standard, and the Treasury with many misgivings had seen millions of pounds' worth of gold shipped to America in payment of war debts. There was a general feeling that an all-round abolition of war debts was urgently necessary in the interests of world recovery; the world economic depression was made worse by " protective " devices, such as tariffs, which deprived countries of the foreign currency which enabled them to buy one from the other.

Two women, meanwhile, followed Eden's progress with eager affection. Beatrice, his wife, would often come to the House of Commons to hear him speak, though at home she tried, not always successfully, to make him forget politics and seek refuge in music and painting, his only hobbies besides gardening. The other lady was his mother, Sybil Lady Eden, who from the peace and quiet of Windlestone followed his career with avid interest and hero-worshipping affection. Each day she scoured the newspapers for mention of him; and comments, pictures and speeches were carefully pasted into a cuttings book. She had always told friends that she was certain Anthony would succeed in anything he tackled. And that was happening rather quicker than either she or Mrs. Eden could have expected.

NINE

Crazy People

THE year 1933 was to offer the rising young politician even more scope for his energies. He had specialised in foreign affairs, and his appetite for work was easy enough to satisfy. Towards the end of 1932 he had helped to sort out an argument with the Persians over the Anglo-Iranian Oil Company. France, in between changing governments (she had four in this year), was demanding security for herself and adducing complicated plans which, although usually rejected, took up time and money in discussion. The Locarno Treaty, Eden reminded the House, already gave France considerable security, so far as support from other powers, and especially Britain, was concerned; and we had further commitments as members of the League of Nations.

Early in March Mr. Eden, the British Delegate to the Disarmament Conference in Geneva, brought gloomy news of its drift and indecision. The situation, he declared, was critical. The collapse of the conference would mean an end to peace and stability in Europe, and intelligence reports from Germany showed beyond doubt that rearmament, both clandestine and open, was being pursued at frantic speed. At a special Cabinet meeting on March 3rd it was decided to send Mr. Ramsay MacDonald, Prime Minister, and Sir John Simon almost immediately, and after further meetings on policy they left London for Geneva six days later, stopping at Paris on the way to sound M. Daladier on his views.

A draft Convention was laid before the Conference by the British Ministers on March 16th. In polite language we said that discussion on detail had gone far enough; it was time to agree on a broad plan acceptable to everyone. The document submitted by the British was far-reaching and even listed the troops which countries might be permitted to have—for France,

200,000 troops for home service and another 400,000 for overseas; Germany, 200,000 for home service and another 400,000 for overseas, and so on. An important clause was that bombing from the air should be abolished. It may seem odd in retrospect that a Socialist should have seriously recommended that Germany should have 400,000 troops for service overseas, but in the present mood of Germany, it was felt that the world would be lucky if military ambition could be limited to that figure.

While in Geneva, Ramsay MacDonald, whose speeches were becoming muddled and obscure and who gave the impression of being a spent force, dashed to Rome for conversations with Mussolini, who wanted to propose a Four Power Pact, including Great Britain, France, Italy and Germany. It was suggested that this was possible within the fabric of the League of Nations although, as events were to prove, Mussolini's motive was to keep other people talking about security whilst he secretly prepared for war.

MacDonald, outlining the plan in the House of Commons, commended it as an example which other powers might well follow. It was a diffuse speech, but was well received except by the redoubtable Mr. Winston Churchill, who said flatly that disarmament conferences did more harm than good (it is certainly a fact that they did no good, and one single conference had cost the British taxpayer £40,000). Better for Mr. MacDonald to stay at home and concern himself with domestic affairs than tinker with matters he did not understand. That should be left to our Ambassadors—trained men who understood foreign affairs.

Pale and tense, Anthony Eden rose to defend the Prime Minister. Facing Winston Churchill, who sat glowering and impenitent, he said that to accuse the Prime Minister of having brought Britain nearer to war through his interventions in foreign affairs, as Mr. Churchill had done, was a " mischievous absurdity," all the more to be regretted because it might be taken abroad as implying the endorsement of the House, which it did not (this was a hit at Churchill who had been given no job in the new Government). Pre-war diplomacy, said Eden, had no very creditable record. He did not subscribe to the theory of the infallibility of Ambassadors, valuable though they no doubt were. New times demanded new methods. Mr. Churchill had admitted the necessity of bringing France and Germany together—what better opportunity than the Prime Minister's visit to Rome?

In fact, the beginning had been made to a disastrous policy of which the fruits were not yet foreseen; Mr. Eden's spirited defence of his chief was loudly applauded by the House, but there was uneasiness about the Pact. Two of the countries concerned, after all, were Fascist—on January 30th Hitler had become Reich Chancellor and on the ruins of the Weimar Republic was raising a totalitarian state. And it was known that both Hitler and Mussolini had been invited to the Disarmament Conference and had refused to come. It suited Mussolini much better for his prestige both at home and abroad, that a British Prime Minister should visit *him*.

On June 7th the Four Power Pact was initialled by Great Britain, France, Italy and Germany. Its purpose was to ensure that the four powers would co-operate and agree on a common policy of peace, not in competition with the League but as part of it. In view of the blatant military organisation of both Germany and Italy and their contempt for the most elementary freedoms, the public in Britain put little faith in the Pact.

On June 12th the World Economic Conference opened in London and the lessons of the world slump were explored in language far above the heads of ordinary people. Japan had been branded by the League of Nations as an aggressor in Manchuria. Unemployment at home still stood at three million. The whole nation was talking, not of war or peace, but the Loch Ness Monster, a strange and elusive sea-serpent of prodigious length which many people claimed to have seen at different times. True, descriptions varied a little, as do the accounts of people who have seen flying saucers. One thought it looked like a bearded eel, another a hippopotamus, yet another like a reptile. The only photograph available showed two large humps in the smooth waters of the Loch, as though a monster black camel had decided to walk under water. Rumour fed on rumour. It had been seen with a sheep in its mouth; it had carried off an old woman whose body was found on the moors. The legend grew, satisfying those with a sense of mysticism and mystery. Then it faded, and people began to worry about Mussolini's increasingly belligerent speeches and heard with misgivings the hysterical rantings of Hitler on the radio.

In October Eden's chief, Sir John Simon, roundly accused Germany of changing her course. Germany was already smarting under a sharp refusal from Britain to sell her twenty-five aeroplanes in July—a request of which we informed France at the time, and, in return, received the reply " We told you so." The rearmament of Germany, one suspects, disturbed Eden far more than it did a large body of Conservative opinion. There was at the time a feeling that a rearmed Germany might be a sort of insurance policy against Communism, whose disruptive interventions in Britain, especially during the General Strike of 1926, had fostered the deepest suspicion of Russia and her intentions. A good many people assume that if two people dislike the same thing, they must necessarily like each other, and that because Mussolini and Hitler were anti-Russian we ought therefore to get along well with them.

The German response to Sir John Simon's accusation was to walk out of the Disarmament Conference and to resign from membership of the League of Nations. It was evil news. Only a few days previously both Ramsay MacDonald and Arthur Henderson had warned the International Peace Society that peace prospects had not increased—an under-statement if ever there was one. But to some extent at least (so far as public pronouncements were concerned) Eden was inclined to soft-pedal on references to Germany.

The Government's attitude towards Europe's dictators seemed far too mild and conciliatory; appeasement in a sense had already begun. Big business executives were inclined to favour Fascism, sensing that it might not only be an insurance against Communism but perhaps Trade Unionism as well. The bulk of Sir Oswald Mosley's British Union of Fascists funds came from such people. But the more liberal minded were shocked at the trend of events, and humanitarian feelings were outraged by the all-too-well authenticated reports of outrage and injustice to the Jewish minorities in Germany.

Yet in a speech on November 3rd, at Skipton, during a by-election there, Eden accused the Labour Party of hysterical exaggeration. The international situation was difficult, but the Labour Party was trying to exploit anxiety. He deplored Germany's action, but there was no need for alarmist language of "scaremongering." The situation could no doubt be redeemed, but to do so the British must keep cool.

Did Eden believe that so far as Germany was concerned, the situation " could be redeemed " ? Were those who saw in Hitler's dictatorship a threat to peace really scaremongers, or were they simply being frank? But Eden had his heart on peace. He had travelled thousands of miles, from capital to capital, often going without sleep, taking scratch meals as he could, drafting and re-drafting, pleading and reiterating. His appeals had always been to reason and humanity, never to sentiment or passion. It was not his fault if the world, after the terrible lesson of 1914-19, had not learned that the only hope for humanity was peace and co-operation.

When he touched on peace and war in a speech to the League of Nations Union held in Birmingham Town Hall, Eden spoke as an ex-soldier:

". . . the generation that knew war, that hated it from intimate knowledge of its blind wastefulness and senseless cruelty, is passing away. There are many of us in this hall to-night whose experience of the war years was not that of grown men and women. Even for those who had that experience, human memory is merciful. The cruel memories, sharp because they are cruel, become blunted, sufferings grow dim, and an ever-deepening haze of years cloaks tragedy in oblivion. There is danger in this. What man ceases to fear acutely, he ceases to guard against actively"

He appealed for coolness. Scaremongers were the satellites of war. Disarmament and collective security machinery ought not to be scrapped because it had produced negligible results so far; there was nothing wrong with the machinery but simply with the use made of it. The death of the liberal-minded Stresemann in Germany had been followed by a drifting apart of France and Germany—a drifting farther apart, actually, as they had neither been very close in aims or spirit—and events in Germany had caused anxiety. He welcomed Hitler's declarations of peaceful intentions, although there were " disturbing evidences the removal of which would do more to reassure us than any number of the most pacific speeches." Eden did not put it stronger or more specifically, for he hoped after all, to keep the door open and not slam it in the face of the dictators. Their belligerence had not reached its climax, sinister though the portents were. Eden preached patience, firmness and hope. And the Prime Minister, in a New Year Message to the Nation, said, " To-day we say good-bye to the old year and turn to face a new one. The last twelve months, despite their difficulties and anxieties, have nevertheless been a time of steadily increasing hope. They have brought us in this country tangible proof that we are travelling on the right road and that our efforts are beginning to receive our reward, We should therefore look forward to the new year with renewed confidence. . . ."

Was Britain " travelling on the right road? " Our Prime Minister and our most senior ministers were going cap in hand to see military dictators who were too arrogant to come to Britain or meet us half-way. We had a vast army of unemployed. There was war in the East. Disarmament had failed. General rearmament had begun. Economically, perhaps, Britain was beginning to see daylight; but the prospects of that peace for which Anthony Eden strove so hard were as remote as ever.

TEN

Lord Privy Seal

THE opening of 1934 found Anthony Eden promoted to the office of Lord Privy Seal, whose antiquated and picturesque title belies its importance. In effect, it made him a Minister without specific duties, but of undoubted seniority and importance none the less, and enabled him to concentrate on League of Nations affairs. In the same year he became a member of the Privy Council.

The promotion meant what Eden had been striving for—full Ministerial rank. It was expected that Eden would continue to be principal delegate and liaison officer to the League of Nations and generally act as plenipotentiary at large. The step was well received by all parties in the House, and by now Eden was as well known in Geneva as he was in London. His immaculate elegance had caught the eye of the gossip writers, and press photographers were used increasingly here and abroad to represent him as a well-dressed Englishman. His black Homburg hat, which he buys at the ancient hatter's shop, Locks of St. James's Street, was the trade mark of an aristocrat, and was avidly copied by lesser-paid bank clerks, confidence tricksters and salesmen intent on promotion; the hat was a veritable symbol of refinement, prosperity and aristocracy.

Eden now left his house in Mulberry Walk in favour of a more elegant house in Fitzhardinge Street, Mayfair, where the servants had blue liveries faced with red. Its furnishings were quiet, but decidedly elegant, one of the most handsome rooms being in brown and gold. He had a study of his own, and would often be closeted in it until the early hours of the morning. His room at the Foreign Office was now larger and more impressive, for the Civil Service had a nice way of registering your ascent or descent in life by furnishings permitted to you from the stores. A larger ink-well, an extra strip of carpet and the ubiquitous coal-scuttle—all these are a barometer by which success is measured.

In his constituency, Eden was now a local hero. He was the Galahad of the thirties, the Prince Charming who would beguile the dictators and stop them dropping bombs on us. The strange thing is that throughout these years, Eden was able to support a Government which was frankly following a policy of appeasement—even in the early thirties Mussolini and Hitler were being chased, so to speak, by British rulers; frank words were not spoken to them. Eden's speeches mention " anxiety " and the rest, but they are masterpieces of understatement when weighed against the infamies for which Mussolini and Hitler were directly responsible. It is ironic indeed that Hitler had no sooner crushed democracy in Germany, but we were running after him, begging him to join forces with Mussolini in the Four-Power Pact; yet, the Chinese saying, " he who lies down with dogs gets up with fleas " never applied to Eden. He had supported the Government through thick and thin and had once contemptuously dismissed critics of the ill-fated Locarno Pact by saying, irritably, that Britain had no wish to be a sort of Special Constable in Europe. He under-played the League's first failure, despite the fact that the localised security envisaged in the Locarno Treaty was bound to weaken the League. The politicians could blunder and meander along, but somehow Eden escaped the opprobrium which was earned by the rest.

On January 6th, 1934, Sir John Simon, who had paid another visit to Mussolini, returned to England and four days later, reported on his conversations to the Cabinet Disarmament Committee. Germany had submitted her demands to France, creating alarm and shock by the sweeping nature of her military estimates. Germany demanded an army of 300,000 and a wide range of weapons. France of course, would have none of it and Britain, as a matter of urgency, drew up revised disarmament proposals which were issued as a White Paper.

The British proposals, however, were hardly " disarmament ". They stated that Germany should be permitted an army of between 200,000 men (the recommended figure) and 300,000 (the number Germany claimed), that the Government was prepared to agree that the period of service should be twelve months instead of eight, and that the new German army should have tanks up to six tons and 155 mm. guns. Further, if the Permanent Disarmament Commission had not suceeded in abolishing military aeroplanes within two years, all countries might have them—including Germany, who was making them in defiance of the Treaty of Versailles anyhow. " Disarmament " which included guns, troops, tanks and planes did not sound like a formula for peace; but in the present state of the world it was considered the only compromise that stood any chance of acceptance by the major powers. It seemed worth trying. The choice lay between an unrestricted arms race or (1) the abolition of certain types of arms, or (2) no abolition of existing arms but agreement not to add to them.

Sir John Simon tried to convince the House that these proposals were sound, that Germany had a rightful claim to equality in armaments. He announced that Mr. Eden would leave as soon as possible for Paris, Rome and Berlin and discover by personal contact what the attitude of the respective governments would be to the proposals. The debate on February 6th was an historic one, and deserves reprinting in full, if only as a warning of how sweet reasonableness may open the gates of terror. War was raging in the Far East, with nothing tangible done to stop it by the League of Nations; Fascism had taken hold of Italy, and Germany was about to engulf Austria. The original idea of a Four-Power Pact was mooted by Mussolini, whose contempt for democratic practice and whose warlike organisation of Italy were well known. Yet Sir John Simon's speech reads as if some great gift were being offered to the British; how good of Messrs. Hitler and Mussolini to consider disarmament—this, despite the fact that both countries were known to be arming to the teeth. The legal sophistry of Sir John Simon makes painful reading. He pleaded for a " spirit of realism " and added:

> " The first proposition is that Germany's claim to equality of rights in the matter of armament cannot be resisted, and ought not to be resisted."

Major Attlee replied, with some truth, that the paper before them was in effect a proposal for the rearmament of Germany. Germany was claiming the right to rearm—which she had already asserted without the approval of her neighbours—and the Government was saying in effect "We must permit her rearmament or there will be no chance of peace." Major Attlee had had experience of prairie fires, and drew on that experience for a strong analogy. " I suggest that when there is a fire, it is unwise to drench all the surrounding area with the highly-inflammable oil of hypocrisy by pretending that there is no danger, and that everything is quite secure if, when you say ' Let the fire burn away there; it will not catch anything ' you have, as a matter of fact, done away with your entire security. That is really what is happening in the Far East. It has happened since, not in deeds but in words, in this House."

And a prophetic warning was uttered by Sir Stafford Cripps:

> "Any country can stand out against our ideals . . . and wreck the whole thing. Then we should find countries going out, putting a pistol to our heads and saying, ' we will not come back unless you give us what we want '; and the thing would be repeated on the next occasion. When anybody wants anything they will go out of the League and say that they will not come back unless we give them what they want. . . ."

Eden, however, was entitled to answer Cripps by saying that in some respects his argument was not logical. Sir Stafford had said " the only possible thing to do is, as has been suggested by several Honourable Members to-day, to set up some sort of international police." The original conception of the League had been a concourse of nations pledged to avoid war and the means of war, and to take collective action against an aggressor. Before long, it had broken down into bickering over the size of guns and the precise degree of sovereignty which it would be safe to yield in the course of peace. And as recently as October 14th, 1933, Germany had walked out of the League of Nations, making the prospect of European agreement more remote than ever. But the Socialists on one hand demanded disarmament and on the other accused the Government of not " policing " the world energetically enough. They insisted on disarmament yet urged the assumption of responsibilities which could only effectively be discharged if Britain were armed.

A careful reading of this debate shows that more faith was being reposed in the dictatorships than could possibly be justified by what had happened so far. That there was danger in the air was admitted, but this was simply an echo of what most people knew. The severity of the assault on democracy in the Fascist countries, and the vigour and determination with which both Italy and Germany had converted themselves into military states, was deliberately under-played. Would plain speaking have been better? Would Britain have gained by saying to Hitler and Mussolini " We don't like your methods. We don't admit your right to rearm and threaten your neighbours. But if you put the whole thing into reverse we shall be glad to welcome you into the League." But that is a matter for the historians. This paper had been produced at a time when the nationalisms of Europe had flared up again. The Government's plan did at least provide for the supervision of arms production. If nations could not be prevented from being armed perhaps, the Government hoped, they might be dissuaded from adding to their present strength. The comments of Attlee and Cripps however, were a warning to the House that " appeasement " (a word coined by diplomats and intended, like most of the jargon of diplomacy, to under-state or dissemble what it means) had already begun—as it had. But in the present state of play Eden would have been content to have achieved *something*:

> " We believe that the general balance of the document is just, and therefore it should be maintained and not be departed from. I should like the House to consider for a moment the position as it would be if the Proposals in this Memorandum were accepted. There would be solid advantages. No country need then greatly increase its armament; many would be able substantially to reduce it. There would be no race in armaments; Nations would know their own commitments, their own programmes and those of their neighbours, for ten years to come. Regulation would take the place of rivalry, limitation of *laissez faire*."

Ten days later Anthony Eden left on a tour of Paris, Berlin and Rome to explain Britain's proposals and solicit support. There was little joy to be had in Paris, where Germany's frantic militarisation was being watched with grim understanding. In Berlin, Hitler received him with some show of friendliness and listened attentively to what Eden had to say. But the exchange of notes had made it clear enough that disarmament was out of the question and that Germany's cooperation, if forthcoming at all, would be based on recognition of Germany's demand for an army of 300,000 men. One reason for his good reception was that Eden was the first representative of one of the Western Powers to come into direct contact with Hitler—to come and see *him*. This flattered his vanity. Further, Eden was an ex-Serviceman; Hitler, who had joined up as a volunteer early in the first World War and enrolled as number 148 in the 1st Company of the 16th Bavarian Infantry Regiment, had been facing Eden during the battle of Ypres. This was not to prove a lasting link, but it did effect some contact between the two, and the conversations lasted much longer than were expected.

What were Eden's impressions of Hitler on that first visit? It would be interesting to know. John W. Wheeler-Bennett, in his book *Munich: Prologue to Tragedy*, says that at this first meeting Eden formed " a not wholly unfavourable view of Hitler." Another consideration in Hitler's mind made it possible for him to appear to be offering some sort of compromise; he talked of disbanding the S.A. or Storm Troopers—the Brownshirts whose quasi-military organisation had brought him to power. He offered to do this because for domestic reasons it would suit him very well. He controlled the army, the machinery of law and order and all the other sources of government. But the Storm Troopers were now an embarrassment to him; two and a half million men now waited for the rewards and perquisites of their long campaign to overthrow democracy. They were well armed. They were a rival to Hitler's army, which itself was restive about the Storm Troopers. Hitler could afford to talk of disbanding them as though it were a gesture of disarmament. Perhaps it sounded like that to Eden.

In Rome Eden had a meeting with Mussolini. Both disliked each other on sight, and Mussolini, smarting under the supposed indignity of being seen by somebody he considered a junior, was offensive and deputed a lesser official to dine with him in the evening. He said that in his view Hitler's offer to be content with an army of 300,000 and an air force half the size of France's was a generous one and should be accepted. In Paris, on his way back, Eden saw the French Premier Daladier, who was horrified at the suggestion that he should meet Hitler. The British habit of bearding the lion in its den seemed to Daladier to imply loss of prestige. Perhaps he was right.

Eden's trip had achieved nothing tangible, but he valued his opportunity of coming face to face with the men who for the moment were an unknown factor in diplomacy. He reported with satisfaction that Hitler attended a lunch at the British Embassy in Berlin, accompanied by Goebbels, his propaganda chief, Hess (an unbalanced individual who, during the second World War flew to Britain in the mistaken belief that he had friends here who would bring fighting to an end) and Neurath. He had met Mussolini. He had been received in audience by His Holiness the Pope and had talked long, hard but without results to President Doumergue and M. Barthou of France.

Hitler had said on many occasions that he had no designs on Austria, but Nazi agents were very active there, financing the Austrian Fascist movement. In February, on the instruction of the so-called " pocket-dictator " Dolfuss, a Socialist rising in Vienna had been suppressed with unparalleled brutality. Austrian Fascists spoke openly of union with Germany, and arms were being surreptitiously smuggled in and stored.

The hope of getting any agreement on disarmament was more remote than ever, but on March 14th, Anthony Eden, in giving the House of Commons a résumé of his tour, did his best to sound a note of optimism. The least agreeable part of his statement is his putting France and Germany in the same category. The French and German people, he said, did " not understand each other's point of view." On one side there was a mistrustful apprehension and on the other an aggravated impatience. "Aggravated impatience" was one way of describing Hitler's attitude; but Mr. Winston Churchill did not share Eden's optimism. In vigorous and forthright language he informed the House—as he had often done before —that international disarmament was a will o' the wisp which it was useless and even dangerous for the nations to pursue. The awful danger of British foreign policy, he declared, was that throughout it had tried to weaken France.

The world was still talking disarmament when Dolfuss, the Austrian dictator, was assassinated in Vienna; his murder was the culmination of a long reign of Nazi terror, although the

Germans kept up the pretence that they were not implicated in it. Talk of limiting arms continued whilst war between Bolivia and Paraguay raged in "pitiless and horrible conditions," to quote the Chaco Commission. It was a war that attracted hardly any attention in Europe; it was also another test case for the League of Nations, which from start to finish of the hostilities failed to intervene in any effective way.

Eden, addressing his constituents at Kenilworth on June 28th, repeated the sort of platitudes with which newspapers and their readers had become depressingly familiar. The Disarmament Conference had so far failed, but we should not despair. One setback did not spell disaster (in fact, there had been innumerable "setbacks"); on this small earth's surface we had got to live together. If the Disarmament Conference failed, Britain could not afford to disarm herself as an example to others. . . .

Early in October Anthony Eden, with his infinite capacity for keeping his head when all around him were losing theirs, helped to avert a European war. On October 9th King Alexander of Yugoslavia disembarked from the destroyer *Dubrovnik* on an official visit to France. He was greeted by the Foreign Minister, M. Barthou, and with him the king was riding through Marseilles in a car. Suddenly, from the dense crowd, a Croat terrorist appeared, jumped on the running board and amidst cries of horror and shouts of alarm, shot the king dead and injured Barthou, who died afterwards. The assassin was killed on the spot by the enraged crowd.

Enquiries showed that he had entered France on a forged passport and was a member of a Croat terrorist organisation headed by Ante Pavelich. Since the headquarters of the gang was in Hungary, an international crisis was precipitated. Yugoslavia, as the country had been called since 1929, was a kingdom of Croats, Slovenes and Serbs with a traditional hatred of Hungarians. Both countries were violently nationalistic and there were numerous cross-currents of hatred at work. Now, it seemed, reconciliation between the two countries would be impossible. Yugoslavia was already aggrieved at Hungary allowing Croat *émigrés* to organise terrorist activities on Hungarian soil.

The matter being referred to the League of Nations, Anthony

Eden was asked to sort out the muddle and reconcile the two countries—not in those terms, of course. Throughout he showed clearness of thought and coolness of head. Both countries levelled accusations against each other; each accused the other of endangering peace. Eden ignored polemics and kept to the essentials of the dispute, helping to draft a resolution which satisfied both parties. To have achieved a settlement in these circumstances was an achievement which enhanced Eden's reputation enormously at home and abroad.

Meanwhile, Hitler had extended his propaganda to the Saar territory, an important and densely populated industrial area of nearly a thousand square miles which the French had acquired during the Revolutionary wars but were obliged to hand over, principally to Prussia by the Treaty of Vienna in 1815. It included the richest coal mines on the Continent and after the first World War France considered they should be ceded to her in compensation for the French coal mines destroyed by the Germans, but the Allies did not favour France's total possession of the Saar basin. The compromise reached at the time was that the coal mines were to be ceded to France, the district was to come within the French customs boundary and after fifteen years the people resident there at the time of the signing of the Treaty should vote as to their future status—electing to be reunited with Germany, become a permanent part of France, or continue to be administered by the League of Nations.

The French had good reason to be concerned at the drift of affairs in the Saar. The Germans were conducting a vigorous agitation there for reunion with Germany. With a programme of rearmament under way, the coal of the Saar would be a valuable impetus to heavy industry. The Council of the League of Nations was busy making preparations for a plebiscite and Mr. Knox, the chairman of the League Governing Commission, tried vainly to secure law and order. Every day Nazi terrorism increased; a Nazi *putsch* seemed quite possible, and France said flatly that she would send troops into the Saar territory if Germany seized it. January 13th, 1935, was fixed as the day for the voting. Britain was not unfavourably disposed to Germany's claim to the Saar; Hitler had implied that it would be an important step towards Franco-German understanding. That the return of the Saar to Germany would increase both her capacity to rearm and the speed with which she could do so was hardly mentioned in any of the British Government's pronouncements. Eden's speech to the Council of the League on December 5th, 1934, simply referred to Britain's willingness to send troops to the Saar to help to maintain order during the plebiscite. "There might be, however great the goodwill on either side, *a certain amount of excitement and ebullition* in the period during and after the plebiscite." The italics are mine. Once again Eden showed his genius for finding anæmic words which make bad things sound so much better than they are. Self-restraint? Caution? Or an uncritical obedience to the Government's policy at the time, the policy of keeping Fascism at bay by making constant concessions?

The year 1934 closed with Anthony Eden's reputation higher than ever; his immaculate clothing, his quiet and harmless manner, his flair for saying things that amounted to nothing but sounded pleasant, but more especially his handling of the Yugoslav-Hungarian dispute and his enormous energy had made him, at the age of 37, one of the best known politicians in the world. The world was one year further from the prospect of disarmament and peace; ironically, the popular song most in vogue as the year ended was "Who's afraid of the big, bad wolf?"

ELEVEN

All Work and No Play

THE year 1935 was an historic one, in the least pleasant sense. The official seal was set upon folly; British prestige waned; the lives of millions of people were to be affected for good and ill—mostly ill—by events that followed fast one on the other.

For Anthony Eden, too, it was to be a momentous year. Not only in Britain, but in the press of the world, his name was now a byword. He had scarcely said a controversial thing in his life; he had created no precedents, and his reputation as an idealist, which was by now well established, had no basis in anything he had ever said. His speeches had no edge to them. Between him and his principal opponent in the House, Mr. Winston Churchill, was an enormous difference of outlook. Churchill disliked euphemisms, evasions, equivocations and compromises. He called a spade a spade. Eden would perhaps describe it as " an implement with which all of us, no doubt, are familiar."

But the world looked upon Eden as somebody young, fresh, neither lazy nor disillusioned, a welcome contrast to the devious scholarship of Sir John Simon, the complacencies of Baldwin, the machinations of the swarthy Laval, the blusterings of Mussolini and the threats of Hitler.

On January 13th the Saar plebiscite was held. The several days before the atmosphere had been tense and explosive, but the presence of the League army, troops sent by the supervising Powers at the request of the League, discouraged outbreaks of violence. There had been a good deal of terrorism organised by Germany, and there is little doubt that had the verdict not gone in favour of Germany the territory would have been seized by force. Such a step proved unnecessary. Ninety per cent. of the people voted for reunion with Germany and on

January 17th the Council of the League of Nations awarded the entire Saar basin to Germany. France received 900 million francs in compensation from Germany for the mines, railways and other assets transferred. The spread of Nazism to the Saar was hardly a matter of rejoicing. For trade unionists, Socialists, Jews and other sects persecuted by the Nazis in Germany it meant that they were now defenceless in the face of highly organised terrorism. But Mr. Eden, broadcasting from Geneva on January 18th made it sound much more attractive than it was:

> "The future of the Saar has now been settled in accordance with the Treaty of Versailles. . . . the League of Nations may justifiably be congratulated upon the peaceful discharge of its anxious responsibility."

But although his smooth words must have sounded like a death knell to certain people in the Saar, the fact remains that League forces did keep order, the plebiscite was held, and the League did in this instance save a certain amount of bloodshed. Eden had worked very hard behind the scenes and was entitled to feel a certain qualified satisfaction.

What of Eden's family life all this time? Travelling this week to Geneva, another week to Rome or Berlin or Paris, his home life was sacrificed to his job. Mrs. Beatrice Eden once described herself as a "diplomat's widow" and the truth is that although she was very patient about it all and encouraged her husband to do whatever would be good for the country and redound to his prestige, she did see, on average, very little of him. He would, when in town, leave early in the morning and arrive back late at night. Even then the ubiquitous red leather despatch boxes would follow him. Sometimes the family—they had two boys now, Simon Gascoin, born in 1925 and Nicholas, born in 1930—would go off to stay at Warwick Castle, and occasionally to Windlestone, the old family seat. But to put it mildly, the atmosphere of Windlestone had changed. There were no longer the servants who kept the place so beautifully in Anthony's boyhood. Sir William was no longer alive to detect a bush whose foliage was juxtaposed inartistically with its neighbours, and to upbraid the gardener for his stupidity. And staying in the house were numerous tramps—over twenty of them. Sybil Lady Eden, who was greatly interested in social work, was President of the Wayfarers' Benevolent Association, a movement which aimed at reclaiming young men from their vagrant ways.

When he was at home, Eden would usually retire to his study and relax. Relaxation did not come easily to him. He taxed himself considerably, and disliked delegating anything to others; he would often be exhausted, often dangerously so. Sometimes he would put aside his books and documents and agree to go to a cinema with his wife; he liked funny films, such as those of the Marx brothers, and considering the strain and boredom of much of his work, one can understand it. A newspaper commentator at the time observed: " I think the most ardent film fan in London must be Mrs. Anthony Eden. She seems to spend much of her spare time in one cinema or other. Her husband is, of course, usually too busy to accompany her. . . ."

On Sundays the family would go to church, sometimes to communion, perhaps simply to morning service or evensong. Anthony inherited from his mother her great love of the Anglican church and he knew every word of the Services by heart.

Sometimes Eden would just drop into the Carlton Club and relax after his own fashion—talking politics, most likely, with the members. Or he would go off for a game of tennis at weekends. He was so fond of tennis that when in Geneva he would wake his secretaries at 7 a.m. so that they could get a game in before the talking-match began. And sometimes Anthony would do as his father did, take his easel and paint-box and give himself up to painting. He is quite a fair artist, Beatrice shared this interest with him—as she had shared most of his interests except politics, which bored her—and is to-day a very passable artist whose works have been exhibited in art galleries in New York. It is interesting, coming back to Anthony Eden himself, how persistently an artistic streak asserts itself in his family. His brother Sir Timothy Eden is also an artist of some merit, whose works have been exhibited in West End art galleries. But Sir Timothy is an altogether more stimulating person than his brother; he has far more wit, is not so inclined to take himself seriously, is more relaxed and is able to express himself with more fluency and colour, both verbally and in writing. His literary gifts, as revealed in *Tribulations of a Baronet*, are far above average; not simply his insight, but his quietly sardonic style and warm-hearted magnanimity make him almost the opposite in temperament to his brother Anthony.

But at this period, 1935, Anthony Eden was certainly one of the hardest worked men in Europe; he loved family life, and also enjoyed every minute of the companionship of his two boys. His devotion to his work was a matter of duty. He did not subordinate his marriage to work. It would be fairer to say his work subordinated him.

Following the Saar plebiscite, the next important event so far as Anthony Eden was concerned, was the state visit of M. Flandin, the French Premier, and Pierre Laval, the Foreign Minister, who after the second World War was tried for treason and executed. Laval had recently been in Rome, where he had negotiated a Franco-Italian understanding. It was hoped to tackle the question of German equality in a system which would provide security for all the nations of Europe. Eden took part in the discussions, the other representatives present being the Prime Minister, Mr. Baldwin, and Sir John Simon. On February 3rd a statement was issued which made known the main points agreed upon. In accordance with the Rome Agreement, Britain would consult with other powers if the independence of Austria were menaced. Britain and France did not acknowledge Germany's right to modify its obligations under the Peace Treaties (in other words, did not admit her right to rearm without permission) but hoped nevertheless for a " general settlement " freely negotiated between Germany and other powers. The same statement referred with misgivings to the potential destructiveness of aerial aggression, and hoped that regional pacts might limit or prevent aerial warfare.

This statement was sent to Hitler, who was non-committal about it. For him the question was how much he could hope to get on the mere promise of co-operation; that being so, the less he did the better—let him do so little that the least thing would look like a concession worth paying for. The German Government agreed to the proposal to conclude an Air Convention but was vague on other points. It contained, however, a hint that the British should enter into a direct exchange of view with the Germans as they had done with the French.

This suggestion was accepted, and Sir John Simon and Eden were to go to Berlin on March 11th. A complication arose, however, through the publication by the Government, only a few days before Simon and Eden were due to leave for Berlin, of a Government Statement of Policy—prepared for an all-round debate on defence scheduled to take place in the House of Commons on March 8th. In that statement Germany was singled out for criticism. " His Majesty's Government," said the statement, " have noted and welcomed the declarations of the leaders of Germany that they desire peace. They cannot, however, fail to recognise that not only the forces, but the spirit in which the population, and especially the youth of the country, are being organised, lend colour to, and substantiate, the general feeling of insecurity which has been incontestably generated."

That was only stating the obvious, but the reference was pointed enough to offend Hitler. He claimed to have a cold, and retired in ostentatious disgust to Berchtesgaden. The British visit arranged for March 11th was postponed. A few days later, on March 16th, Hitler tore up the Treaty of Versailles, as he had openly planned to do for so long, and introduced conscription. Immediately the news broke, Sir John Simon, who was on a visit to South Wales, hurried back to London while the Prime Minister came up from Chequers. On March 18th there was a full Cabinet meeting. The result was an ill-balanced note of " protest " to Germany—a development which one can be sure Hitler took for granted. But the the note was basically one of pained surprise. " We were going to give you lots of the things you wanted anyway," the note said in effect, "and now you go and do a thing like this," the language was a little more devious; but that is what it added up to. What had been contemplated was " a general agreement " freely negotiated between Germany and other powers " (this ignored the fact that German pressure on anyone weaker than herself made " free " negotiation an impossibility) and " agreements regarding armaments which in the case of Germany would replace the provisions of Part V of the Treaty of Versailles." In other words, nobody was going to insist on the provisions of the Treaty of Versailles, which had specifically prohibited German rearmament. The note added that the Government wished to continue with discussions. To this Hitler agreed, and the news was received with satisfaction in the House of Commons. The dreamy, benign, pacifistic Mr. Lansbury urged that Britain should sacrifice her Air Force as a gesture. Members spoke of alarm and despair, but were careful to avoid saying anything which could spoil the Foreign Secretary's chances of reaching agreement with Hitler.

It was a forlorn hope that took Sir John Simon and Anthony Eden to Berlin on March 23rd. The talks were to be " exploratory "—a word by which nobody was committed in advance to achieving anything concrete. What was privately hoped was that Germany might be tempted back into the League of Nations. Sir John went straight to Berlin; Eden broke his journey in Paris to consult with Laval, the Foreign Minister and Signor Suvich, of Italy.

Neither Simon nor Eden made the slightest impression on Hitler. There is pathos in the official picture of them in Hitler's Chancellery. There was the absolute ruler of Germany, his shoulders tense and defiant, his thin lips set, his toothbrush moustache contrasting absurdly with his carefully arranged hair style. There was Simon, listless, unanimated; and there was Eden in his impeccable morning coat and grey trousers carefully pressed. Not a match, one feels, for the sharp-witted fanatic who knew only too well the advantages of surprise and decision.

Hitler's language at this interview was very different to his conciliatory talk at his first interview with Eden. He would have nothing to do with an Eastern Pact—he distrusted the Russians and hated Communism, which he said was the main danger in Europe. He wanted no truck with collective security or disarmament—on the contrary, the German Air Force had now reached parity with Britain's. Hitler talked the language of war; of absorbing Austria and recovering Germany's lost colonies. It was obvious that, to quote Simon's words, there were " considerable divergences " of view.

On March 27th Simon returned to London. Eden, tired and depressed, went to Moscow. His health was breaking under the strain of constant journeys, scratch meals and long hours of discussion and mental work. In the train he tried vainly to snatch a few phrases from the Russian grammars which Beatrice had bought for him before his departure, but gave it up. He must have been inwardly very excited. It was the first time a British Minister had been asked to the Kremlin, and in all the troubled events which were taking place, Russia was the great enigma.

The special train from Berlin crossed the frontiers of the Soviet Union, and by March 28th Eden was in Moscow, where an enthusiastic welcome awaited him. It was a bizarre occasion. Stalin, the 55-years-old dictator of Russia, had never before received a Western statesman or ambassador.

Eden was accompanied by Ivan Maisky, Russian Ambassador to the Court of St. James. From the moment of his arrival he was caught up in a round of visits and discussions. He lunched at Molotov's house and there met Ismet Bey, the Turkish Premier who remembered with gratitude Eden's championship of the new Republic in the House of Commons. At Voroshiloff's flat there was an " accidental encounter " with the American Ambassador, Mr. Bullitt; then to the British Embassy, then occupied by Lord Chilston.

At 3.15 p.m. came what must have been one of the most exciting moments in Anthony Eden's life. Accompanied by Lord and Lady Chilston and Mr. Strang (now Sir William) the Foreign Office expert on League of Nations Affairs, and various members of Chilston's staff, the procession of three British cars, each flying the Union Jack, entered the " holy city " of Communism. The golden domes and eagles of the Kremlin glinted brightly in the sun. At the ancient Borovitsky gate no sentry scrutinised their documents. For an hour they enjoyed a tour of the Kremlin monuments and museums and at half past four Eden, Lord Chilston and Mr. Strang saw Stalin in Molotov's office on the third floor of the Kremlin. Stalin was accompanied by Molotov and Litvinoff, who acted as interpreter and had met Anthony Eden a good deal at Geneva and knew, presumably, how to translate some of Eden's wordier statements into intelligible Russian. In contrast to his callers formal clothes, Stalin wore his famous grey gabardine blouse, blue trousers and soft black top boots. Portraits of Karl Marx and Lenin looked down impassively as the Georgian and the Durham man talked of pacts, security and the rest. Stalin had received the news of Eden's Berlin visit with considerable suspicion; did it presage a free hand in the East for Nazi Germany? Or would Britain come in with Russia, supporting her in the event of an attack by Germany? Stalin showed a ready grasp of world affairs and is reported to have been favourably impressed with the young statesman. The atmosphere was cordial. Stalin, as usual, toyed with his pipe without using it. Russian tea was served in glasses and Russian cigarettes handed around.

Nothing very new was said. Stalin's comments were a reiteration of everything his ministers had previously declared. Eden was at pains to disabuse Stalin of any idea that Britain favoured German rearmament. We were, he assured him, only concerned with peace and trying to secure it by local agreements. Stalin thought that (since it was obvious Britain did not wish to be involved with such a pact) a mutual defence treaty between France, Russia and Czechoslovakia ought to be attempted. Eden gave his assurance that Britain, although not participating in such an Eastern Treaty, would not discourage it or disapprove of it. Stalin outwitted Eden on one question. He had asked him whether the risk of war was greater or less than it had been in 1914? Eden thought the danger of war was less, but Stalin contradicted him. In those days, he pointed out, there had been but one menace to world security—the German nation. Now there were two great powers determined to expand—Germany and Japan. Stalin motioned to a map showing the sprawling continent of Europe and Russia and a small red dot indicating Britain. " Strange, isn't it," said Stalin, " that the peace of Europe should depend upon that tiny country?"

In the evening Eden found himself the principal figure in a scene of unimaginable splendour and colour. He entered the former Imperial box of the Grand State Opera House to see Tchaikovsky's ballet, *Swan Lake*, performed before a glittering assembly of Communist rulers and foreign diplomats. Seminova, Russia's greatest ballerina, had been brought back specially from Turkey to do justice to the occasion. The great gilt and red plush opera house was crowded to the roof. The audience stood to attention whilst the orchestra thundered out *God*

Fox Photo

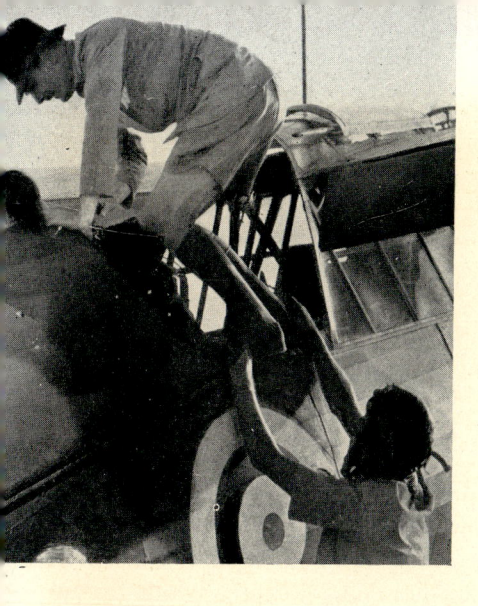

Touring the Middle East war zone in November, 1940. Anthony Eden, then Secretary of State for War, was visiting advance positions. A small two-seater was used because a larger plane would have attracted notice from the enemy.

With Mr. Harriman (*left*) and Mr. John Winant, American Ambassador (*right*), at a Thanksgiving Day Luncheon of the American Society in 1941.

Fox Photo

Photo: *Associated Press*

Mr. Anthony Eden, his wife and his elder son Simon (killed on active service in Burma, 1945) outside the Foreign Office, 1943. The Foreign Minister had just returned from a tour of the U.S.A. and Canada.

As Honorary Air Commodore of No. 500 Auxiliary Squadron of the R.A.F., Anthony Eden prepares to lead his squadron through the skies (1947). Eden has flown more miles than any other diplomat.

Photo: *Harris*

Save the King, followed by *The Internationale*. Eden was loudly cheered for several minutes.

Two more days were spent in conversations and sight-seeing; chats with Molotov; reports to Lord Chilston; vague answers to the newspaper correspondents he saw in front of the fire at the British Embassy, in a room made cosy with chintz; a glimpse of Lenin's embalmed body, pink and stately in its polished granite tomb; the Cathedral of the Assumption, with its five gilt domes; a banquet at Litvinoff's home, at which a showpiece was a monster slab of butter with the inscription " Peace is Indivisible! "

All very exciting, but there was more work to do, and after a crowded three days, with the satisfaction of knowing that one of the stations in the palatial new underground railway had been named after him, Eden left for Warsaw, where President Pilsudski regaled him with twelve of Poland's national dishes and some Polish mead, which had been hidden in the castle ever since Napoleon occupied Warsaw in 1806. There was more general talk of peace and goodwill, and Colonel Beck, the Foreign Minister, reminded Eden of how Sigismund Augustus of Poland had written to the first Queen Elizabeth of England promising fair play for English sailors in Polish ports. But the diplomatic atmosphere was icy. Eden was hob-nobbing with two of Poland's potential enemies, Russia and Germany. Pilsudski was too old and tired to be interested in British vacillations. Beck explained that Poland already had agreements with both Russia and Germany, and that the proposed Eastern Pact seemed a needless complication.

On to Prague, capital of Czechoslovakia, and to the fantastic baroque splendour of Hradcany Palace, home of the Hapsburgs and now the residence of President Masaryk. More discussions, most of them with Dr. Benes. Then on to Leipzig and by plane to Cologne.

The plane journey from Cologne was so rough that Eden, his heart already strained by the rush and the long journeys, was made thoroughly ill by it. The plane ran into a snow storm over the Black Mountains, and was tossed in the air currents like a celluloid ball on a water spout, at one moment dropping into a void, the next being pushed upwards by unseen hands, the snow beating against it in fury.

At Cologne Eden broke down. His wife was shocked when at last he returned to London, and the doctor who examined him made up his mind at once. Eden was working too hard. He must rest completely for six weeks; his heart was badly strained. When, therefore, Sir John Simon left with the Prime Minister for the Stresa Conference, at which co-operation with France and Italy was to be discussed, he was not accompanied by Eden. The conference was also to discuss the Franco-British Declaration of February 3rd on the subject of arms, disarmament and security. The Prime Minister reported to the House on April 17th that despite the shock of Germany's provocative announcement of her intention to rearm, Britain, France and Italy would do all they could to promote international agreement on arms, and the door would be left open for Germany—meaning that the British Government still hoped that Germany might yet be persuaded to limit, if not to abandon, her rearmament programme. Germany's recent action was not condoned; but it was still hoped that Germany might play an active part in a system of collective security. A forlorn hope indeed!

Whilst it is an historic fact that the Government pursued a policy of appeasement with Fascist dictators, it is also probable that the policy of any alternative government at the time would have been equally disastrous and perhaps more immediately so. A White Paper on Defence issued on March 4th had evoked furious opposition from the Labour opposition, despite the fact that the suggested increase in Service Estimates was a mere $10\frac{1}{4}$ million pounds, and that the rest of Europe was frantically rearming. The feeling of pacifism was very strong, and easily exploited for political ends. When the Labour Party—or rather the Labour majority of the London County Council—withdrew the L.C.C. grant from the School Cadet Corps, the move had the sympathy of a very great number of people.

The financial situation at home was gradually improving. The accounts showed a surplus of ordinary revenue of nearly 20 million pounds more than had been estimated, and a saving in expenditure of over nine million. The number of unemployed was, very slowly, being whittled down, although a conference of churchmen called the Government's attention once again to the tragic plight of the miners of South Wales, to the " physical, mental, and spiritual deterioration of the people of Wales, who are sinking into bitterness and despair owing to their long continued unemployment."

In May, the nation took time off to celebrate the twenty-fifth year of King George's reign. The garlanded streets, gaily bedecked lamp-posts, triumphal arches and illuminations, and the magnificent processions in the course of which the King and Queen were greeted with tremendous enthusiasm, showed that in an age of revolutions the British Monarchy still exerted its old spell. The bonfires and floodlighting and ceremonial drives were scarcely forgotten when Eden, now recovered from his attack of heart strain, spoke to the East and West Fulham Conservative and Unionist Association on May 16th, 1935, on the subject of foreign affairs. The difficulties in Europe were " formidable " but Britain should pursue a foreign policy that was " frank, stalwart and above all firm in support of the League of Nations and the collective peace system ". He appealed, in a roundabout way, for Germany to rejoin the League. No progress had been made with Germany regarding security of armaments, nor had she rejoined the League. But " public opinion in the country would warmly welcome the return of Germany to the League of Nations ". Germany's demands for a high rate of increase in her armed forces could not be agreed to, despite " her anxieties in Eastern Europe ". But touching on Russia, he doubted whether she could have serious designs on any other country, especially Germany. " The distances which separate the greater part of Germany from Russia are truly vast. They have to be travelled to be understood " (here Mr. Eden could speak with some feeling) and for that reason and many others he found it " difficult to share the apprehension of military aggression by Soviet Russia which appears to exist in Germany to-day."

A few weeks later Anthony Eden was promoted to Cabinet rank. It was felt, and it was surely true, that he understood the swiftly-moving events in Europe better than any other member of the Government, and certainly knew more about the workings of the League of Nations than anyone in the Cabinet. Ramsay MacDonald, whose health had begun to break down, resigned with a certain feeling of thankfulness and handed the reins of office to Stanley Baldwin. Sir John Simon went to the Home Office, and Sir Samuel Hoare, who had privately hoped he would be sent to India as Governor-General, a post for which, by virtue of his many years in that country, he was well suited, was made Foreign Minister. Anthony Eden was made Minister without Portfolio for League of Nations Affairs, with his headquarters at the Foreign Office. Some wondered if this arrangement would work—was it not like having two Foreign Ministers? In a sense, it was. But the two men, it was hoped, would work closely and harmoniously together; and foreign affairs could scarcely be divorced from activities in the League of Nations.

Eden's patience and hard work in the face of continual discouragement had impressed members of all political parties. The public recognised that although a Tory he was not one of the "old guard". Here, it was felt, was a man who really cared about collective security, who would secure peace if he was given his head—which, for good or ill, was something that never happened. His popularity was greatly increased in Europe and America by virtue of the fact that the Italian press singled him out for special abuse; it is always a compliment to be abused by the unscrupulous, implying as it does that they are convinced they have no common ground with you. It was a hall-mark of Eden's integrity that the Fascists saw in him one of their principal enemies.

A few days before his appointment, *The Spectator* paid this tribute to the up-and-coming statesman:

> " In the last three years, when with each month the international situation has worsened and the prospects of disarmament have become increasingly remote, and Europe is again as it was in 1914, an armed camp, one man has stood out with courage and consistency for the translation of the ideals of the post-war peace system into realities. . . . at thirty-seven he has won a position for himself abroad and in his own country that no man of comparable age has achieved in our time."

The fundamental cause of his success, the writer claimed, was Eden's " deep sincerity." In this he differed from most statesmen, who had ceased to believe in anything at all. One could, I suppose, summarise the drift to war between 1919 and 1939 by calling it a chaos of contradictory expediencies. Even nations that were themselves to be the most tragic victims of nationalistic aggression—Poland, for example—were obsessed with nationalistic ambitions of their own. When Eden had been in Warsaw the dying Pilsudski was more concerned with squabbling with the Czechs over the ownership of the industrial district of Teshin (part of Czechoslovakia) than with trying to avoid the large scale tragedy of a war in Europe.

Meanwhile yet another war was simmering. Mussolini had made up his mind to attack Abyssinia, and Italy's language, both on the radio and in the state-controlled press, became steadily more menacing. On December 5th, 1934, there had been a clash between Abyssinian and Italian border patrols at Walwal, an oasis between Abyssinia and Italian Somaliland. All the indications were that Mussolini was determined to make war. For years his speeches had been filled with bluster about the invincibility of Italian forces, the heroic stature of the Italian, and the glories of militarism. But with Italians this talk could not sound real until one humiliation had been wiped off the slate of history—Adowa. For fifty years Italy had longed for the control of Ethiopia, or Abyssinia as the world preferred to describe the country. Late in the nineteenth century Italy had secured a foothold on the East African coast and in Somaliland. In an attempt to secure a firm hold on Abyssinia, Italy, in 1889 had bribed and supported a chieftain known as Menelek to usurp the Imperial throne. In return he was persuaded to sign a Treaty which the Italians claimed made his country a protectorate. Two years later Menelek denounced this treaty. In 1895 Italian forces invaded from Eritrea and suffering a devastating defeat near Adowa; they were forced to retreat, to pay a heavy indemnity and to recognise Menelek's absolute sovereignty.

Abyssinia had joined the League of Nations in 1923, and in 1928 had signed an agreement with Italy by which the two countries were pledged to friendliness and co-operation. But Mussolini knew that scientific advancement in offensive weapons made a repetition of the Adowa fiasco unlikely; Menelek's men had relied on strategy, familiarity with the terrain, cunning, surprise and a clever exploitation of the Italian's excessive confidence. Then the Abyssinians had not suffered from any great inferiority in arms, but if they had to face armoured tanks, bombs and machine-gunning aeroplanes it might be another story. Besides, a successful colonial enterprise would not only bolster up Fascist morale, but distract the minds of the population from the grievous economic ills from which Italy was suffering at the time. As for the League of Nations—what could it do to restrain him? Had it stopped the Japanese invasion of Manchuria? The war between Bolivia and Paraguay? German rearmament? As for that young chap in the British Foreign Office—that " dandified popinjay " as Mussolini sneeringly described him—he could achieve nothing. Eden was out to make the League of Nations work, but could he succeed? Meanwhile, Mussolini made the Walwal incident an excuse for a display of naked force intended to intimidate Abyssinia. Tanks, guns, planes and ammunition were poured into Italy's East African colonies, and a force of a quarter of a million soldiers and labourers established there.

Eden, Sir Samuel Hoare and Sir Robert (now Lord) Vansittart, permanent Under-Secretary at the Foreign Office, had done some hard thinking, and talking in private, usually at Vansittart's quiet country home at Denham in Buckinghamshire. Eden disliked Mussolini intensely—he had never forgiven the dictator for bursting into uproarious laughter when, advancing over the huge polished floor of the dictator's study in the Palazzo Venezia, Eden tripped on a rug. Another report has it that to emphasise his points Mussolini thumped the desk with such effect that ink had been splashed on Eden's immaculate waistcoat. A simpler explanation is that Eden had seen Mussolini for what he was—a gross, bullying, insensitive unscrupulous man intent on war and power.

Baldwin had adroitly dodged a request to define the respective duties of Anthony Eden and Sir Samuel Hoare. Their work was bound to overlap, and unless there was to be indecision at a time when events moved fast, each should know where his duties lay. Luckily the two were able to talk it over together. Hoare entertained some hope that he could influence Mussolini in favour of British foreign policy. The two had co-operated during the first World War, when Hoare was a young Lieutenant-Colonel on the General Staff on the Italian front, and Mussolini was a young agitator and editor of a paper in Milan. Britain at that time was worried at the possible defection of Italy from the Allied cause. The Italians were sick of war, and there was a strong pacifist and pro-German element in Milan. On that occasion, at least, Mussolini had promised to make short work of the pacifists. " I will mobilise the *mutilati* in Milan," he declared, " and they will break the heads of any pacifists who try to hold anti-war meetings in the streets." Perhaps, thought Hoare, this fortuitous and short-lived acquaintanceship might make the nucleus of a new goodwill between Britain and Italy. Mussolini was reputed to dislike Hitler and distrust his designs in Austria. Hoare entertained the hope that Britain might split the Axis, but Eden was more reserved. He had no faith in the value of Mussolini's promises, and felt the only reliable way of coping with him was to bring League pressure to bear on him, and to impose sanctions.

While the Italians stirred their witch's brew in Abyssinia, a pale and arrogant ex-salesman of champagne, Herr von Ribbentrop, arrived from Berlin to discuss a naval agreement between Britain and Germany. The suggestion had come from Hitler during a meeting with Sir John Simon in April. The plan which Ribbentrop brought with him provided that Germany could build up a naval strength in the proportion of 35 per cent. of that of the British Commonwealth. This was conceded in the agreement which was speedily reached. Further, Germany was to be allowed to build a submarine tonnage equal to that of the British Commonwealth, provided the proportionate strengths of the Navies were not affected, though she undertook not to exercise this right unless in exceptional circumstances.

The First Lord of the Admiralty, in a broadcast, commended the Anglo-German Naval Agreement as a first step to a general agreement on naval strength. The plan evoked the fiercest criticism in France, Italy, America and, of course, at home. Germany had shown contempt for her promises by tearing up the Treaty of Versailles; now she was being encouraged to build a navy.

Anthony Eden scored a personal triumph at Geneva by helping to remove, if only temporarily, the threat of war to Abyssinia. The League put forward compromise terms, which amounted to a reaffirmation of Article 5 of the Italo-

Abyssinia Treaty of 1928 which provided that there would be no recourse to force. In Italy itself there was no diminution of militarism, whilst the Italian press seethed with vituperation and abuse of Britain. Mr. Eden, in a speech to the League Council, hoped that the action would lead to a " friendly and equitable settlement of the question."

But that matter was hardly disposed of when at the request of the Government he undertook another tricky and unpleasant assignment. Because the Anglo-German Naval Agreement had aroused consternation in France and Italy Eden was asked to placate them both. Accordingly he set off on a tour of Paris and Rome to sooth injured dignity and ruffled tempers; neither France nor Italy had been consulted over the Agreement, the British Government's attitude being that the opportunity might have been lost if Hitler's gesture had not instantly been accepted.

In Paris, Eden saw Laval, the French Foreign Minister, who in the agreement negotiated with Mussolini in January had offered Mussolini the use of the Addis Ababa railway in Abyssinia and other concessions, including an unofficial promise not to obstruct Italian ambitions in Abyssinia. No wonder Mussolini remarked: " It is a pleasure to talk to him. I venture to believe that there is personal sympathy between us, because our tormented youths had something in common, because our similar evolution has led us away from a somewhat Utopian universalism to profound and indestructible national realities." *The Times* in a despatch from their Paris correspondent on June 23rd, said that " at yesterday's meeting . . . Mr. Eden, who had been in touch with London earlier, and M. Laval were alone, and profited by the intimacy of the occasion to discuss their respective points of view." That is, one imagines, one of the points of such a meeting. However, although it was agreed to regard the Naval Agreement as " a bit of past history," that did not imply French approval of it. He was able to assure Laval that Britain did not seek separate air agreements with Germany.

On June 23rd Eden was in Rome again. One feels he cannot have relished his mission, which was two-fold—to explain the Anglo-German Naval Agreement and to discuss the Abyssinian question with Mussolini. The interview with Mussolini was quite fruitless, and all the more galling to Eden because of the mutual antipathy between them and the fact that he had to offer the dictator a strip of British territory—in Somaliland—as an inducement to abandon his ambitions in Abyssinia. Appeasement had been carried a stage further, and Eden was the unhappy instrument of this humiliating overture. Luckily for Britain, and perhaps for the Somalis, Mussolini rejected the offer with contempt. There were angry exchanges between them, and for a while Anthony showed something of his father's fiery temper.

A few days later came a demonstration of the extraordinary background against which British statesmen and legislators were expected to do their work. The Peace Ballot, organised by the Labour and Liberal Parties in conjunction with the League of Nations Union, published the results of its enquiries.

Eleven and a half million people had taken part in the Ballot, but the issues were hopelessly confused. Ten and a half million people declared that they were in favour of an all-round reduction in armaments and nearly ten million wanted to see military aircraft abolished altogether—yet ten million people also advocated the application of sanctions to an aggressor—nearly seven million approving military sanctions. The ballot was confirmation of the confusion of which the public itself was guilty; of wanting opposite things. On one hand, disarmament; on the other, power to restrain an aggressor who, being interested in nothing but force, could presumably only be restrained by force. How the unarmed nations could apply sanctions against an aggressor was never explained. The ballot proved the hunger of people for peace—an understandable hatred of war. It also proved their complete unwillingness to face the facts as they were. With a public demanding collective security on one hand and disarmament as well, the lot of statesmen having to deal with people like Hitler and Mussolini was unenviable.

Giving the House of Commons an account of his talks with Mussolini, Eden said " I said that British Foreign Policy was founded upon the League. His Majesty's Government could not therefore remain indifferent to events which might profoundly affect the League's future . . . it was through collective security that in our judgment peace could be preserved and only through the League that Britain could play her full part in Europe." He continued:

> "I then described to Signor Mussolini what His Majesty's government had in mind . . . To obtain a final settlement of the dispute between Italy and Abyssinia, His Majesty's Government would be prepared to offer to Abyssinia a strip of territory in British Somaliland giving Abyssinia access to the sea. This proposal was intended to facilitate such territorial and economic concessions by Abyssinia to Italy as might have been involved in an agreed settlement. . . . Only the gravity of the situation could justify the cession of British territory with equivalent return. . . ."

The suggestion did "not commend itself to Signor Mussolini." Nor did it commend itself to the House, which did not like parts of British territory being offered as baits and bribes. But as Mussolini had rejected the offer the matter was allowed to rest.

On July 22nd in the House of Commons Anthony Eden defended, at some length and with some vehemence, the Anglo-German Naval Agreement. At one time Germany would have been content with an army of 300,000—now she was organising an army of 550,000. Wouldn't it have been better to have agreed to the smaller figure when one had the chance? Would one wish to see the lost opportunity of the limitation of land forces repeated in respect of naval armaments? The logic of that argument was not infallible, since it ignored a point of principle. Eden denied, at the same time that the agreement which amongst other things, permitted Germany to build submarines, had diminished the prestige of the League of Nations. Considering that the League had been brought into existence to abolish armaments and outlaw war, one would have thought that the rearmament of a military dictatorship, and negotiations entitling or even encouraging it to increase its naval forces, would have weakened the League.

Eden denied indignantly that he and Sir Samuel Hoare had gone behind the back of the House of Commons in respect of the offer made to Mussolini. The purpose of the offer, he said, was to obtain a final settlement of the dispute between Italy and Abyssinia. The object was to give some *quid pro quo* to Abyssinia for territorial and economic concessions by her which the settlement of the dispute with Italy might entail.

Had it been welcomed, the next step would have been consultation with France, with Abyssinia and with the House of Commons.

The public was depressed at the drift of things. So, too, were those closer to events. Neville Chamberlain, then Chancellor of the Exchequer, recorded in his diary: " . . . it does seem barbarous that in these days it should still be in the power of one man, for a whim or to preserve his personal influence, to throw away the lives of thousands of Italians." And King George V was saying to Sir Samuel Hoare: " I am an old man. I have been through one world war. How can I go through another? If I am to go on, you must keep us out of one."

Eden continued his efforts to prevent a war in Abyssinia. In August 1935 representatives of Great Britain, France and Italy met in Paris with a view to negotiating a settlement. The talks broke down, and on September 11th Sir Samuel Hoare delivered a speech to the League Assembly making it plain that Britain stood by collective security and the application of the League Covenant. In other words, aggression would be met by sanctions.

Before making this statement Hoare had consulted with Laval in Paris, despite the fact that he was suffering from arthritis and had been obliged to fly to Paris lying on his back. Sir Samuel, a good judge of character, was not attracted by Laval's " greasy hair, dirty white tie and shifty look " but admired his nimble mind.

But Mussolini, in spite of all warnings, had no intention of backing out. On October 3rd, Italian troops invaded Abyssinia and with bombs and tanks and mustard gas wiped out the memory of Adowa. Four days later the League named Italy an aggressor. Later, sanctions were applied under Article 16 of the League Covenant, the decision being agreed to by 47 nations. Britain applied her sanctions from October 29th—prohibiting the export of some things which could help Italy in her attack. But oil, the precious commodity without which planes could not fly, tanks would be immobilised and troops could not be transported to the front, was not cut off from Italy. Mussolini had made it clear that oil sanctions would be treated as an act of war, and neither France nor Britain was willing to risk war at that time.

Whilst the Abyssinian war was raging, the Government's lease of life was drawing to a close and a General Election was necessary. The Government's efforts to adhere to League principles was one of the Conservative's main electioneering points, and Eden, as the principal spokesman on League matters, got back to Parliament easily with a large majority. Ramsay MacDonald lost his seat. The Conservatives were returned. The half-hearted sanctions applied to Italy in no way lessened the deadly impact of her attack.

At this time a drama was being enacted which was to prove of crucial importance in Anthony Eden's career—the Hoare-Laval Pact. Sir Samuel Hoare had negotiated with Laval, who was so friendly with Mussolini that he had a direct and secret line to him in Rome.

By the evening of December 8th agreement had been reached between Hoare and Laval. In effect, Italy would be getting what she wanted without war. The plan allowed for the cession to Italy of huge areas and exclusive economic rights in Southern Abyssinia. Abyssinia would be given an outlet to the sea " with full sovereign rights " over all the districts ceded to Italy —a sovereignty which, it goes without saying, she could not have asserted against an armed dictatorship. The plan would have been put to the League of Nations for approval or rejection, but it never got that far. Although the discussions had been secret, news of the scheme leaked out and a wave of disillusioned horror and indignation swept across Britain. That a dictator whose airmen were dropping mustard gas on children should be given parts of the country he had attacked was sheer capitulation.

So it had seemed to the public. Actually Britain was the first country to apply sanctions to Italy, to try to prevent the raw materials of war from reaching her. A League committee recommended an embargo on oil exports to Italy after Britain had taken action—but it was a half-hearted gesture that could come to nothing. A neutrality resolution passed by Congress in the United States gave the president no authority to stop oil, steel or iron going to Italy, and if British and Dutch companies had cut off Italy's oil supplies, America would have supplied the need.

The Hoare-Laval plan, as it came to be known, was a compromise—an attempt to condone something evil so that greater evil might not result. As Lord Templewood has put it in his memoirs:

> The proposals were in striking contrast with Mussolini's earlier demands. His minimum terms had been the cession to Italy of all the non-Amharic districts, and an Italian mandate for the rest of Abyssinia, and he had threatened, if these were not accepted, to wipe Abyssinia off the map. The war had since started with a series of Italian victories, and it seemed certain that unless we could end it in the immediate future, incalculable suffering would be inflicted on the population, and the whole country annexed, the Emperor deposed, Mussolini inevitably driven into Hitler's arms, and the League hopelessly disrupted, and German aggression everywhere encouraged.

That was as Sir Samuel Hoare saw the problem at the time. Whether Eden protested to him or to Sir Robert Vansittart at this attitude to Italy we do not know. The policy, in a nutshell, was that the only way to keep dictators from joining forces was to make common cause with one of them, which might be good strategy but bad principle. In all this muddle and drift, Eden was almost the only man to care about the League of Nations as a matter of principle rather than a question of expediency. When the Cabinet discussed and approved the Hoare-Laval plan, it is said that he threatened to resign. In answer to anxious questions in the House of Commons, Eden was still the spokesman for the Government, but his manner betrayed his uneasiness. He stressed that Hoare and Laval had been trying to find a basis for peace at the request of the Co-ordinating Committee of the League. There were inaccuracies in press reports, he said, without specifying what he thought they were. He admitted that the proposals went beyond what people might have expected. The exchange of territory he described as conveying " definite advantages to both sides ". It was not the speech of a man whose feelings were outraged, or whose heart was moved by the plight of the Abyssinians; it did not sound like the speech of a man who had thought or was thinking of resigning.

The news of the Hoare-Laval deal had been flashed across the world. Neville Chamberlain was recording in his diary:

> " When Sam left for Paris . . . we had no idea that he would be invited to consider detailed peace proposals. I believed, and

my colleagues believed also, that he was going to stop off at Paris for a few hours on his way to Switzerland. Instead of that, a set of proposals was agreed to, and enough was allowed by the French to leak out to the press to make it impossible for us to amend the proposals, or even to defer accepting them, without throwing over our own Foreign Secretary. Our whole prestige in foreign affairs has tumbled to pieces like a house of cards. . . ."

Eden, meanwhile, hurried to Geneva to try to undo some of the damage to British prestige. His presence there had some calming effect; the proposals, he explained, were not final and were subject to League approval. But his work was undone a few days later by the publication of the proposals, which proved even worse than had been forecast. Public opinion at home reached a crescendo, and on December 18th Sir Samuel Hoare submitted his resignation to King George V.

The debate in the House of Commons on December 19th earned Mr. Baldwin the nickname of "Old Sealed Lips", a term of derision used by his opponents for the rest of his days. He said that if his lips were unsealed he was sure nobody in the House would vote against him. The matter was made no better by Sir Samuel's unrepentant speech of resignation. But the conscience of the nation had been thoroughly roused, and Baldwin knew he could not gainsay it. Now he needed a Foreign Minister, somebody who would be acceptable to the public; someone whose reputation was unsullied abroad; somebody with the necessary experience, charm, tact, artifice. Who could it be? Only one man in the Cabinet could answer this description. That was Anthony Eden.

TWELVE

Foreign Secretary

AT last "Lord Eyelashes", as Eden had become known to the Italian press, occupied one of the most important positions in the whole Cabinet. Home affairs were dwarfed by the threatening aspect of foreign affairs; and Britain's part in them was now very largely in the hands of a young man whose name was a byword but whose personality was elusive. His quiet confidence and aristocratic bearing seemed a tonic in a Europe torn by strain and distrust. His caution commended himself to the older politicians; his somewhat indeterminate idealism encouraged the young; his dandyism and good looks appealed to women.

Yet there were always two Edens. That immaculate clothing, for instance; his mother always maintained that he did it to get on, because it was expected of him. A man making his way in the world could not afford to look slovenly.

His wife Beatrice was delighted when he broke the news to her. It was what he had always wanted; it was what he had been working for. However, it meant that in those days of crisis, that she would see even less of him, and the rift which was in time to separate them was to widen just a little more. A degree of mutual tolerance had become a feature of their relationship. If, after a dinner party at home, he chose to go to his study and relax over a book of Shakespeare, she did not mind; it was well understood that his work was demanding, and that he might not be inclined, as she might be, to go off to a dance hall or night club with the guests. He had no wish that her life should be as heavily burdened as his own; nor was he willing to unload any part of his own burdens in the interest of his own pleasure.

Soon Eden, dressed in impeccable morning suit, drove to Buckingham Palace to be received by the dying King George V.

King George, who was a good judge of men, had met Eden many times before and respected him greatly. One suspects that he was never over-stimulated by his conversation. Eden does not mind telling against himself of the occasion when he had called to give the King a report of recent happenings in the field of foreign affairs. The King received him in a room immediately above the bandstand at Buckingham Palace. He apologised for receiving him there but explained " It's all right, however. I have told the band not to play until I give the word." The King then delivered a long harangue on foreign affairs, at the end of which Eden began to say what he had come to say. The king reached for a small gold handbell. " Just a second," he said. A page appeared. " Tell the bandmaster," he instructed the page, " he can start playing now." Then, turning to Eden, ". . . you were saying? "

On this occasion, however, the King was attentive and serious. He was very worried at the drift of affairs, and longed to save his country the horrors of another war.

And so to the Foreign Office, whose air of sleepy gentility is, perhaps, conducive to that degree of detachment necessary for the handling of serious matters. Eden's new office was a large well-furnished room looking out over St. James's Park, reached by means of a lift through a side entrance. Soon he was in conference with Sir Robert Vansittart, the quiet, almost anonymous Permanent Under Secretary whose shrewd and tough mind was behind almost every transaction of the Foreign Office in the inter-war years.

Both Press and public welcomed his appointment hoping it would mean an end to drift. Actually, this was an illusion. Until his job became untenable, Eden continued as the willing servant of the Government, loyally fulfilling his responsibility by being reticent on matters about which he personally felt strongly, committing himself to nothing without the most careful consultation with the Ministers concerned.

Eden, at 38, was the youngest man to hold the post for 84 years. Ever since he entered the House of Commons twelve years before he had worked and waited for it. He was two months younger than Lord Rosebery was when he became Foreign Minister in the Gladstone ministry of 1886. In the past 100 years there had been only one younger Foreign

Minister—the Earl of Granville, who became Foreign Minister in 1851 at the age of 36.

What Eden did not do was to make any direct or human contact with the worried British public, which for years had been self-deluded, expecting a League of Nations to work miracles with governments and with human nature without any force with which to back their arguments. This fallacy had never been exposed by any statesman speaking plainly and factually on behalf of the Government as Churchill knew so well how to do during the war. A plain statement of the gravity of the situation and the facts behind the rearmament and expansionist plans of Germany, Italy and Japan might have rallied the public and encouraged the Government in a completely new programme of sane preparation and plain speaking. But the Government was not changed. The attitude of which the Hoare-Laval Pact was merely a symptom had not changed; the monstrous plans of Hitler and Mussolini—plans which were by now obvious to the world—were hidden behind polite euphemisms, elaborate under-statements and pious hopes.

A few weeks after Eden's appointment King George V died at Sandringham, and an elaborate and moving homage culminated in a simple but beautiful service at St. George's Chapel, Windsor.

For Eden the year began with a rush of work which continued unabated throughout the year. A whole procession of important people had to be seen; von Neurath of Germany, the pleasure-loving King Carol of Rumania, King Boris of Bulgaria, Flandin of France, the flashy millionaire Fascist, Prince Starhemberg of Austria. Flandin was worried about the Rhineland, as well he might be. There were reports that Germany was planning to invade it, a step which years ago would have meant war, but which would in any event add to the mounting tension in Europe.

Von Neurath, speaking for Germany, assured Eden that Germany was not planning to occupy the Rhineland; Eden had information to the contrary, and requested an urgent audience with the new King, Edward VIII, an impetuous and often opinionated man who did not understand the legislative limits imposed on a modern monarch, and lacked his father's intimate knowledge of foreign affairs. Whereas his father knew much and interfered little, he knew little and interfered much. January and much of February, 1936, were taken up with "exploratory talks" of every description, including attempts to strengthen the Anglo-French-Soviet bloc.

In the House of Commons on February 25th, 1936, Eden was able to find words to defend the Government's tediously slow, half-hearted attitude in face of Italy's invasion of Abyssinia. The Opposition, not very reasonably, in view of their refusal to see Britain strong enough to assert herself, demanded oil sanctions against Italy. In a week's time the Committee of Eighteen of the League of Nations would decide whether sanctions would be imposed against Italy or not, and the world would know whether the League had any means of implementing its moral judgments.

Eden denied that the Government had been dilatory, using heavy sarcasm against his Socialist critic, Mr. Lees-Smith. Mr. Eden went on to say that the Government had taken every step in its power. . . . Italy had been declared an aggressor by a number of States on the League Council . . . *what was remarkable was the rapidity of action* and not the dilatoriness of the League. He added a speculation of his own which proved wide of the mark. "The effect," he said, "of those sanctions which have been imposed is in effect cumulative and continuous, and the effect must ultimately have an important influence in achieving what is the main objective of the League—the cessation of hostilities." Meanwhile, bombs were raining down on the Abyssinians.

Once more this debate makes me feel that Eden encouraged a faith in the effectiveness of the League which his own observations of its working, and its history, could not possibly justify. Yet again he showed his unhappy knack for making bad situations sound better than they were. It is axiomatic that to cut off oil supplies from an aggressor is the first and most urgent thing to do. Eden knew that tanks need oil, cars need oil, planes, cruisers and submarines need oil. Yet despite that he could talk as though there were some doubt about the potential effectiveness of oil sanctions against a warring nation—as though the question of whether to stop exporting oil to an aggressor was a matter of academic uncertainty, demanding long discussion. "Oil," he said, "is a sanction like any other, and must be judged by the same criterion, *whether its imposition will stop the war.*" My own view is that it might not have stopped the war, but it would have made it more difficult for Italy to wage it. However, said Mr. Eden, the Government would play its full part in any collective action agreed upon. There was a hint to Italy that sanctions were an unpleasant problem of which Britain would like to be rid. " I wish to say—for it is my duty to return to Geneva to resume the discussions of further sanctions . . . that His Majesty's Government and this country, while playing their full part with others in the imposition of sanctions, desire first and foremost to see the re-establishment of a just peace between Italy and Abyssinia." Of the general outlook in foreign affairs, Eden made a statement which might be used in text books as an awful example of a platitude:

> " It would be equally idle to deny that there is anxiety which we must all share on the Government Bench, an anxiety which is not minimized, though it is mitigated, by reflection that the course which this country pursues in the next year or two may well be the decisive factor on events."

The war generation, he continued, had thrust upon itself the obligation to prevent the tragedy of another war . . . an obligation only to be discharged by adherence to the League and Collective Security. For that to work, the system must be truly collective, powerful enough to deter an aggressor, and Britain strong enough to play her part—a self-evident condition which did not, however, make sense to the Opposition, from whom came cries of " the old, old story." Shouting down interruptors, he made no bones about collective security: " . . . if you want to get disarmament you will only be able to get it through increased power and authority of the League."

Provoked, Eden always speaks with more feeling and clarity, One of his troubles in life is that he has had too much authority and influence whilst subject to too little criticism. This time he really created an atmosphere of hope and enthusiasm in the League; Britain could, he said, take the lead in maintaining the authority of the League, and in inspiring others to work for its full development . . . Britain had taken the lead in the past by giving the world Parliamentary Government; it could, and it was the Government's intention that it should build up a new world order.

But there were still men who could under-state the enormity of war, such as Mr. Amery, who sneered at the " arid pedantry " of those who would " deal with a great nation on the lines of a stipendiary magistrate who fined it forty shillings and costs for starting a war." Major Attlee was " profoundly disappointed " with Eden's speech and alleged that Britain was buying off the aggressor.

Eden's honeyed words were delivered in poor voice for the occasion, for he was somewhat hoarse. Signor Grandi, the Italian Ambassador, listened attentively from the Distinguished Strangers' gallery. The Ambassadors of France, Germany and Russia were also present. This galaxy of diplomats may have accounted for Eden's reluctance to commit himself to any course of action except that which might generally be agreed upon by the League. Allowing for that, his debut as Foreign Minister was counted a success.

No man, it is safe to say, ever carried a weightier burden than Eden in those first few months of his office. Even had there been no routine administrative work to bother about—and of course there always is—Eden would have found the pressure fierce enough. A Naval Conference had drawn to its close at the beginning of March. Eden thought the moment propitious to approach the German Ambassador in London and remind him of a proposal put by Hitler in December, that nations which had signed the Locarno Treaty—including, of course, Germany—should proceed to negotiate an Air Pact limiting Air Forces and their uses.

Germany's reply to this was a diplomatic bombshell. She repudiated the Locarno Treaty and announced that her troops were already occupying the Rhineland, which was now " restored to unrestricted sovereignty with Germany." She offered at the same time to conclude Non-Aggression Pacts with her neighbours, to discuss an Air Pact and to rejoin the League of Nations. Eden warned the Ambassador of the grave effects of this " unilateral " action in Europe, then hurried to Paris to consult with representatives of the Locarno powers. Feeling ran high in Paris, too high for calm thinking, especially as France had no intention of backing her indignation with positive action. In Britain too, feelings on the subject were mixed; there were many people who approved of Germany's action, but few would have risked war to maintain the Locarno Treaty. *The Times* in particular was strongly pro-German. But the appeasers were not simply in the Government. The public equally refused to face the facts. Most people wanted " them " to do something; few would have been willing, at the time, to back their clamour with personal action.

Speaking in the House of Commons on March 10th, Eden admitted that the German repudiation of Locarno was a severe blow to the sanctity of treaties, but that whilst this could not be condoned, it was " a manifest duty to rebuild " (an echo, interestingly enough, of pro-German *Times's* own phrase, which had been "A Chance to Rebuild "). Next Eden saw the German Ambassador and urged him to ask Hitler to withdraw all but " a symbolic number " of troops from the Rhineland and to take no steps, such as fortification of the Rhineland, until there had been discussions and agreements. Conversations between the Locarno powers continued in London, with Eden presiding, and a statement was issued making it plain that in the event of aggression Britain would honour her obligations under the Locarno Treaty. And so Germany, without firing a bullet, had gained her first round and brought her frontier up to the Maginot Line.

In this crisis, as in so many others, Eden worked feverishly —often until two in the morning—arriving home exhausted. It was rumoured that in the Cabinet he was the only man who demanded firmness in face of German threats, but it was not as simple as that. The Dominions, for example, had never ratified the Locarno Pact, and in any warfare arising from it, Britain could not expect automatic help from that quarter.

The pro-German element in Britain grew stronger. Constant changes of French Governments, France's vacillating policy, coupled with the distinctly unpleasant impression conveyed by press photographs of Laval, tended to make the Germans seem better by contrast. With France so divided, some argued, the only sane policy would be to make terms with Hitler.

The heavy strain of diplomatic activities at this time was described by Mrs. Beatrice Eden. Her husband often arrived home at 4 a.m., yet had to be at the Council table (for discussion with the Locarno powers) at 10.30 a.m. the next day with all the preparation and scrutiny of documents done in between meetings. Taking three days, she described his hours as being from 10 a.m. until 1 a.m., 10 a.m. to 2 a.m., 10 a.m. to 4 a.m.

Meanwhile the Abyssinian war continued with unabated fury. The forces of Haile Selassie were in retreat, and when Mussolini announced plans for the " total annihilation " of the Abyssinian military formations he was announcing to the world the total inadequacy of " collective security ". On April 8th Eden took a firm line at Geneva. The talks, he said, could not drag on as they were, without something being done. He appealed to both parties to arbitrate. What the British Government wanted was the " immediate cessation of hostilities " and peace negotiations within the Covenant of the League. But it was a vain hope. Italy had almost won the war. Mr. Eden added with " unmistakable emphasis " that if the efforts of the Chairman and Secretary-General produced no results the British Government " must reserve their attitude as to any subsequent steps which they might feel compelled to take in the matter." This highly non-committal statement was described by one correspondent as " this blunt declaration " and added that it caused " great excitement " at Geneva! But Eden did condemn in the strongest language the Italian's use of poison gas, and his complaint of delay did hasten things up. But too late. At a later meeting Eden was even more critical of Italy and insisted that British sanctions, so far as they had been applied, must continue. But he knew, as everyone knew, that Italy had got what she wanted and that the existing sanctions could not save Abyssinia.

Hardly a fortnight later the problem solved itself. Addis Ababa, capital of Abyssinia, was captured by Italian troops, the war was ended and Haile Selassie, the diminutive " Lion of Judah," left for exile in England. Many people, including Austen Chamberlain, Stanley Baldwin and Samuel Hoare, felt that there could be no point in continuing sanctions, which could only further embitter Britain's relations with Italy, lock up part of our naval forces in the Mediterranean area in case of some warlike act from the Italians, and at the same time fail to benefit Abyssinia.

Shortly after this came Neville Chamberlain's famous "midsummer madness" speech, in which he unwittingly revealed not simply how he was thinking, but how many of his colleagues must be thinking too. He made it abundantly plain that his main worry was to avoid offending Italy:

"I see, for instance, the other day that the President of the League of Nations Union issued a circular to its members in which he ... urged them to continue a campaign of pressure ... with the idea that if we were to pursue the policy of sanctions, and even to intensify it, it is still possible to preserve the independence of Abyssinia. That seems to me the very midsummer of madness...."

Chamberlain had not consulted Eden about that speech. "I did not consult Anthony Eden, because he would have been bound to beg me not to say what I proposed. At the same time as I was urging on Anthony the reform of the League, I said sanctions must come to an end...."

Chamberlain's speech made a sensation. In retrospect it is not as scandalous as it sounded then. He was not condoning the conquest of Abyssinia. Furthermore, Britain had done more in the way of sanctions than any other country. Russia, a Communist country, had by contrast actually increased her oil exports to Italy during the Abyssinian war.

Chamberlain's "midsummer madness" views had shocked the public, but more was to come—this time from Eden himself. For years he had spoken hundreds of thousands of words, about collective security. His words had fallen as ineffectually as a mild shower of rain on a concrete roof, but he was committed irrevocably by his own words to collective security and the stern treatment of aggressor nations. Now it became Eden's unpleasant duty to put his own ideas into reverse. The Government, to appease Mussolini, wanted to see an end of sanctions as soon as possible. The change of policy came as a shock, and some were disappointed that Anthony Eden was (seemingly) the willing and uncritical instrument of this abandonment of League principles.

Speaking to the House, Eden pointed out that Britain had taken the lead in proposing League action in the "dispute" (the word "war" was tactfully avoided). Therefore it was right and proper that Britain should take the lead in raising the question of removing sanctions at the next League meeting. Sanctions had failed. They could no longer restore Abyssinia's position. No member of the League—including Britain—would take military action to free Abyssinia, (or " restore the position " as Eden put it). "*For the sake of the League and in the interests of collective action*" Britain would at the next meeting of the League propose the dropping of sanctions.

The speech came strangely from a crusader. Abyssinia had been attacked. Throughout, the word " dispute " had been used to describe a cruel and unjust war. Throughout, Ethiopians were being killed—men, women and children—whilst statesmen talked in the palatial League headquarters at Geneva, or the comfortable Beau Rivage lounge where so many diplomatic conversations were conducted, the stone dignity of the Foreign Office or the gilded pretension of the Quai D'Orsay. Now Abyssinia lay prostrate, her people enslaved, their Emperor an exile, received in Britain without the attention due to his office and greeted with a minimum of formal politeness. Italy, gloating and triumphant, was to escape even nominal condemnation; the half-hearted sanctions must be removed lest Mussolini be offended. It was an occasion where moral indignation and mere humanity could have been expressed in glowing words, words of leadership which could have awakened the sleeping conscience of Britain. But in tone and manner Eden might have been addressing Clapham Rotary Club on the mating habits of the little owl. There was, as Mr. Greenwood told the House of Commons, no word of sympathy for a broken nation, no word of condemnation on a nation that had deliberately used poison gas. Greenwood made the mistake of claiming that this " betrayal " of the League was deliberate. Lloyd George was more effective in his attack. Mr. Eden, he said, had spoken of the " well-ordered ranks of the League " and now was himself going to the League to break them.

Eden, with what amounted to near genius, made a sell-out sound like an achievement. He said that now the League was " perplexed " it was Britain's duty to lead again. " No doubt it would be easy, quite easy for us not to do so, and to leave it to someone else and to follow after someone else's lead, but I do not believe that that is the right attitude for this country to take. I am quite convinced that so far from this lead, which we are going to take, embarrassing others, it will be welcomed in many quarters." Those quarters might include Rome, as one Member of Parliament suggested; it would certainly not have been true of Addis Ababa.

The " sanctions," Eden continued, had been ineffective because of a "military miscalculation." It had been assumed, why it is difficult to imagine, that the Italian campaign would take longer than it did, and that the limited restraints imposed on Italy would take time to be effective. The situation in Abyssinia could not be retrieved without military action, which nobody was willing to take. A war, if it started, could not be confined to the Mediterranean. At the next meeting of the League the Assembly of fifty nations would consider the question, " but His Majesty's Government, after mature consideration, *on advice which I as Foreign Secretary thought it my duty to give them*, have come to the conclusion that there is no longer any utility in continuing these measures as a means of pressure against Italy."

There were cries of " Shame! " and " Resign! " from outraged Members. The Parliamentary Labour Party published a manifesto to the nation headed "The Great Betrayal!" and on June 23rd Mr. Attlee moved a vote of censure accusing the Government of lowering the prestige of the country, weakening the League and endangering peace. Sir Archibald Sinclair, for the Liberals, refused to accept the summing-up for the Government by Sir John Simon. The struggle was still going on in Abyssinia, he said; sanctions, limited as they were, had made themselves felt and the better thing to do would be to intensify rather than to lift them.

Abyssinia was to be left to her fate. There were plenty of excuses—wordy, obscure and tortuous—but the main fact is that Abyssinia was deserted. The tiny, dignified figure of Haile Selassie, in his flowing cloak, appeared before the League as a very symbol of the fate of small nations in a world of force. " What has become of your promises to me? " he asked them, " God and history will remember."

We do not know what Eden's innermost feelings were about all this. We can only go by what he said and did. The

Government's policy was to stop Mussolini joining forces with Hitler; the Italians had little in common with the Germans and the Italian dictator was contemptuous of Hitler. But sanctions had alienated Mussolini irrevocably and Hitler, who had himself defied world opinion with such success, had been able to see how powerless the League was to prevent naked aggression or to punish it. The League, everyone knew by now, was a talking shop, the world's worst insurance—all premium and no protection.

Eden lost prestige over Abyssinia, but it would be unfair to impute the failure of the League to him; his mistake, if there was a mistake, lay in over-stating its prospects and in under-stating its shortcomings. But so much emphasis has been put on his resignation later in his career, that there is a point worth making; that to a man of conscience there were plenty of opportunites for resignation beforehand.

During all this, Anthony Eden's life was becoming more restricted with each passing week. An unremitting routine of work, only occasionally enlivened by a visit to a cinema, a session of painting, or a visit to an art gallery, strained his stamina dangerously. But those around him maintained that his vitality was extraordinary. He would work until he was all in, but with a few hours' sleep he would be vigorous and fresh again. He could be quick with criticism, and many a junior learned that his temper could be short and sharp. He was then, and is still said to be, patient in public and impatient in private.

Mrs. Beatrice Eden supported her husband in every possible way, playing the hostess to his friends, who were few, and his official contacts, who were often intolerable bores. She had the home to run, the boys to bring up, meetings to visit with her husband, speeches to prepare for occasions over which she was asked to preside on her own account. She had also— despite Anthony's troublesome and dangerous plane journey from Moscow—taken enthusiastically to flying and seized every opportunity to go by air instead of by train or car. She had been involved in a plane accident the year before when the aeroplane in which she was returning from Yorkshire skidded on landing and went into a fence. But she made history on

June 30th, 1936, by being the first woman to fly to launch a ship—the motor tanker, *British Fame*, at Newcastle.

Eden's experience coming back from Moscow had not cured him of air travel either; in any case, it would have been impossible for him to have kept all the dates he did without aviation. To visit three capitals within three days was nothing unusual for him. And his secretary knew the telephone numbers of the airlines and aerodromes by heart, they were so frequently used.

In July the Eden family decided that it was time to sell Windlestone Hall, the family seat in Durham. Lady Sybil, now nearing her seventies, her hair the most brilliant gossamer silver, went to live in a four-roomed cottage on the estate, for she was too attached to the district to want to live anywhere else. She still pursued all manner of activities, including church social work, the reclamation of tramps and the Royal Society for the Prevention of Cruelty to Animals. " Sometimes," she said to a meeting, when speaking of her son, " I feel like bursting with pride." On another occasion she had said to a friend: " Anthony will be Foreign Secretary one day— you'll see." Now there were more cuttings to enter into her famous album, to be produced on special occasions and shown to visitors—all carefully annotated and dated. Lady Eden also set about writing a book of her own, a work eminently readable and describing a vanished world of security, elegance and late Victorian splendour. The pages exuded a last whiff of Feudalism, but unfortunately Lady Sybil had not acquired the caution of diplomacy. Some of the book was too frank, and even her own husband's letters, written to her before their marriage, were considered to be too revealing of his temperament. With Anthony making a career at the Foreign Office, her family pressed her, in later years, to abandon all idea of publication. Lady Sybil never agreed with them that publication could do any harm; there was and could be nothing in it which discredited anybody living or dead. But she bowed, regretfully, to the judgment of her family.

In July yet another war was to darken Europe and demonstrate the impotence of the now discredited League of Nations. The Spanish Civil War began. A left-wing Government under

President Azana had begun a weeding out of right-wing officers and leaders in the army, and had exiled General Franco, then unknown to the outside world, to the Canary Islands. On July 17th several regiments in Spanish Morocco revolted, and Franco flew there to give them leadership. The insurgents drew into their ranks most of the officers and about two-thirds of the organised military forces, and received backing in arms, men and planes from Germany and Italy. Forces of the " Popular Front " Government were badly organised and ill-disciplined, but volunteers were recruited from many countries, mainly, though not exclusively, through the local Communist Parties. Russia sent technicians, advisers, planes and tanks to the Republicans. The war was characterised with peculiar cruelty on both sides and the horrors were accentuated by the thought that countrymen were fighting each other, and that some of the worst atrocities were committed against the background of natural scenery of unimaginable beauty.

Most of the Left groups in Europe favoured the Republicans, whilst Franco found most of his moral support abroad from those who, on principle, favour a right-wing regime because they feel that their investments are more likely to be respected.

Eden from the outset, favoured neutrality, and when the French Government suggested that the western powers agree between themselves that they would favour neither side with moral, financial, technical nor military support, and that war materials should not be exported to Spain, Eden was their firmest supporter.

Despite the feverish excitement in Britain at the time—trade unionists, aware of the strong-arm methods of Franco and his men against trade union members, were strongly anti-Franco —a Committee of Non-Intervention met in London late in August 1936. Its job was to work out plans for, and apply, an agreed policy of non-interference in the Civil War. At all costs Eden wished to localise the conflict and prevent it developing into a European war. Britain, France, Italy, Germany and Russia were represented on the Committee but of those countries only Britain attempted to keep her word. All of the other countries were guilty of intervention, the last three being engaged in actual warfare on one side or the other. Unhappy Spain, supposedly the country of sunshine and music, became a testing ground for all the infernal weapons of modern war. The Civil War was, for the Fascist countries and for Russia, a mere manœuvre with real human beings as targets. But the farce of " non-intervention " was continued in London, whilst Eden was forced to make the same sort of justification for its continuance as he had for the League discussions during the attack on Abyssinia. Non-intervention might not work as one had hoped, but at least the principle was still maintained. Intervention, Eden insisted, would be " bad humanity and bad politics " and he was supported in this view by Mr. Winston Churchill who counselled keeping clear of " this dismal welter." In London the cigarettes were passed round, and at the conference table sheets of foolscap paper were filled with desultory notes scribbled by Maiski, the Russian Ambassador, Herr von Ribbentrop and Count Grandi, the Italian Ambassador. Until the very end of the Civil War they argued on legal niceties and questions of definition or method. It was a tragic farce.

A brighter moment came in August when Eden signed the Anglo-Egyptian Treaty at the Foreign Office; it strengthened Britain's foothold in the Middle East, but attracted very little interest at home. But the Spanish Civil War absorbed the public, for it was so near home and was reported by correspondents on the spot with a wealth of detail that harrowed the feelings and fed partisan arguments.

On October 14th, 1936, Eden spoke on the war in Spain at the Cutlers' Feast at Sheffield. His speech told the listeners nothing they would not have known already. It did not retrace what had happened, explain the issues involved, describe the present state of the opposing forces, examine the implications of a victory one side or the other and state any firm policy on the part of the British Government. He started by saying that " Preoccupation with the international situation is wide and deep." He went on to the not very original observation that " . . . so far as I can observe there exists a very general and widespread feeling in this country of distaste for those extreme political doctrines which are being preached and fostered in different forms in different countries . . . " Oh, the vagueness of it!

Later, in the House of Commons, Eden gave a review of the

international situation. His statement "All must have noticed in the last year the factor in international events that speed has become," is a classic of platitudes.

Eden put forward some proposals for improving League machinery, but to his listeners they sounded too complicated and at best an academic quibble. On foreign relations, he considered Britain's relations with France " close and cordial." As for Germany, he had made " repeated declarations " of a desire for friendship with her. He repudiated Germany's complaint that Britain was responsible for her economic difficulties—Britain had lent to Germany as much as she had received in reparations, whilst a trade agreement was in Germany's favour. He denied Germany's allegations of being encircled by hostile nations, including Britain. He had a word of warning for Mussolini, who was threatening to push our ships out of the Mediterranean—or into it. Suddenly he emerged from the labyrinth of words and was doing some straight talking, as on occasions he can do so well:

"Almost every nation in the world—every nation in Europe—is rearming steadily, vigorously or feverishly . . . once again marching men have become a common feature of the landscape. . . ."

The daily newspapers carried pictures of Spanish cities in ruins, of weeping and terrified refugees, with trailing children and awkward bundles of their humble belongings, fleeing from the battle zone, of people looking with fearful eyes at the sky. On the radio the hysterical voice of Hitler could be heard haranguing his troops, and their robot-like response: *Sieg Heil!* The ranting of Mussolini made headlines every day. The lonely figure of King Haile Selassie of Ethiopia paced the streets of Bath in silent reproach. Indeed, Eden's listeners in the House of Commons *had* noticed " the factor in international events that speed had become."

To his constituents at Leamington Eden talked in November of the need to rearm. British weapons would be used only for purposes approved by the League or for defence—defence of the British Commonwealth of Nations and of France and Belgium. The last was a hint to Germany.

Later in the month the Belgian Prime Minister, Mr. Van

Zeeland, came to London, and Eden made it clear that Belgian independence was of " vital interest " to the British.

For Anthony Eden his first year of office had been one hectic rush from one crisis to another. He had inherited a long legacy of drift and incompetence—for which the public, unwilling to face facts and constantly demanding irreconcilable opposites, such as collective security and disarmament (a world police force and no weapons with which to keep order) were certainly as much to blame. Eden knew that Britain was unarmed, and that whatever the merits of the matter, we could not risk a war. What can never be proved is whether appeasement only postponed a war or made it worse when it did arrive. Had appeasement paid, say, in respect of the Rhineland? Germany, in invading it earlier in the year, had been prepared to withdraw her troops if the French met them with force. Instead, there had been no opposition whatever, and Germany had extended her boundary to France without firing a shot.

But in the closing weeks of 1936 another topic, a domestic one, dominated all others. The King's infatuation for twice-divorced Mrs. Simpson, a matter of drawing-room gossip for months, now blazed into a first-class constitutional crisis. The Abdication crisis shook the country at a time when unity and strength were Britain's greatest need.

A review of international affairs, which Mr. Eden delivered at Bradford on December 14th, reiterated that Britain would stand by France and Belgium if attacked; that our agreement with them need not stop other nations from coming in with us, that rearmament was necessary, that non-intervention had saved a general war from starting in Europe; and that non-intervention was not being properly observed.

Anthony Eden will remember his first year of office as Foreign Minister as one of the busiest in his crowded life. A less idealistic man might have been disheartened by Britain's lost authority in foreign affairs. But Eden did not despair.

THIRTEEN

Conflict in the Cabinet

THE year 1937 opened with an emphasis on foreign affairs. Events had moved with such speed that now everyone opened his morning newspaper to see what Mussolini or Hitler had said. It was so obvious that everything revolved around their activities.

The temper of the public had changed a little, too. The outcry over Abyssinia (much of it based on the false assumption that sentiment alone could achieve anything) had to some extent died down. Certainly the British Government considered the whole thing over and done with, and was mainly concerned with agreeing with Italy on British interests in Ethiopia. So anxious was the British Government to avoid ruffling Mussolini, that our Ambassador in Rome informed Count Ciano, Mussolini's son-in-law and Italian Foreign Minister, that five trunks belonging to the ex-Emperor Haile Selassie had been deposited with the British Embassy for safe keeping. The British would have been entitled to transport them to England in accordance with the accepted rules of diplomatic immunity. But as a sign " of good faith and confidence " the British Ambassador asked for permission for these possessions of the emperor's to be sent to England. Four of the trunks contained nothing of value. The remaining one contained gold worth about four or five thousand pounds. Ciano did not give the permission asked for.

Britain, meanwhile, was worried about the drift of affairs in the Mediterranean, where Russian, Italian, German and Spanish shipping were pursuing their illicit missions and blaming their piratical activities on somebody else. Italians and Germans did not trust each other, and together were hostile to the Russians; the Russians disliked Italy, Germany and Franco Spain; the British maintained an attitude of studious diplomatic

Photo: Kemsley Picture Service

On Bondi beach, Sydney. With Eden is Commander Alan Noble, M.P. for Chelsea, who accompanied him on a two months' tour of Australia in 1949.

ther and Son. Anthony Eden th his son Nicholas who d come to meet him at the port. Mr. Eden had been on visit to Canada, New Zealand, stralia, Malaya, India and Pakistan (1949).

Photo: Keystone

Photo: Picture Post

In thoughtful mood. At a United Nations Conference in November, 1951, Mr. Anthony Eden considers a point from the U.S. Secretary of State, Dean Acheson. Eden was renewing international contacts after six years in the Opposition.

With his son Nicholas, at his coming-of-age party in 1951.

Photo: Picture Post

politeness, but privately were concerned lest full-scale war should break out in the Mediterranean, as it might do at any minute. Eden managed, however, to negotiate a " gentlemen's agreement " between Britain and Italy on rights of way in the Mediterranean.

Eden had also pressed the British Ambassador in Rome to sound the Italians about volunteers fighting in Spain, but Ciano refused to consider the withdrawal of Italian " volunteers " in Spain unless every other country agreed to do likewise; otherwise Italian volunteers would continue to leave Italy for Spain in the proportion of ten to every one Communist. That the Italian Government could state what proportion of volunteers would leave compared with that from other countries showed, of course, that the " volunteers " were organised by them.

The next day Eden addressed the Foreign Press Association in London at some length on the subject of foreign affairs. There could be no better motto for a Foreign Secretary he said than " perseverance and understanding." He agreed that it would be foolish to pretend that we open the new year without many disturbing and indeed menacing factors in Europe. Britain, he continued, recognised the right of countries to chose their own governments, and did not sit in judgment either on Fascism or Communism. It was taken for granted that the outcome in Spain must be one of these two things, but neither form of government was "likely to endure." (He was speaking in 1937, and eighteen years later General Franco is still the unchallenged dictator of Spain.) Britain repudiated any division of Europe into rival ideologies. There was a reminder that Britain wanted peace:

> We do not believe in conflict. We believe in co-operation. The world has surely learnt enough, in its long history, to know that by patient collaboration can man steadily increase his standard of living.

Those who believed in international co-operation did not wish to see any nation excluded—a hint to Germany to rejoin the League. Regretfully, he admitted that rearmament was under way. He appealed again to the nations of the world to co-operate with each other for peaceful and pleasant ends, because

" There may have been a time when nations could be independent and self-sufficing, but that day is long past."

The same month was chosen for a visit to Rome by General Goering, who was sent by Hitler to discover whether anything serious lay behind the " gentlemen's agreement " with Britain. Goering pretended that Germany was pleased Italy had been able to find something in common with Britain, to which Ciano replied that both Italy and Germany had reason to be indignant at Eden's references to Germany and Italy in the House of Commons on January 19th. The speech objected to was a survey by Eden of the international situation, when he had emphasised the Government's wish to prevent the Spanish conflict from spreading, and warned other powers that the Mediterranean was " not a short cut, but a right of way "—a hint to Italy to stop threatening British shipping in the Mediterranean.

Count Ciano's diary throws an interesting light on the Fascist Government's attitude to the League of Nations. Goering, in enquiring when Italy would be leaving the League of Nations, told Mussolini that " it had been perfectly understood in Germany that during the Abyssinian undertaking it was to the advantage of Italy to remain in the League "—a grim admission that far from the League of Nations being regarded as a deterrent to aggression it was considered a means of restraint on those who wished to prevent war. Mussolini replied that he was personally not interested in the League, but was disposed to wait until it was forced to recognise the Italian conquest of Abyssinia—" a dose of castor oil which the League will have to swallow later on." The same interview records Mussolini as telling Goering that there were at the time 44,000 Italian volunteers fighting in Spain, even whilst the so-called " Non-Intervention " Committee was sitting in London. Goering told Mussolini that although willing to come to terms with Britain, Germany was staking all she had on a spectacular increase in armaments. Of this the Duce expressed his warm approval, adding that the next great surprise for England would be the growth of English Communism. That would be a good lesson, particularly for Eden himself. It is interesting and a little bizarre that Eden should have been dubbed a radical.

In the House of Commons on March 2nd, 1937, Anthony Eden dealt with three related things; the war in Spain, the position of the League and the British programme of rearmament. He said once again that the Non-Intervention Committee, for all its limitations, was better than nothing, in the sense that it had stopped the contagion of war from spreading; that the League had still some life left in it, having prevented a dispute between France and Turkey over Alexandretta from becoming too serious; and although the League could not guarantee security as one had hoped, and a Western Pact seemed a hopeless mirage, rearmament was the only answer. Everyone knew that Britain would never make war contrary to the terms of the League of Nations covenant. His speech was praised in the House of Lords as having defined British policy more clearly than it had ever been defined in the last two centuries.

Many politicians of both parties had remarked that all through 1936 Eden had been gaining in stature. He spoke more confidently, he stuck to the League of Nations and the conception of collective security—despite sneers from abroad, lack of support from some of his colleagues, and a constant barrage of criticism from the Beaverbrook and Rothermere newspapers. Furthermore, his championship of collective security was not with him a political device; everyone who had any contact with him at the time is firm on this point—Eden was sincere, honest and persevering. He suffered more inwardly than he would ever have admitted, for the conflict was always with him; should he hang on to his job in the hope of making things better, or recognise that the odds were too much for him, that the old complicated game of diplomatic chess was being played according to pre-1914 rules and that a foreign policy that looked to the future would be unacceptable both to Government and public? His occasional outbursts of temper and his cavalier treatment of subordinates—he always made amends for any discourtesy of which he was aware, but could give offence without knowing he had done so—were less a symptom of ill-nature than of strain. There is absolutely nothing petty or mean about Eden. His sense of honour always has been completely opposed to double dealing. And he was more observant than his speeches would indicate. Official position necessarily imposes restraints—although, as I have said, he was more restrained on occasions than he need have been, and too ready in defence of a Government whose policy of drift was to prove disastrous—but we have it on the authority of no less a person than Lord Templewood (then Sir Samuel Hoare) that Eden was not disposed to truckle to dictators, and was most of the time dealing with Government members who were.

> I had a great respect for Eden, my successor at the Foreign Office, and the last thing in the world that I wished was to embarrass his conduct of foreign policy. From the day when I had listened to his maiden speech from the back benches, I had always admired his easy grasp of international questions and his readiness and courage in debate. As his influence increased, he had not only come to represent the Canning tradition in the Conservative Party, but also to express the emotions and aspirations of many men and women on the Centre and Left. I had, however, been forced to the conclusion that whilst our personal relations were never impaired, our outlooks differed. If I described this difference in a sentence, I would say that I was more inclined than he to move step by step in the international field, and more ready to negotiate with the dictators until we were militarily stronger.

Templewood also refers to " Eden's sensitive temperament, which was bound to react to any appearance of disagreement".

It is interesting that Templewood confirms what the public had intuitively grasped—that Anthony Eden, despite the cautious, courteous and often platitudinous wordiness of his speeches, was a young man who—however pathetically—believed that collective security could be made to work in a world riddled with political fanaticisms of all kinds.

In April, when attacks on shipping in the Mediterranean area were becoming almost a daily occurrence, Eden sent a note to General Franco warning him that British shipping would be protected if attacked outside the three miles limit. Later, in a speech on April 12th in Liverpool, Eden praised Non-Intervention:

> No doubt many gibes can be hurled at the policy of non-intervention and at the work of the Non-Intervention Committee. It can be said—and said with truth—that there have been breaches, flagrant breaches, of the Agreement. Despite the Agreement both sides are using materials from abroad; despite the Agreement there are foreign nationals fighting on both sides.

But the flow of help had been partly stemmed by the Committee's work, he said. And " even more important " the policy had " greatly reduced the risks of general war."

Later in April the British public—and the whole world—was shocked by reports of the bombing of the Spanish town of Guernica by German planes fighting with General Franco's forces. On April 24th, 1937, the war front was at Lequeitio and Berriatua. Behind the lines, over twenty miles away, market day was in progress in the town of Guernica. Peasants from surrounding villages roamed the streets making purchases. Suddenly the church bells began to ring in warning, and people ran for such shelter as they could find. The first bomb fell in Station Street. German planes were circling above the town, but these surprised nobody, as they had been seen many times before. Suddenly shops, houses and buildings came crashing down on their occupants in an infernal mixture of smoke, flame, masonry and timber. Incendiary bombs fell with the high explosive bombs. Machine-gunners swooped low and fired at everyone—men, women and children—with calculated impartiality. In a short time Guernica had practically disappeared, with no more than a handful of houses, and those still standing on fire. The air was filled with the screams of the wounded, the moans of the dying, and suffused with the peculiarly revolting stench of burning flesh.

While that was happening, the deliberations of the Non-Intervention Committee continued the same as ever.

The following month, in futile contrast to these happenings, Anthony Eden was chosen at the Paris Exhibition as the ideal Englishman on whom the model could be based for the display of English clothes; his handsome looks and athletic figure showed Savile Row clothes off to the best advantage. Eden, of course, could do nothing about these frivolous and inappropriate uses of his name; the incident is just symptomatic of his popularity in Europe.

In welcome and striking contrast to the unfolding tragedy in Europe, Britain went gay for the Coronation of King George VI in May. Whilst factories worked on day and night shifts in fulfilment of Britain's monster (though belated) arms programme, one Birmingham firm was turning out a million flags a month, stands were being constructed along the processional route to Westminster Abbey, illuminations were being installed and every community in Britain and the Commonwealth was arranging some festivity to celebrate the occasion.

The celebrations were hardly forgotten before 4,000 Basque children—refugees from the Spanish Civil War—arrived in Britain, after difficult and protracted negotiations with the Spaniards. Their presence in England was a tangible reminder that war was going on nearby, a war not to be estimated in military but in human terms. Eden, a few weeks earlier, had prophesied that whoever won the Civil War in Spain, the ultimate victory would be for neither Communism nor Fascism. " The Spanish people will, after this civil war, as for centuries before it, continue to display that proud independence, that almost arrogant individualism which is a distinctive characteristic of that race." As for the lesson of that war, he continued, it had proved to everyone, that " a war of long duration means the ruin of victor and vanquished alike." Eden denied that the Government pursued a policy of drift, quoting Lord Kitchener's aphorism: " One cannot conduct foreign affairs as one would, but only as one can".

The physical and mental strain of his work as Foreign Minister was heavier during 1937 than it has ever been, yet Eden accepted it in good part and showed great physical resilience. He could be utterly exhausted by excessive hours of work, yet after a few hours' sleep would be fresh and alert again. His speeches may at times have been diffuse and vague, but he never lacked resolve in other matters; he had become a first-class administrator who would not shirk a decision. Mrs. Beatrice Eden said of him at this time: " A day away from London —involving two train journeys and two political meetings is nothing less than a welcome rest cure. In all seriousness, the pressure of work at the Foreign Office, the Cabinet and the House of Commons at this time is such that it is almost a superhuman task . . . "

An important thing to remember about Eden is that he is capable of greater warmth and friendship than his disciplined exterior suggests. There was always, too, a considerable degree of political tolerance in his make-up. He never did parcel the world out into opposite halves and align himself irrevocably with the half he preferred. Men like Major Attlee, the fiery Maxton and even the Communist William Gallagher instinctively trusted and respected him. Gallagher once told Eden that there was nobody he liked less to interrupt than Anthony Eden.

Maxton was convinced of Eden's idealism, although regretting that, as it seemed to him, it was dribbling away into the wrong channels. Attlee recognised Eden as a courageous man with strong Liberal leanings, who in other times would almost certainly have been a Liberal and never a Tory.

Stanley Baldwin, too, had a high opinion of Eden. "Do what you think best, my boy," he would say when asked for advice, "I'll back you to the hilt." The fact was that Baldwin, a homely, kindly man, was inclined to live in the past. He came of a fine old Shropshire family, and his heart was more with the countryside and the pigs than with the devious speeches and machinations of politicians. His mind was better stocked than he pretended; even as a boy of nine he could read nine of the Waverley novels. He had worked with an old family business in Birmingham as an ironmaster—worked in those happy, halcyon days when, to quote his own words, "strikes and lock-outs were unknown . . . where nobody got the sack." Basically he disliked foreign affairs and it is interesting that he gave Anthony Eden a free hand to back the League of Nations. It was because the nation was strongly pacifist at the time that Eden, as the chief champion of the League, enjoyed such enormous popularity; he was at once a symbol and instrument of their hopes. But the title of the League was deceptive, implying a unity and an all-embracing purpose it never from the outset deserved; the League was in the practical sense Britain and France, and a handful of smaller nations simply out to get protection at the expense of the greater.

That there were members of the Cabinet who were worried at this championship of the League is now an accepted fact, confirmed by the memoirs of Lord Templewood and many other politicians of that period. Both Templewood and Sir John Simon, to both of whom Eden had been subordinate, looked askance at Eden's faith in the League. I think they were quite right to do so. But even if the Government would have been wise to have seen the ineptitude of the League earlier than it did, it does not follow that its attitude of appeasement to dictators was the only one possible. On this, however, there is complete agreement amongst those who knew Eden at that time. He was transparently sincere in his wish to keep firm to the principle of collective security. By talking of Communism and Fascism as though they were simply different systems of government—as distinct from nationalist hysterias very difficult to confine within borders—he hoped that from Russia or Germany or Italy there would be some positive contribution to collective security.

Strangely, he was more mild in his comments on Hitler than on Mussolini. Hitler had received him courteously. Mussolini had been studiously offensive, and it is certain that both Eden and Mussolini allowed their personal feelings to colour their attitudes to each other's countries. In this respect Mussolini was certainly the worse culprit. Unlike Eden, he controlled his country's radio and newspapers, both of which poured out contempt and vituperation on Britain in general and Mr. Anthony Eden in particular. This propaganda was very much more effective in Britain than the public or Mr. Eden realised. Mr. Eden, an honest man who assumed that a firm stand on principle must gradually rally support to his cause, underestimated the sympathy with Mussolini in influential British quarters. The barrage of anti-Eden propaganda from Italy and Germany made it possible for some members of the Conservative Party to talk of Eden as an " obstacle " to an understanding with the Fascists.

While Germany became more menacing to her neighbour Austria, and through her fifth column inside the country did her best to foment revolution there, Hitler paid a state visit to Rome and in return invited Mussolini to come to Germany to be impressed—as he was—with a display of military might.

But something else happened which was to have a profound effect on Anthony Eden's career. In May, Stanley Baldwin retired, his reputation somewhat shaken by the indiscreet speech in which he had admitted that he had been obliged to promise not to rearm during the last General Election, because a frank statement of the international situation as he understood it then, would have caused his Party to have lost the election. It was a fantastically stupid thing to have told the House of Commons, and it did him less than justice. What he surely meant was, that knowing the country to be in no mood to face facts, he saw little sense in labouring the point about rearmament then. However, his statement that an election promise had been made at a time when there was no intention in his mind of fulfilling it made a bad impression.

And so " Honest Stanley " retired, to be suceeded as Prime Minister by Neville Chamberlain, a man of persevering if flat personality, who had entered Parliament in 1918, been Minister of Health from 1924 to 1929 and Chancellor of the Exchequer from 1931 to 1937. He was decidedly more negative in appearance than Baldwin, who wore like a cloak an air of self-satisfied competence. Chamberlain's gaunt figure, eyebrows like neglected hedgerows, his batswing collar and sombre clothing—reminiscent of a not very prosperous undertaker—scarcely marked him out as a suitable captain for a leaky ship in troubled waters. His job was unenviable and probably nobody would have made a great name as Prime Minister at that particular time. Even Sir Winston Churchill records with satisfaction that he was lucky to be passed over at that time— " over me beat invisible wings".

Chamberlain was a Birmingham business man who had started as an apprentice to a chartered accountant, worked for a time on his father's sisal plantation in the West Indies, returned to Birmingham to set up in business and eventually entered politics and became Lord Mayor of the City. Chamberlain had followed foreign affairs with considerably more interest than some of his critics have suggested. Although he had not himself, like Anthony Eden, experienced the full horrors of war, he had been quick to grasp, during Hitler's first year of power, that Germany was " encouraging bloodshed and assassination for her own selfish aggrandisement and pride." In 1932 he had pressed for the abolition of reparations from Germany, so that the country should not drift further into despair through economic strains, and the liberal elements in that country be thereby discouraged. As Chancellor of the Exchequer he had encouraged rearmament, a step he knew to be necessary in face of the ever growing menace from Germany and Italy.

That much needs to be said as an introduction, because his later mistakes were those of a man no less sincere than Eden.

Lord Templewood, in his memoirs, *Nine Troubled Years*, makes it clear that when Chamberlain was appointed an underlying divergence of outlook undoubtedly became more definite . . . As soon as he succeeded Baldwin, I became increasingly conscious of two distinct points of view in the Cabinet. For the time being the general relief at the advent of a very efficient and vigorous Prime Minister preserved its outward unity. Eden in particular seemed delighted with a change that gave him the support of a more active chief who was always ready to help him in Cabinet discussions."

Not everyone would subscribe to this mild assessment of Neville Chamberlain, but that he has been generally underestimated because of his futile efforts to appease the dictators is proved by his own diaries. They show that he was a hardheaded man trying to extract the best he could from a difficult situation. His methods were to prove wrong but his motives were right.

From the outset he intervened in foreign affairs more than his experience justified, and often without consulting Eden. Technically Sir Samuel Hoare was First Lord of the Admiralty, but in practice Chamberlain turned to him for advice on foreign affairs. The two men were almost every day to be seen walking round the lake in St. James' Park before going to their offices, followed behind by their two wives and, last of all, by two detectives. One feels that this was a situation which Hoare might have done something to discourage, but the two were old friends and fellow members of the same party, the same government and the Cabinet.

Sir John Simon, former Foreign Secretary, was yet another member of this " inner nucleus " of the British Cabinet. Chamberlain's ambition was to establish friendly relations with Mussolini so that in the event of a war with Germany our communications in the Mediterranean would not be cut off. He would have preferred to get on good terms with Germany: " If only we could get on good terms with the Germans, I would not give a rap for Musso," he is credited with saying.

Chamberlain believed that the machinery of the Foreign Office, with its numerous traditions and elaborate hierarchy by which responsibility was passed from one level to the other, was too long-winded to deal with a situation which daily grew more menacing. Direct contact with Ambassadors seemed to him quite proper, although it was bound to create confusion and embarrassment at the Foreign Office. But Eden, always a loyal colleague, was slow to see the implications of the new situation. When the smiling, bearded Count Grandi, Mussolini's envoy in London, called to see Eden and asked that he might be granted an audience with the Prime Minister, Eden fell right into the trap—for trap it was. He granted Grandi the request and made the mistake of not insisting on being present at that and all subsequent discussions between the two. Thus began a personal exchange between Chamberlain and Mussolini. Eden was repeatedly ignored and by-passed, a situation which was of Mussolini's making and which suited the dictator very well.

Italy was, in fact, very well informed on what went on in the British Cabinet. To an astute man like Grandi the differences in the Cabinet were obvious—the mere fact that Chamberlain had received him and discussed international affairs with him without inviting his Foreign Minister to be present spoke for itself. And there was a leakage to Rome of information about Britain and British intentions through the unloved and unlovely Laval, who was in constant contact with Mussolini by direct line from Paris. Sir Robert Vansittart, who accompanied Eden on so many of his visits abroad, had the poorest opinion of Laval, who at the time of the Hoare-Laval Pact, when Vansittart called at the Quai D'Orsay, " descended in some sort of soiled night-gown, edged with pink. His eye-lids were heavier, his *bonhomie* more unpleasant, than ever." Vansittart asked if he might telephone confidentially to London. " I performed the operation," he said, " in an adjoining cabinet, with a bevy of audible eavesdroppers between me and Calais." We can be sure that the substance of his conversation was duly transmitted to Rome.

On July 8th full-scale warfare by Japan against China began. On the 19th Eden gave the House of Commons a summary of the international situation, including the somewhat extraordinary claim that in the Far East " the indications encouraged us to believe that the present situation, grave as the possibilities are, was not deliberately provoked by either Government." Considerable troop movements had taken place on either side. He referred sympathetically to Japan's problems and hoped for understanding with both Japan and China. Of the Non-Intervention Committee, he reiterated its usefulness. At last the basis for a plan had been agreed. " No nation," he said, " wants the Spanish Civil War to be a European War, yet if the nations will not now co-operate . . . we shall drift perilously nearer to it." Finally, a word about the League of Nations, a subject with which most people were completely bored and cynical. It was, Eden said, " neither dead nor moribund. The field of action may be restricted by the limitation of League membership and by the absence from Geneva of many powerful States, but the League still exercises a valuable political influence . . . " He maintained that Britain was not concerned with what a Government did in its own country, but how it behaved abroad, and added a word of tribute to the German and Soviet Governments for their " helpful and statesmanlike attitudes " in concluding naval agreements with Britain.

As for Foreign Office policy, he quoted Sir Edward Grey, who as Foreign Secretary once said, " Foreign Office things are always in a mess; they are not as if one were doing constructive work or writing a book or lecture, or reading up a subject, and they can never be put aside for a day ".

While Eden was saying all this, Chamberlain was making friendly overtures to Mussolini, whose shipping was engaged in piratical attacks in the Mediterranean. Chamberlain's letters avoided such contentious topics, however, whilst Mussolini's were personal and quite long.

FOURTEEN

Was it a Plot?

WE now approach one of the most important periods in the life of Anthony Eden and in the history of Britain during the twentieth century.

Was Anthony Eden the victim of a deliberate plot by Germany and Italy to remove him from office because of his advocacy of collective security and his opposition to Fascist expansion? There is plenty of evidence that he was. There is no evidence that the Prime Minister or any members of the Cabinet knowingly assisted in this plan—there was no such need, because Mr. Chamberlain, by his outlook and methods, was playing straight into the hands of Italy.

In July, 1937, Chamberlain had begun direct talks with Count Grandi, the Italian Ambassador in London. He did not invite Eden to take part in these meetings, or keep him informed of what transpired. In this he was encouraged by both Sir John Simon and Sir Samuel Hoare, whose respect and personal liking for Eden were tempered by their disapproval of his policies.

Italy at the time was drawing closer to Germany and reconciled to the thought that war with Britain, *in the future* was a virtual certainty. She was privately encouraging Germany to seize Austria—or rather, offering no obstacle to its seizure. She had by now no fewer than 100,000 men fighting in Spain, and Italian planes were to bomb Barcelona to remind the world that, as Mussolini put it, Italians could do other things besides play guitars. She was drawing closer to Japan, poised at that moment for an attack on China.

But with all her aggressive plans, Italy might have been brought to book by a firm stand. Eden's uncompromising attitude to Italian aggression could have restrained them, as the diaries of the Italian Foreign Minister, Count Ciano, show only too well. Ciano was Mussolini's son-in-law, a man of bluster, insincerity and cunning. Whereas Chamberlain based his policy on the assumption that it would be disastrous to provoke Mussolini or Hitler, neither of the dictators was prepared for a European war at that time.

The Italian Government, however, was from the outset well informed about British intentions. The tirade of abuse poured out against Anthony Eden in the Italian press and on the Italian radio—and the hostile impression so carefully conveyed both to the British Ambassador in Rome and by Count Grandi in London—was due to the fact that Eden meant business. His speeches might be diffuse, his exterior might be smooth and gentle, but so long as Eden was at the British Foreign Office, Mussolini could not be sure that his plans for expansion would be unopposed or his conquests recognised. The radio and press were therefore told to keep up a campaign implying that Eden was the main obstacle to Anglo-Italian understanding. The propaganda campaign was intended to unseat Eden—and it succeeded. There were several reasons for this, one powerful reason being the vanity of Neville Chamberlain himself. His vanity was flattered by Grandi's personal approach to him. His ego was stimulated by the thought that he could write personal notes to the Italian dictator and receive personal replies. He was convinced, as a good many other people have been and will be again, that so long as *he* was in control of things everything would be all right.

Chamberlain was genuinely anxious to avoid war. He thought that in her present state of military weakness Britain must play for time and at all costs keep out of trouble. Appeasement seemed to him a practical policy, despite the fact that some problems are more difficult to face later than earlier. His plans were based on the assumption that war could break out at any moment. A minor war was actually being fought by Italian submarines in the Mediterranean; the British destroyer *Havoc* was attacked by an " unknown " submarine off the Spanish coast. Other shipping had suffered, too, and although protests were addressed to General Franco, all the evidence indicated that the attacks were Italian in origin.

Piracy in the Mediterranean had, by September, become so common that the British Government, due almost entirely to

Eden's energetic action, called a conference at Nyon in Switzerland. France and Britain issued invitations jointly, Germany and Italy refused to participate, although the site of the conference had been changed from Geneva to Nyon so that it should not be associated with the League of Nations and so offend Italian susceptibilities.

The Conference, under Eden's direction, quickly got down to work and achieved what it sought. Great Britain and France undertook to patrol the Mediterranean, and once again it became safe for merchant shipping. As Russia had accused Italy outright of sinking two of her freighters, a highly dangerous situation had been averted. Italy, who had refused to take part in the conference (quite understandably, since her submarines had been very active in the Mediterranean) was asked by Britain and France to accept patrol of the Tyrhennian Sea. She refused, demanded equality of status with France and Britain and finally, after a meeting with both, was awarded custody of a zone between the African and Italian coasts—an ironic situation, as Italy was the chief pirate.

This Conference was a triumph for Mr. Eden and contrasted with the futile and heartless pretence of the Non-Intervention Committee, which had proved quite powerless to stop countries supplying arms and men for one or other of the belligerents in Spain. The Italians were annoyed, one of their newspapers complaining that "As long as Mr. Eden is at the head of the Foreign Office we must be on our guard."

And Ciano's diaries show that Italy's resources had been strained almost to breaking point by her efforts in Spain and Abyssinia. Ciano records in his diary on September 16th, 1937: " Considerable anxiety in industrial circles. They say our stocks are exhausted and we could only keep a war going for a short time." The previous day there is a significant entry: " Bova (Renato Bova-Scoppa, official in the Italian Foreign Ministry) telephones from Geneva that Eden and Delbos (French Foreign Minister) are ready to accept our demands, but would like us to take the first step. Impossible. We mustn't move an inch. They will come to us."

The conviction that England was the suppliant and could be relied upon for concessions—the English Government, of course, and not Mr. Eden—was due to Mr. Chamberlain's habit of ignoring his own Foreign Minister. Furthermore, the Italian dictator knew for certain that Eden meant what he said when he talked of collective security, discouraging aggression and the rest. For some time the Italian Foreign Ministry had had constant access to secret documents from the British Foreign Office, including directives sent to Rome by Mr. Anthony Eden and Sir Robert Vansittart.

In the autumn Senator Scalata, Italian Ambassador in Vienna, informed Dr. Schuschnigg that the Italian Government had a secret despatch that Sir Robert Vansittart sent from Geneva to Anthony Eden in London. In this despatch the Austrian Under-Secretary of State was credited with saying disparaging things about Mussolini. The Italian Government demanded the resignation of Dr. Schmidt, Austria's Foreign Minister—a move really made to please Hitler, who was planning to invade Austria.

Dr. Schuschnigg, in his book *Austrian Requiem* claims that Italy had access to secret files of the British Foreign Office in return for " several million gold lira." A million gold lira was worth about £10,700 at the time. This matter was raised in the House of Commons after the war, when it was stated that a servant in the British Embassy in Rome had admitted to receiving considerable sums for information, and had been able to remove documents from the Embassy " over a considerable period."

We need not wonder, therefore, why Mussolini and Ciano felt sure that their best bet was to see Eden out of the British Foreign Office. Mussolini knew that Chamberlain was apprehensive, that he over-estimated Italian strength and that he negotiated from a sense of weakness. Hence that telling phrase in Ciano's diary: *They will come to us*.

Chamberlain recognised that Eden had scored a great triumph at Nyon by making the sea comparatively safe for shipping again; at least it seemed great because in almost every other field attempts to restrict rearmament and aggression had been a dismal failure—a situation by no means the exclusive responsibility of English politicians and statesmen. The League of Nations was in advance of its time. Nations had not outgrown their nationalisms, and most people found it impossible to think in any terms except immediate advantage and survival.

Chamberlain, still hoping for an agreement with Italy, noted in his diary:

> We have had a great success at Nyon, but at the expense of Anglo-Italian relations. . . . now with intense chagrin, they see collaboration between the British and French fleets, of a kind never seen before. . . . It would be amusing, if it were not so dangerous.

And he was worried about Anthony Eden's remarks about Fascist bluster. To Chamberlain's ear they sounded too militant or untimely:

> Mussolini has been more than usually insolent with his offensive remarks about the bleating democracies . . . but Anthony should never have been provoked into a retort which throws Germany and Italy together in self-defence, when our policy is so obviously to try and divide them.

What Chamberlain did not realise was that his attitude to foreign affairs, and his constant intervention in them without proper discussion with those responsible, and especially with his Foreign Minister, was upsetting the whole of the Foreign Office machinery. If Anthony Eden had not been so loyal to his chief, or so mild in his relations with Cabinet members, he would have seen this danger sooner; there are reasons for thinking that, when Grandi had asked to see the Prime Minister, Chamberlain would not have refused Eden had he insisted on being present. Once the precedent of direct contact between the Prime Minister and the Italian Ambassador had been established, there was nothing he could do about it. Chamberlain, at the time, was a little surprised and no doubt relieved at Eden's complaisance. "Anthony," he noted in his diary at the time, " made no complaint."

The handling of foreign affairs demands that Parliament should be kept abreast of the Government's policy by occasional statements—usually by the Foreign Minister—and answers to questions put by Members of Parliament. The Foreign Minister is expected to be the Cabinet's chief advisor on foreign affairs and chief executive of the Foreign Office. It is imperative that, with very rare exceptions, directives, instructions and advice to British Ambassadors abroad should come through the Foreign Office. The machinery may look cumbersome, but is founded on generations of precedent and experience, and the general level of education demanded in the most junior Foreign Office appointments is extremely high.

Two things are essential if the Foreign Office is to do its job; contact with Ambassadors should in general be left to the Foreign Minister and his staff, and Ambassadors should be consulted when weighty decisions are taken respecting the countries to which they are accredited.

It is easy to imagine the confusion brought about by the Neville Chamberlain regime. Directives and guidance were sent to Ministers by the Foreign Office, but Chamberlain approached Ambassadors direct. Britain had in effect two foreign policies, one directed to the appeasement of dictators and the other, championed by Eden, of adherence to League principles. In the opinion of Sir Walford Selby, who has been private secretary to six Foreign Secretaries, and was later British Minister in Vienna and Lisbon, Foreign Office machinery had broken down. The Foreign Secretary was no longer master in his own house, and the Foreign Office had, he said, lost its authority as a department in Whitehall. In *Diplomatic Twilight* he says flatly:

> In the years of the rise of Hitler the British ship of state had been at sea in stormy waters with all its invaluable cargo on board but with its navigational control thrown out of gear by sabotage and its charts out of date, while incompetent and palsied hands alternated at the wheel.

Sir Walford lists example after example of confusion and lack of confidence. Vital information from abroad was pigeon-holed, reaching neither departmental chiefs nor the Service departments. Ambassadors were ignored while matters on which they were best informed were discussed. Sir Walford is extremely critical of Sir Robert Vansittart, the permanent head of the Foreign Office during those crucial years. Vansittart has implied in his memoirs that he had constantly warned the Foreign Office of the dangers of truckling to dictators. Selby maintains that, on the contrary, warnings and advice from Ministers abroad went unheeded.

It is too easy to accuse permanent civil servants of faults and incompetence, because whilst in office they must keep away from public discussion affecting their work, and on retirement public memory is too short to appreciate fully the implications of the explanations they make; the events are too far distant, the issues too vague. Nor are they ever free to adduce the documents which might sustain them in their own defence. What is certain is that Neville Chamberlain's by-passing of Eden was bound to lower the Foreign Office in the esteem of foreign governments and of other British Government departments.

Meanwhile, the complete breakdown of the League was further exemplified by the war between Japan and China, which had started in July and had now resulted in the wholesale slaughter of civilians. The British public, bewildered by one war after another, read with horror of bombing attacks in the East. A Nine-Power Conference, with British support, was summoned by the League to discuss the matter, but nobody expected anything of it. The League had become a lazy watch-dog with no teeth. Nobody even heard it bark.

Eden was feeling the increasing strain of trying to work with his hands tied. He was standing up to the dictatorships, whilst the Cabinet, including Chamberlain, were not supporting him. The duties of Foreign Secretary are onerous enough at any time, but they are made impossible if, added to ordinary worries, there is the frustration of having your decisions negatived and the humiliation of having your work undone.

Not only was Eden worried at the manifest breakdown of collective security and the encouragement of aggression by British servility in the face of it; he was alarmed at the tardy progress of rearmament. In the chaos of world affairs Britain was almost unarmed. But Chamberlain, to whom he confided his misgivings, gave him no more than a snub. " Go home and take an aspirin " was his comment.

Speaking at Llandudno on October 15th, 1937, Eden welcomed a recent speech by President Roosevelt in which he showed that the United States was watching with growing concern the collapse of civilisation. It was a call to nations to respect the sanctity of treaties, and such a speech was an opportunity to strengthen resistance to the dictators by American influence and authority. Chamberlain called Roosevelt's speech " a clarion call, as welcome as it was timely " although he continued as energetically as before to court the dictators who despised agreements and flouted humanity. Mr. Eden said:

> If there is anything else a Foreign Secretary lacks, he does not lack advice. Unhappily this is somewhat contradictory. On the one hand I am urged to make the League work ... on the other hand I am advised that we should have done with the League and its unrealities and come to terms with the non-Member States.

To the latter category Chamberlain certainly belonged. Unknown to him, of course, Ciano had recorded in his diary:

> Is it advisable to embark on action which may lead to conflict? I say No. In the first place, because Germany is not ready. In three years she will be. Secondly, we are short of raw materials and munitions.

Here again is interesting confirmation of Eden's stand. Italy was short of raw materials and munitions, unwilling to risk a real conflict with Britain. Nor was Germany ready. Real sanctions against Italy could have been effective—even the half-hearted embargoes imposed had at least found Italy, at the end of the Abyssinian War and towards the end of the Spanish Civil War, unready for a real show-down.

Nyon and the combined Anglo-French patrols of the Mediterranean had been intended by Mr. Eden as a warning and a deterrent. But Mr. Chamberlain's obsequious little notes to Mussolini took the sting out of anything Anthony Eden might say. Eden had lost all faith in the pledges of the dictators, whose intrigue and threats boded ill for the future of Europe unless they were met with stern resistance. "I am as anxious as anybody to remove disagreements with Germany and Italy or any other country," Eden said, "but we must make sure that in trying to improve the situation in one direction it does not deteriorate in another." But without support from the Cabinet these words were not going to worry Hitler or Mussolini. As Lloyd George remarked in the House of Commons, Eden could be likened to a first-class chauffeur trying to drive a car whilst a load of nervous wrecks pulled constantly at his elbow.

The long-drawn-out tragedy of Spain still troubled the

conscience of some questioners in the House of Commons, and on November 4th, Eden defended the continued activities of the Non-Intervention Committee. Its deliberations, as he knew quite well, had not stopped the war, but he firmly believed that it had to some extent limited the scope of the war. Without underestimating the part played by volunteers in Spain, he reminded Lloyd George, who declared that non-intervention operated to the advantage of General Franco, that the lifting of non-intervention would handicap the Spanish Government even further. At present it was receiving large quantities of war material from Russia. If the Non-Intervention Committee packed up, belligerent rights, at present withheld from the insurgents (Franco's forces) would have to be granted. The flow of war material to Franco's forces would almost certainly increase.

Soon afterwards Anthony Eden received further evidence that Chamberlain was taking decisions affecting foreign affairs without consulting him or even informing him. Sir Winston Churchill who was present at a Foreign Office dinner held in October, 1937 for the Yugoslav Premier, M. Stoyadinovitch, describes in *The Second World War* how Anthony Eden was informed, casually and with no opportunity to express an opinion or prevent such a thing happening, that Lord Halifax, the Lord President of the Council, was going to Germany on an " unofficial visit ".

> Early in October I was invited to a dinner at the Foreign Office for the Yugoslav Premier, M. Stoyadinovitch. Afterwards, when we were standing about and I was talking to Eden, Lord Halifax came up and said, in a genial way, that Goering had invited him to Germany on a sports visit, and the hope was held out that he would certainly be able to see Hitler. He said that he had spoken about it to the Prime Minister, who thought it would be a very good thing, and therefore he had accepted it. I had the impression that Eden was surprised and did not like it; but everything passed off pleasantly.

Neither Chamberlain nor Halifax had consulted Eden beforehand, despite the fact that, informal or not, such a visit was bound to receive publicity in the world press, and lead to speculation, and that visits by leading English statesmen to dictators who were violating their international obligations and threatening the peace of Europe were bound to give them a prestige they did not deserve. Lord Halifax did go to Germany in his capacity as a sportsman. The Nazi press made a great fuss of him, and he visited Hitler at Berchtesgaden, where he failed entirely to estimate the character and intentions of Hitler who, for all his mental instability and evil character, did have a sort of dynamism with which he could so often sway visitors. A quiet, contemplative high churchman was scarcely a foil for this scheming, sadistic ex-house-painter who was at that very moment perfecting his plans for the invasion of Austria. Hitler told Halifax that there were no differences with Britain except Germany's shortage of colonies. Halifax reported this to Chamberlain, adding that Germany was not likely to force the pace.

The fearful war in the Far East, with its massacre of civilians and large-scale bombing, had spurred Eden to try the hopeless experiment of the Brussels Conference, attended in November by representatives of nineteen nations to consider how the war in the Far East might be terminated. It was from the outset a fiasco. Japan refused to be represented. A declaration was made regretting Japan's resort to force and describing her action as illegal, but nobody would agree to withhold war materials and credits from Japan. There were too many troubles in Europe to contemplate getting embroiled in what looked like being an endless large-scale war in the Far East.

Anthony Eden was immensely depressed about the turn of things. The drift of affairs, the muddle, the uncertainty, the feeling of impotence—but far worse, the feeling that he was not supported in all he had tried to do, and that his work at the Foreign Office was subject to constant interference, were telling on his health. The work, at the best of times, is exacting; but the disillusionment and constant sense of frustration made his position increasingly insupportable. He was disgusted with Halifax's visit to Germany. He was not edified by reports—perfectly true reports—that Lady Chamberlain, widow of Sir Austen Chamberlain and sister-in-law to the Prime Minister, was acting as a sort of go-between, conveying messages from Chamberlain and receiving messages from Ciano in return. Ciano welcomed these evidences of a weakening resolve, although he despised Britain for it. In October, Ciano was "surprised" to find that Chamberlain was willing to consider recognising Italy's conquest of Ethiopia and noted in his diary:

> "After the threats of the last few days this withdrawal is enough to make one speculate about the decline of the French and British peoples".

After Eden's stern reprimand about piracy in the Mediterranean, Chamberlain's dulcet wooings must have come as a bizarre and comforting contrast. And now the sister-in-law of Britain's Prime Minister was constantly on Count Ciano's doorstep in Rome, currying favour by wearing the Italian Fascist badge. Even this childish and ill-conceived gesture had the opposite effect to that which she supposed, for Ciano said of this, in his diary: "Lady Chamberlain wears the Fascist badge. I am too much of a patriot to appreciate such a gesture from an Englishwoman at the present time."

And a significant little note in the same month:

> We are reading everything the English send—are we to believe that other people are less good at the game than we are?

Ciano was referring, of course, to the constant leakage of official documents from the British Embassy in Rome. These were making their way almost automatically to the Italian Foreign Ministry; the culprit was not apprehended until 1944, and could not then be punished as he was an Italian national. It has never been disclosed by whose carelessness confidential despatches could be taken away from the Embassy by a comparatively minor Italian employee.

Eden was feeling the nervous tension all the more because there were few people to whom he could unburden himself. His wife Beatrice, of course, heard of his difficulties, sympathised with and supported him. But she never really understood what it was all about. Politics frankly bored her, and there is an unconscious touch of irony in Anthony Eden dedicating his book of speeches—speeches which although important in their general intention, are undeniably tedious to read—to "B.E. from A.E. In gratitude to a patient listener to each one of these pages."

But at least in Beatrice, who admits that she was never cut out to be a politician's wife, he had a listener and a sympathetic one. In the Cabinet Eden was isolated. His staff at the Foreign Office was loyal to him, but as he was not master in his own house this was small comfort to him.

Sick at heart, and feeling very tired, Eden decided to snatch a holiday in France. Before leaving he had made it clear to Chamberlain that he disapproved of Halifax's visit to Hitler, but Chamberlain was now too obsessed with the thought of himself as the Perfect Answer to Difficult Dictators to bother with this objection. They did not quarrel; both men respected each other. But both were pursuing the same end by totally different and irreconciliable methods.

Eden chose an unhappy time to be absent from the Foreign Office. Whilst he was away, President Roosevelt, depressed and alarmed by the war in the Far East and the drift to war in Europe, decided to take an initiative which he hoped might limit war and lessen tension elsewhere. The British Ambassador in Washington, Sir Ronald Lindsay, was asked to convey to Mr. Chamberlain a vital and highly secret message from the President. Roosevelt thought that to stop the drift he would invite representatives of the various governments, including France, Germany and Italy, to a conference in Washington. Here was a momentous step—what amounted to an offer of active intervention in European politics by the head of a Republic strongly isolationist in outlook. The democracies might have been supported in their stand for collective security by the weight and authority of the United States.

But Chamberlain failed entirely to see its import and give its sender encouragement. Acting on his own initiative and without proper consultation of the Foreign Office, Chamberlain poured cold water on the proposal and sent an unimaginative and unappreciative reply which disgusted and disappointed the President of the United States. Chamberlain declared that whilst he appreciated Roosevelt's interest he had to be careful that his proposals did not cut across other negotiations being conducted by Britain. He spoke of his efforts to reach agreement with Italy and Germany and said that he would be willing for Britain to recognise the Italian conquest of Abyssinia in return for " evidence of their desire to contribute to the restoration of confidence and friendly relations ".

The Foreign Office was, of course, aware of the receipt of

the telegram, which it had passed to the Prime Minister as requested by the Washington Ambassador. Sir Alexander Cadogan, shocked at the manner of its handling, telephoned Anthony Eden in France and pressed him strongly to return to England and assert his authority before more damage was done to Anglo-American relations.

Eden arrived at Dover to find the faithful Sir Alexander Cadogan waiting for him. On the way back to London, Eden realised that all he had struggled for over the years was being undone. Eden believed that Britain and the League nations should try, however impossible it seemed, to limit the spread of aggression by sanctions, condemnation and group action. Chamberlain felt that the condonation of aggression might prevent more widespread attacks on liberty later on. Eden believed that once a principle is foregone, it cannot be invoked as a restraint; when the principle is lost, all is lost. Chamberlain thought—and was fully supported by all his Cabinet colleagues except Eden—that principles could be forgotten because there was no hope of the most powerful nations in Europe acting in accordance with them. But above all he hoped to drive a wedge between Italy and Germany, to split the Rome-Berlin Axis by getting on good terms with Italy.

Chamberlain had not asked Eden to come back to London, and had been quite content to act on his own. Mussolini had succeeded in impressing on the Cabinet that Eden was the main obstacle to Anglo-Italian understanding, and the theme was reiterated by Italian propagandists. While Eden was in France Signor Gayda, Mussolini's official mouthpiece, had published a provocative and impudent article in the *Berliner Tageblatt* attacking Mr. Eden and laying down—as much for the information of Italy's friends in London as for his German readers—the essential preliminaries to "Anglo-Italian understanding." Fully armed and well disciplined, Italy demanded four things as a condition to agreement: a recognition of the Italian Empire (in other words, of Italy's conquest of Abyssinia); British approval and support for, Italy's attack on the Spanish Government; a recognition of " new historical realities "—the Rome-Berlin Axis, Fascism and National Socialism, and the absence from the League of Nations of Germany and Italy. In a nutshell, Italy was asking for approval and support for aggression;

the abnegation of neutrality in Spain; support for Fascism and all its evil tyranny, including the persecution of Jews, concentration camps, one-party government and the complete suppression of freedom; and the overthrow of collective security as a safeguard to peace.

On the day that article appeared, Lord Perth had an audience with Count Ciano in Rome, and the following day it was announced that Italy had accepted the Franco-British proposals for the strengthening of naval patrols in the Mediterranean. This gesture was intended further to delude London into thinking that all was goodwill and that only Mr. Eden's office as Foreign Minister prevented further concessions.

That Eden stood alone in the Cabinet was well known to the Italians, and all their efforts were now concentrated on unseating him from his position. In conversations with Count Grandi in London, Eden insisted that Italy must make some gesture of good faith before an Anglo-Italian Agreement could be reached; for example, there must be a withdrawal of Italian volunteers in Spain. The Italian Government lost no time in rejecting Eden's condition, knowing, of course, that Eden's colleagues did not support him and that he spoke, not for the British Government but simply for himself. Eden considered the attitude of the Italian Government to constitute a threat.

On February 10th Count Grandi saw the Prime Minister and Anthony Eden and said that Italy was agreeable to holding conversations. It was obvious to Grandi that the Prime Minister was conducting the negotiations, that Eden was present as a mere formality and that his position was completely undermined. Two days later Eden, speaking at a crowded meeting of the Junior Imperial League at Birmingham Town Hall, made a long speech on foreign affairs which, like most of his speeches, lost much of its impact because of its long-winded phrasing and sprinkling of clichés. Yet concealed in it was a plain warning to Grandi—a warning Grandi could afford to ignore—that there could be no sacrificing principles and shirking responsibilities in order to obtain quick results.

In the meantime Germany was increasing its pressure on Austria. It had organised and financed a Nazi movement inside Austria, and its uniformed and armed thugs organised provocative meetings so that any attempt to suppress them might be interpreted as persecution and an invitation to Germany to protect its nationals. The German General Staff had, on Hitler's instructions, drawn up plans for invading Austria in July, 1936. Under the Stresa Agreement of 1935 Britain, France and Italy had guaranteed Austria's integrity.

On February 12th, Schuschnigg, the Austrian Chancellor, was invited by the German Ambassador to visit Hitler at Berchtesgaden, and left by a special train. He had accepted on the distinct understanding that the sovereignty of his country would not be in question, and as an understandable though futile precaution he informed the governments of France, Italy and Britain of his visit.

On arrival, the dumb-founded Chancellor found himself threatened, insulted and told to sign an ultimatum giving the Germans the right to Nazify Austria, and to instal a Nazi as Minister of the Interior and Chief of Police in Austria. As Hitler raved and stormed, without asking his visitor to sit down, he used the only language he understood, the language of force:

> HITLER: I need only to give an order, and overnight all ridiculous scarecrows on the frontier will vanish. You don't really believe that you could hold me up for half an hour? Who knows—perhaps I shall be suddenly overnight in Vienna: like a spring storm. Then you will really experience something. I would willingly spare the Austrians this; it will cost many victims. *After the troops will follow the S.A. and Legion!* No one will be able to hinder their vengeance, not even myself. Do you want to turn Austria into another Spain?
>
> SCHUSCHNIGG: ... naturally, I realise that you can march into Austria, but Mr. Chancellor, whether we wish it or not, that would lead to the shedding of blood. We are not alone in the world. That probably means war.

Poor Schuschnigg, head of a small state, face to face with a dictator who had not the manners to offer his visitor a seat, and who called him to his face " murderer ", and " a dwarf ", realising that now the Germans intended to invade, bringing with them into once-happy Vienna the whole evil apparatus of Nazism. Their entry would be the death knell of freedom and the signal for organised persecution of Jews, Catholics, Freemasons, Socialists, trade unionists and all free associations.

"We are not alone," he said, pathetically, for in 1938 all small states were alone. They always have been and probably always will be, in the sense that their defence is never undertaken by any stronger power except for strategical or economic reasons. But there was the Stresa Agreement; Britain and France and Italy. . . . He did not mention this Agreement specifically.

In a flood of abuse Hitler swept aside Schuschnigg's hint that German force would be met with force:

> HITLER: Don't believe that anyone in the world will hinder me in my decisions! Italy? I am quite clear about Mussolini: with Italy I am on the closest terms. England? England will not lift a finger for Austria . . . and France? Well, two years ago when we marched into the Rhineland with a handful of battalions—at that moment I risked a great deal. If France had marched then we should have been forced to withdraw. . . . But for France it is now too late!

Schuschnigg was given no choice. The ultimatum was for the Nazi, Seyss-Inquart, to be made Minister of the Interior, all Nazis to be released from Austrian prisons (they included a big percentage of terrorists) and complete freedom for the German-subsidised Nazi party in Austria. Reluctantly Schuschnigg signed, and made his way back in deep gloom to Vienna.

Soon the Nazis were in control of the key ministries dealing with security and foreign affairs, and minority groups of pro-Germans were encouraged to demonstrate for union with Germany.

All these signs were plainly understood in London. Hitler had been right in his low assessment of the "protection" which Austria could expect from Britain, France and Italy under the Stresa Agreement of 1934. France was too busy courting Italy. Mussolini had a tacit understanding with Hitler to let him have his way with Austria. And Anthony Eden, in the House of Commons a few days after Schuschnigg's meeting with Hitler, agreed that Britain had given an undertaking to protect Austria's independence in conjunction with France and Italy, but was not called on to act in the matter unless she was approached by one of these powers.

It is strange to reflect that Eden made no public statement in defence of Austria at this hour, nor did he hesitate to abandon Austria to her fate. Three major powers had agreed to protect a small country, but Britain did not feel compelled to do anything unless requested by France, who was indifferent, or Italy, a country in complicity with the German aggressors. A strange interpretation of an obligation. But Eden was simply the mouthpiece of the Government, and had no active hand any more in shaping British policy.

Italy had decided that the moment had come to unseat Eden. The campaign against him was intensified. *Regime Fascista* on February 11th, 1938, carried an article by Signor Farinacci, Secretary of the Fascist Party, who declared that there was no hope of improvement in relations with Britain so long as the control of British Foreign policy remained with Mr. Eden.

Lord Perth reported from Rome that he had seen the Italian Foreign Minister, who had instructed Count Grandi in London to urge an early start in the conversations with Britain—an instruction which by implication rejected Eden's condition that Italian troops should be withdrawn from Spain as a preliminary.

Then followed what must be the most humiliating week ever to be endured by a Foreign Secretary. On February 16th and 17th Eden telephoned the Italian Ambassador in London as he wished to discuss the Austrian crisis with him—no doubt to sound him, as it was his duty to do, on Italy's attitude to its obligations under the Stresa Agreement. Each time Grandi stalled. It has been said that he had been informed that Eden was not going to last long at the Foreign Office, and that he saw no point in discussing policy with him. As Chamberlain's policy was out of step with that of his Foreign Minister, and as the former suited Italy better than the latter, this reponse was only to be expected. But for Eden to be told that Grandi could not come and see Britain's Foreign Minister on a matter of urgent importance, simply because he had to play a game of golf, must have been a bitter pill to swallow.

On the 18th Grandi saw Chamberlain and Eden together. Grandi's despatch to Count Ciano, describing this meeting, shows that Chamberlain was privately in touch with him through an intermediary.

> ... after my having refused ... to present myself at the Foreign Office, there came to see me on Thursday afternoon the confidential agent of Chamberlain, who, since the month of October

last year, has been functioning as a direct and secret link between myself and Chamberlain, This agent, with whom, as I say, I have been in almost daily contact since the January 15th told me that he was instructed by Chamberlain to draw my attention to the fact that it would be opportune not to avoid the conversation requested by Eden, since " it was ' very probable ' . . . that the Prime Minister, Mr. Chamberlain, would himself take part in the conversation. . . . "

Mr. Chamberlain received Grandi " very cordially ". He broached the question of Austria, which Grandi brushed aside as irrelevant to the question of Anglo-Italian conversations. Eden intervened " observing that, after all, Italy has never denounced the Stresa Agreement which provided for consultation between Italy, France and England on the Austrian problem. I answered Eden drily," says Grandi, " that between Stresa and the event in Austria to-day there had intervened exactly three years, during which some events had taken place of considerable national importance. . . . "

Grandi, refusing to give any undertaking about Austria or to discuss it, then delivered what was a thinly veiled threat. If agreement was not reached with Britain, including recognition of Italy's conquest of Abyssinia, " the Duce would definitely have to direct Italian policy in a spirit of frank, open, unshakable hostility towards the Western powers."

Chamberlain repeated this, to be sure he understood correctly. Unless agreement was reached now, Italy would be hostile in the future? Grandi confirmed the accuracy of this interpretation.

Eden had been sitting through this exchange in grim silence. At last he intervened. He insisted on the Austrian crisis being discussed as an urgent matter; on the Spanish business being settled, for " it is useless and dangerous to ignore this problem, which is of fundamental importance to Anglo-Italian relations . . . " As Eden enlarged on his theme, Chamberlain showed irritation and disappointment. Eventually he began to lecture Eden as though Grandi were not there. " What the Italian Government is asking," he said, " is that England recognises Italian sovereignty of Ethiopia and that thereafter one could pass on to the examination of all the problems which must form the subject of the general agreement between the two countries. . . . I am in agreement and accept this. . . ."

Eden insisted that no concrete goodwill had been given on

the Italian side. " He had been waiting for an answer for ten days to a formula for limiting the war in Spain. . . . "

At this point Chamberlain intervened, " this time with the air of being thoroughly annoyed. . . . "

The conversations were continued in the afternoon. Chamberlain gave way to everything. He would recognise Abyssinia, lend Italy £25,000,000 and even present himself to Mussolini in Rome (Grandi resisted any suggestion that the talks should be in London). Eden tried vainly to prevent this undignified surrender. At times he and Chamberlain, in Grandi's presence, were arguing with each other. Grandi was shocked that disunity could go so far, and reported to Ciano: " It was one of the most paradoxical and extraordinary meetings in which it has been my lot to take part. Chamberlain and Eden were not a Prime Minister and a Foreign Minister discussing with the Ambassador of a foreign power a delicate situation of an international character . . . but two cocks in true fighting posture . . . the questions and queries addressed to me by Chamberlain were all, without exception, intentionally put with the aim of producing replies which would have the effect of contradicting and overthrowing the basis of argument on which Eden had evidently previously constructed . . . his miserable anti-Italian and anti-Fascist policy. . . . Eden did not scruple to reveal himself fully in my presence as what he has always been and what I have always described him as: an inveterate enemy of Fascism and of Italy."

In these accounts of Grandi's, one sees a different Eden—an Eden more outspoken, more firm and less compromising than the spokesman in Parliament, the Party man, or Foreign Minister.

From this moment, events moved swiftly towards a crisis in Anthony Eden's career. He had kept silent so far, feeling that to reveal a deep cleavage between his policies and those of the Prime Minister would encourage Britain's enemies and discourage her friends. But to by-pass these international crimes, the rape of Abyssinia, the war in Spain and now the betrayal of Austria, and to curry favour with a bullying dictator whose promises were worthless—this was a final humiliation in which he would play no part. He demanded a Cabinet meeting, which was held on Saturday, February 19th. Chamberlain sent his secret agent to Grandi to tell him of this, saying, in effect, "Don't worry. All will go well". And it did—from Chamberlain's point of view. Eden argued with his colleagues on the fatal policy of feeding titbits to the lion. It was useless.

The Cabinet crisis had aroused intense public interest. On Saturday crowds waiting in the bitterly cold evening, cheered Mr. Eden when he arrived at Downing Street, tense and preoccupied but as dapper as ever. Sunday newspapers carried banner headlines of the crisis, and crowds on Sunday thronged Downing Street. On this occasion the crowds seemed more organised. Inside No. 10 other Ministers pleaded with Eden to stay, but his mind was made up. At 6.30, accompanied by his Parliamentary Private Secretary, Mr. J. P. L. Thomas, and greeted with cheers and the cry, in unison, "NO PACT WITH ITALY", he walked across to the Foreign Office.

There, in his office, his back to a blazing coal fire, whilst a portrait of George III looked down at him quizzically, he dictated his resignation:

> "My dear Prime Minister, The evidence of the last few days has made plain a difference between us on a decision of great importance in itself and far-reaching in its consequences. I cannot recommend to Parliament a policy with which I am not in full agreement . . ."

That day the Sunday newspapers, realising that his resignation was imminent, had kept staffs waiting to print a special edition. At 7.30 p.m. Eden went back to No. 10, staying only four minutes in order to hand over his letter of resignation. At No. 17, Fitzhardinge Street that night a liveried servant heard the newsboys shouting: "SENSATION! ANTHONY EDEN RESIGNS!" and rushed out to buy a paper. Nicholas Eden, in the act of undressing for bed, heard the newsboy's cry from an open window and rushed inside yelling "Nanny, Eden's resigned! Eden's resigned!" "Come and have your bath" was her cryptic reply, and the routine of the Eden household continued as placidly as ever.

Tense and bitter, Eden came home and told Beatrice the news. The previous night they had sat up until the early hours, whilst he confided his reasons for a decision he knew would be inevitable.

Photo: Harris

Meeting with Tito. Anthony Eden was the guest of honour at a reception given to him by Marshal Tito, the Yugoslav Chief of State, and Jovanka, his third wife (1952).

Sir Anthony Eden, photographed with Rita Hayworth at a London film première.

Photo: P.A.-Reuter

Photo: Graphic Photo Union

Off for their honeymoon. Mr. Anthony Eden with his bride, Miss Clarissa Spencer Churchill, niece of Sir Winston Churchill, at the door of 10, Downing Street before leaving for their honeymoon in Portugal (1952).

Good luck, Tony! The British Foreign Secretary kisses his wife good-bye before leaving for his lightning tour of West European capitals to discuss German rearmament. It was this tour which saved the European Defence Community from collapsing.

Photo: Associated Press

Lord Halifax was at once appointed in Eden's place, and when, late at night, the telephone rang in Winston Churchill's home at Chartwell, Britain's future Prime Minister was sunk in unaccustomed gloom. Whilst he had never entertained any hope in the League of Nations, he admired young Eden's efforts, his integrity and general bearing. He recognised in Eden something out of the run of ordinary politicians, and knew that behind the smooth diplomatic manner and the flow of platitudes there was something tough. Churchill writes:

> Late in the night of February 20 a telephone message reached me as I sat in my old room at Chartwell (as I often sit now) that Eden had resigned . . . sleep deserted me. From midnight till dawn I lay in my bed consumed by emotions of sorrow and fear. There seemed one strong young figure standing up against long, dismal, drawling tides of drift and surrender, of wrong measurements and feeble impulses. My conduct of affairs would have been different from his in many ways; but he seemed to me at this moment to embody the life-long hope of the British nation, the grand old British race that had done so much for men, and had yet more to give. Now he was gone. I watched the daylight slowly creep in through the windows, and saw before me in mental gaze the vision of Death.

FIFTEEN

Into the Wilderness

ANTHONY EDEN'S resignation as Foreign Minister caused a world sensation. He became a hero overnight in the eyes of millions of people throughout the world, who felt that somebody ought to stand up to the dictators and take a stand on common humanity. In the excitement of the moment it may be that Eden was invested with an exaggerated altruism and credited with a spirit of defiance in the face of tyranny which, it must be confessed, he had never shown before. He was at variance with the appeasers, according to the statement he was to make; but he did nothing to rally the anti-appeasers and proved ineffective as a leader of moderate or liberal opinion. He had extricated himself from an untenable job, after enduring without complaint the most extraordinary interference in his functions and those of his staff. He had not burned publicly with indignation at the imminent threat to Austria and had sought refuge from the responsibilities of the Stresa Agreement, by which Britain was bound to aid her in collaboration with France and Italy, by saying that it was not for Britain to take the initiative—this, despite the fact that he had no reason to suppose France would do anything, and less reason to imagine that the Italian dictator would risk the enmity of Germany by standing in Hitler's path.

Press reaction to his resignation was mixed, but on the whole mostly pro-Chamberlain. Idealist Eden might be, but after all the League of Nations had been a costly waste of time, and could boast nothing but a miserable record of drift, evasion and vague alibis; Eden's championship of an impotent institution to which no intelligent State would trust its defence may have been admirable, but was certainly not practical. However, to his credit let it be said that he had seen the need to rearm, and had actually been snubbed by the Prime Minister for warning him that Britain had as yet insufficient weapons to defend herself in a Europe which grew hourly more menacing. The *Daily Telegraph* paid Eden a back-handed compliment. " The man who will sacrifice a great position for his convictions deserves respect if he cannot command agreement," it said generously. The *Daily Express* made appeasement sound like a practical policy:

> The easy thing to say in this matter is that Eden is the idealist and Chamberlain the realist. He wants to establish peace in our time and that is a high ideal. Also, he tries a practical way of achieving it. Chamberlain will recognise Abyssinia as Mussolini's because it is Mussolini's and not even the League of Nations can make it Haile Selassie's again. Chamberlain does not believe that the cause of peace in Europe would be helped by insisting that Mussolini should get his troops out of Spain before we begin to talk. Mussolini will take them home of his own accord when there is nothing more to gain by keeping them there, and that time is about now . . . "

The *Daily Herald* accused Chamberlain of coming out " stark and nakedly on the side of the system of power politics." The *News Chronicle*, too, supported Eden. The *Star* thought it was " a bad bargain by a business man in a panic. The international principles on which this country had stood are surrendered by an uncertain protection to a man to whom treaties are a scrap of paper. The humiliating thing is that in yielding to bluff there is no finality. The impudence of the demands increases in proportion to the weakness of the surrender."

The *Manchester Guardian* epitomised the reaction of many thoughtful people:

> In the public mind of this country Mr. Eden is associated with a genuine and active belief in the principles in which the Government formally professes. As long as Mr. Eden was at the Foreign Office the outside world thought, and was right in thinking, that whatever unpleasant compromises were sometimes forced on him he would never abandon principles or shirk responsibilities in order to obtain quick results. Other countries know him as a British Minister who in spite of all discouragements kept his faith in the League and what it stood for. They will draw their inferences now.

In Rome and Berlin news of Eden's resignation was received with delight. "They carried a corpse from Downing Street," one Italian newspaper headlined exultantly. In Berlin the man in the street was convinced that Eden's resignation was a reaction to a violent speech by Hitler the day before, in which he had denounced Eden in scathing terms.

In the House of Commons on Monday, February 21st, 1938, every Member was in his place, the press gallery was crammed to the last inch, diplomats filled the galleries reserved for them. Neville Chamberlain, entering from behind the Speaker's chair, was loudly cheered by his supporters. Just before question time Eden entered from the opposite end of the House, took a seat at the end of the third bench above the gangway on the Government side, and next to Lord Cranborne, his Under Secretary at the Foreign Office, who had resigned with him.

In a hushed House, Anthony Eden rose to give a "personal explanation."

> This is, for me, both on political and personal grounds, a most painful occasion. No man would willingly sever the links which bind him with colleagues and friends. . . . But, Sir, there are occasions when strong political convictions must override all other considerations. On such occasions only the individual himself can be the judge; no man can be the keeper of another man's conscience. . . .

The immediate issue, Eden said, was whether official conversations should be opened in Rome. "It is my conviction," he said flatly, "that the attitude of the Italian Government to international problems in general and to this country in particular is not yet such as to justify this course. Propaganda against this country by the Italian Government is rife throughout the world. I am myself pledged to this House not to open conversations with Italy until this hostile propaganda ceases."

During the last 18 months he had tried for better relations with Italy. They had failed mainly, though not wholly, because of the war in Spain. In January 1937, after delicate negotiations, the Anglo-Italian Agreement had been signed, yet within a few days Italy was shipping Italians to Spain. Eden was concerned with performance as opposed to promise and uttered a warning about appeasement of dictators:

> The events of the last few days . . . have merely brought to a head other and more far-reaching differences . . . in outlook and approach. I do not believe we can make progress in European appeasement, more particularly in the light of the events of the past few days . . . if we allow the impression to gain currency abroad that we yield to constant pressure. I am certain in my own mind that progress depends above all on the temper of the nation, and that temper must find expression in a firm spirit. That spirit, I am confident, is there. Not to give voice to it is, I believe, fair neither to this country nor the world.

Not once did Eden look up above the Speaker's chair, where Lady Chamberlain, Lady Halifax and Beatrice Eden watched the dramatic scene. The hushed silence with which he was heard told of the sympathy for him on both sides of the House —for when he had entered the crash of cheers came more from the Socialists than from his own party. Not once did Beatrice Eden take her eyes off her husband whilst he made his moving statement, in which he studiously avoided references to himself but stuck to points of principle. In some ways it was a disappointing speech, containing more compromise than some had hoped. His condemnation of the Government policy could have been more direct, more detailed and more strongly worded. But his restraint was that of a man who disliked the policy of his party but saw no political future outside of it. He had resigned his office, but was still a party member owing it allegiance and support.

Viscount Cranborne, who followed Eden, was more outspoken. He had been forced to resign because he was in the fullest agreement with Eden. " I am bound to him not only by those natural ties of affection which will be felt by anybody who has had the privilege of working with him . . . it has been suggested in some quarters that this is a question not of principle but of detail, and that on questions of detail Ministers should not resign. I cannot agree with that assessment. This is not a matter of detail, but a matter of fundamental principle. That is not to say that I accept the thesis that we should not enter into negotiations with authoritarian states in any circumstances whatever . . . the principle involved is . . . of good faith in international affairs. In the international sphere the very existence of civilised relationships is dependent on a high standard of good faith. To my mind it is absolutely essential that this country should do all it can to maintain the highest possible standards of good faith in international affairs."

To enter into conversations with Italy without insisting on the withdrawal of " volunteers " from Spain would be not a gesture of peace but a surrender to blackmail.

Mr. Chamberlain put up a defence of his policy which was made easier by Eden's mildly worded reproach. It was essential, he said, to understand the Italian point of view. Relations had deteriorated between Italy and Britain. It would have been reasonable to accept their invitation to discuss various questions. As to surrendering to blackmail, there had been no threats from Italy.

At this point Major Attlee asked if the communications between Italy and Britain might not be published as a White Paper, so that Members of Parliament might judge for themselves?

The peace of Europe, Chamberlain declared, must depend upon the attitude of four major powers—Germany, Italy, France and Britain. (Interesting to note the order in which he gave these countries). Chamberlain was right. With Germany planning war, and in collaboration with Italy actually fighting one in Spain, whilst planning an attack on Austria; with Italy emboldened by the success of her conquest of Abyssinia and drawing closer to Germany; with France vacillating and divided, with Britain pacifistic and undecided, the outlook for peace, if it depended upon these four countries, must be poor indeed—as it proved to be.

Mr. Attlee said he had listened to Eden's speech with " profound sympathy ". He would have had even keener sympathy with him if he had resigned at the time of the Hoare-Laval Pact. But he admired Eden's stand, and regretted that all over the world the story would be spread by Germans and Italians: " You see how great is the power of our great leader. He says that the British Foreign Secretary must go, and he has gone." Major Attlee continued:

> I do not think that there is any parallel for that in our history. I do not know of any case where a Foreign Secretary, acting professedly with the support of the Cabinet, has been subjected

to most outrageous abuse by foreign countries ... it looks rather curious to us that when a colleague is being attacked by people overseas, by foreign countries, when, week after week, he is abused in every possible way, his colleagues do not stand by him.

In the foreign affairs debate on the following day Mr. Winston Churchill rose to support his friend Anthony Eden: "I say that he is an irreparable loss to the Government, being one of the very few men on that bench whose name is widely known throughout this island, and I feel personally, as an older man, the poignancy of his loss all the more because he seems to be the one fresh figure of first magnitude arising out of the generation which was ravaged by the War."

Mr. Churchill read to the House a threat, published in Field-Marshal Goering's newspaper, the *National-Zeitung* clearly directed at Mr. Eden: "... the time is coming when those who bear the real responsibility will no longer be protected. An organisation through which, in some cases, a blow can be struck with lightning speed and with probable success has, it is stated, fortunately long been ready." "It is quite clear," said Mr. Churchill with emphasis, "who is the individual in this country."

Was Eden the victim of a plot to unseat him, because his policy was an obstacle in Fascist aggression? There is, I feel, plenty of evidence that the campaign to remove him, initiated by Italy and Germany, achieved a great measure of support in London. It is the essence of good propaganda that people do not realise when they are affected by it. Mr. Duff Cooper, (later Lord Norwich) who was First Lord of the Admiralty at the time, has said:

> The Prime Minister was, in fact, deliberately playing a part throughout the Cabinet discussions. While allowing his colleagues to suppose that he was as anxious as anyone to dissuade the Foreign Secretary from resigning, he had, in reality, determined to get rid of him, and had secretly informed the Italian Ambassador that he hoped to succeed in doing so. Had I known this at the time, not only would I have resigned with Eden, but I should have found it difficult to sit in the Cabinet with Neville Chamberlain again.

Eden's resignation is a highlight in his career, and was taken as a hall-mark of his uncompromising attitude towards disturbers of the peace.

Was he specifically against appeasement, or was he annoyed at Chamberlain's interference with the functions of the Foreign Secretary? The answer to that, I feel, is that Eden did all he could both to prevent war and to see that, if it did come, Britain would be able to defend herself. He had tried to make the League of Nations work, holding fast to its ideals long after the League had proved itself impotent to stop aggression. He had warned Chamberlain of the need to rearm in face of the growing of militant and irresponsible dictatorships. He had tried to be firm with Mussolini and Hitler, but he had not been supported.

Against this, his critics adduce these facts: (a) when the Locarno Treaty, the first break with League principles, was originally mooted, it was Eden who defended it and asked irritably if Britain was expected to act as a special constable to the world; (b) he did not resign at the time of the Hoare-Laval Pact; (c) just before his resignation, when questioned in the House of Commons as to whether Britain would stand by Austria in the event of invasion, as pledged to do under the Stresa Agreement, Eden had said that it was not for Britain to take the initiative—she could only do this if requested by the other two signatories, France and Italy. He must have known that France was indifferent and Italy in league with Germany.

For many of his followers, his speech in the House of Commons seemed too mild, but Eden, very decently, had no wish to make capital for himself out of the discomfort of his late chief and his old colleagues. His resignation had made him the hero of the hour. On the following day he received no fewer than 6,000 letters. Over thirty M.P.'s including Lloyd George and Lady Violet Bonham Carter, urged Eden to form a new party, but he was not interested. He had made his stand, he had stated his reasons; that was enough. If he made common cause with all who supported him at that moment he would have found himself in some queer company.

On February 25th, 1938, Eden returned in triumph to his constituency at Leamington. The Winter Hall was crowded to capacity and his words were relayed to an overflow meeting in the Pump Room. His supporters sang " For He's a Jolly Good Fellow " and there were cries of " Recall Eden ". But

Eden himself had no battle-cry. He refused to align himself with any opposition. In a mild speech, he praised his Under-Secretary Lord Cranborne, who had resigned with him, he denied that his decision was due to ill-health and insisted that his decision was taken, not because he was tired, but because no other course was open to him. " I am more than ever convinced," he said, " that I was right. If I had not resigned it would have been my duty to stand up in the House of Commons and say ' I believe that this is the best method for dealing with the problem of Anglo-Italian relations . . . ' unhappily I cannot believe this." To have advocated a policy in which he had no faith would have made him a hypocrite. As to Italian pressure, " I stand by every word I said in the House of Commons . . . the meaning of certain communications received from a foreign government was ' now or never '." But this contentious point he had no intention of pursuing, for " I appreciate that it is impossible to make public the relevant documents at this moment". Britain must stand by her conception of international order . . . and Britain must not weaken in her ideas of liberty.

It was a harmless speech which pleased his supporters if it did not satisfy them. Eden kept aloof of the " Recall Eden " agitation. Too many of those who did the shouting had refused to vote for the arms or military training which might have enabled Britain to speak with authority to Germany or Italy. Meetings were held under the auspices of the League of Nations Union but the high-sounding resolutions were not backed by any positive plan.

Chamberlain noted this with satisfaction. "After reading your speech to your constituents last night," he wrote to Eden, " I should like to send you a few friendly words. You had a very difficult task. You had to say enough to justify your resignation, and to vindicate your views, and perhaps the most popular way would have been to emphasise differences and call for support . . . the dignity and restraint of your speech must add further to your reputation. I won't say more now than that my personal feelings towards you are unchanged, and I hope they will always remain so."

Eden had much to be annoyed about in his relationship with Neville Chamberlain, but he was totally without personal rancour. When Chamberlain died Eden penned this personal note to Mrs. Chamberlain:

Beatrice and I have thought so much of you and felt so much for you in these sad days that I would like to send you these few lines of sympathy from us both.

Neville was so vital and courageous a personality that, even after his return to work from his operation, it was difficult to believe how ill he was. I found such a charming note from Neville waiting for me on my return from Egypt, that I feel doubly distressed that I was not back in time to answer it for him. He wrote then such generous words of our political association and friendship, that I should have deeply valued the chance to say " thank you " to him, and to tell him of my gratitude for his kindness ... we shall all miss him and his wise counsel; for my part I know that I have lost a friend whose unwavering personal friendship I have ever deeply valued.

Beatrice joins me in renewed and heartfelt sympathy.

SIXTEEN

The Path to War

ANTHONY EDEN was now 41; he had reached his prime, yet looked much younger. His carriage was erect, his manner firm and decisive, his step springy, his general bearing quietly confident. At 41 he had thrown aside one of the highest offices in the land. He could have clung to that office, continued to draw his £5,000 a year and could have challenged Chamberlain's policy in the House of Commons whilst he was still Foreign Minister.

Instead he had made himself a Conservative back-bencher, with no certainty that he would be able to ascend the political ladder again. Yet his following was enormous. In a world of force it was good to see somebody, at least, standing up to the bullies. The Council of Action, formed to organise support for Eden, was getting 1,000 recruits a day—but Eden was too concerned with the realities of the situation to bother about such agitation.

Eden had made a sacrifice which must affect his family, too. His own inheritance had been modest; Beatrice, reputed at one time to have inherited £150,000 from her father, Sir Gervase Beckett, had in fact been left scarcely more than £20,000. The upkeep of their house in Fitzhardinge Street was expensive, and there were two sons, Simon and Nicholas, to educate. The loss of his income was no small matter.

For a while, Eden disappeared from the public scene, to the great relief of Mrs. Eden, who had seen so little of him because of his long hours at the Foreign Office and his frequent journeys abroad. Together they left for the South of France, and Anthony could forget his cares, for the time being, by playing tennis. He was flooded with offers of directorships and business propositions of all kinds. All these he refused. He had a mortal dread of anything that might look like an exploitation of his unique position—a situation not of his seeking, which had given him so much anxiety. He could have made a fortune—I use the word advisedly—by writing signed articles for the press, or publishing a book giving his views on Foreign Affairs. Many such offers were made, also to be refused. He needed the money; a sense of honour and concern for what was best for the country made him refuse it. He had no wish to give the enemies of Britain delight by showing how deep was the division between his policy and that of the Cabinet. His resignation had shown this enough as it was.

In March Hitler seized Austria. Schuschnigg, his voice breaking with emotion, had made his last broadcast for many years, ending with the heartfelt words: " God Protect Austria! " Soon German tanks had crossed the border, Roman Catholics, Jews, Socialists, Communists, trade unionists and others were being dragged from their homes and hustled into prisons and concentration camps. A wave of despair swept over the Jews, whose freedom had disappeared overnight and who could look for nothing but oppression and terror. In one day there were seventeen suicides. Austria had been deserted by all the signatories to the Stresa Agreement, including Britain. Schuschnigg, her Chancellor, who could have escaped had he chosen, preferred to remain with his tortured country, and was removed to Dachau concentration camp. Mussolini had deserted Schuschnigg, whom he had, by personal promise and by the Stresa Agreement, undertaken to protect. He had not even sent his troops to the Brenner Pass, as he had done in 1934, feeling by now that he could trust Hitler, who would appreciate this gesture from his Fascist neighbour. He was right in supposing this, for when on the day of invasion Prince Philip of Hesse, Hitler's special envoy to the Duce, telephoned Hitler to assure him that the dictator of Italy would support him by remaining neutral, Hitler was beside himself with joy. " Please tell Mussolini I will never forget him for this. Never, never, never, whatever happens. . . . You may tell him that I do thank him ever so much . . . never, never shall I forget that . . . "

While the rape of Austria was proceeding, Field Marshal Goering was assuring the Czechoslovak Ambassador that " Czechoslovakia had nothing to fear from the Reich." Strangely, that country accepted German protestations of good faith and did not mobilise her army or take any steps for her own protection. Perhaps she felt that her treaties with France and Russia were a sufficient insurance against potential German aggression. But Czechoslovakia was next on the list of Nazi conquests; the awkwardly-named country which was once the ancient Kingdom of Bohemia straddles Central Europe. Bismarck once said that who controls Bohemia controls Europe, a fact of which Hitler was well aware.

President Benes, co-founder of the Republic, put his faith in France, in Russia and the League of Nations.

Eden and Churchill—the two had become the firmest of friends over the years—both saw the writing on the wall. So did Chamberlain. But whereas the first two would have stood firm in face of aggression and made it clear that an attack would mean reprisals, Chamberlain hoped that " appeasement "— or submission—would postpone crisis for Britain. He noted in his diary:

> You have only to look at the map to see that nothing that France or we could do could possibly save Czechoslovakia from being overrun by the Germans, if they wanted to do it. I have therefore abandoned any idea of giving guarantees to Czechoslovakia, or to the French in connection with her obligations to that country.

In Italy the fall of Eden was yielding dividends. " Chamberlain is much less strong than he was ten days ago—we must not create new difficulties for him ", Count Ciano, the Italian Foreign Minister, records in his diary on March 19th. Italy had been asked for the help of two Italian destroyers in the Spanish Civil War, an obvious intervention which might cause an uproar and, the Italians feared, the return of Eden to power. The following day Lord Perth called to protest at the bombing of Barcelona. Ciano disclaimed responsibility, although the order to bomb the city was given by Mussolini without even informing Franco.

In April an Anglo-Italian Agreement was signed in Rome. It was held in suspense until there had been a withdrawal of volunteers from Spain, which Italy, however, was not bound to do unless other nations did the same. The war in Spain dragged on and not until later in the year, when Lord Perth presented new letters of credence addressed to "The King of Italy and Emperor of Ethiopia"—formal recognition of Italy's conquest—did the Agreement begin to operate. It did not appreciably affect relations between Britain and Italy one way or the other. The die was cast long ago, as Eden knew.

On St. George's day Anthony Eden made one of his now rare public speeches. He warned of the dangers ahead and said that the democracies, to survive, must show the same energy and determination as the authoritarian States; in general a sensible warning, although dictators do not require any popular mandate to train and mobilise armies or make arms, which gives them an advantage over the democracies in times of peace. In this speech he gave a hint why he had not raised the flag of revolt against Chamberlain or the Conservative Party. "Only as a united nation," he said, "can we give of our best. Party warfare for its own sake should have no place in the scheme of things to-day. The need of the hour is for the spiritual and material rearmament of the nation."

In June Eden, speaking at Haseley Manor in Warwick, made it clear that war was a possibility. Not a profound remark, perhaps, when one considers that two full-scale wars were in progress, one in Spain and the other in China, and that two countries—Abyssinia and Austria—had been successfully invaded. But at least Eden admitted the possibility of war, whereas the appeasers continued to pretend that their policy could avert it.

His silence, said Eden, was deliberate. He wanted to avoid embarrassing the Government. But he said plainly that the situation was bad and gave no scope for optimism. "There is to-day less liberty in Europe than there has been at any time for centuries." He appealed for national unity, in a country that still did not appreciate her danger. He pleaded for voluntary co-operation between states, for continued support for the League of Nations and reproached the country for its listlessness. Even when disarmament had failed, statesmen had not seen the risk of being unarmed in a hostile world.

And he defined Conservatism as he saw it—certainly something different from the old guard, something decidedly more liberal and more modern. "The conception of modern Conservatism" implied "a virile progressive force determined to uphold our national traditions, attached to our age-old liberties and democratic institutions . . . if our own Party is to retain its position it can only be as the interpreter of all that is most progressive in our creed." Britain's national affinity lay " with the great democracies of Europe and America."

Mr. Chamberlain, meanwhile, was conducting foreign affairs almost single-handed. The Germans were putting pressure on Czechoslovakia, using the exaggerated grievances of the Sudeten German minority to utter threats of invasion. Hitler had told General Keitel that he wished to invade Czechoslovakia, but had decided not to march if France intervened—an eventuality that could, of course, have involved Britain. In this instruction to Keitel—of which Chamberlain was naturally unaware—we have startling confirmation of Eden's clear foresight. Firmness could have prevented the invasion of Czechoslovakia, for a time at least.

The threats to Czechoslovakia intensified—abuse in the press, on the radio; movements of troops; fomented riots and demonstrations inside Czechoslovakia. Convinced of his own intuition, Chamberlain brought the strongest pressure on President Benes to accede to German demands. Runciman was sent to Prague to soften their morale. Chamberlain intervened personally with Hitler, who must have enjoyed being chased by a British Prime Minister, who was willing to come and see him irrespective of where it suited him to be.

Then came the Munich Agreement, the betrayal of Czechoslovakia. Chamberlain, Mussolini and Daladier, Premier of France, met Hitler at Munich and granted him all he wanted without even a representative of Czechoslovakia being present. Benes was told—" you must accept it." The Germans were given great stretches of the country without the trouble of firing a shot, although Czechoslovakia had one of the finest armies in Europe. Overnight the young Republic was gripped by terror and despair. The people of Czechoslovakia were stunned. France had betrayed her promise; and Britain, with France and Italy, was helping Hitler to get what he wanted.

In the debate in the House of Commons that followed this terrible news—terrible, that is, to those who could see the writing on the wall; for Chamberlain, who talked of "peace in our time" had received a great ovation from the crowds, and had been wildly praised as a hero—Churchill expressed the sorrow and shame of this episode:

> All is over. Silent, mournful, abandoned, broken, Czechoslovakia recedes into the darkness. She has suffered in every respect by her association with the Western democracies and the League of Nations . . . this is only the first sip, the first foretaste, of a bitter cup . . ."

Eden, characteristically, prefaced his remarks by praise of his old chief, the Prime Minister. " I have a natural sympathy for Foreign Secretaries and I can imagine something of the burden which must have been his . . . now for the moment we can breathe again and it is the duty of each one of us to devote what time we can to stocktaking." For a few moments his indignation was lost in a maze of compromise. The Prime Minister's reception in Germany was " a manifestation of the deep desire of the German people for peace."

But his tribute to stricken Czechoslovakia was sincere. " In the practice of self-discipline we have been set a remarkable example by this brave people." He thought that the Czechs had been asked to make all the concessions. Eden understood the real tragedy of the situation, in human terms. " . . . the time allotted to these proposals is cruelly short. I was trying to put myself in the position of a German Jew or a German Social Democrat in those areas, knowing that by the 10th German troops would enter. What is happening to-day is something like a panic flight of these unhappy people from a rule which they dread." His speech lacked the punch and clarity of Churchill's, but in his own guarded way he was expressing sympathy with Czechoslovakia and concern at the implications of an Agreement he despised.

In December Eden and his wife visited the United States, All the world loves a celebrity, but the Americans have their own special, warm-hearted way of showing it. No Hollywood star has ever been greeted with such acclaim, and he was received on arrival like a visiting potentate. It had been a stormy passage over the Atlantic, with cold north-east winds and a thick belt of fog. As the *Aquitania* entered the New York harbour, a coast-guard cutter arrived to take Eden off. With an escort of police motor cyclists the visitor was rushed off to the palatial Waldorf Astoria, where 4,000 members of the American Congress of Industry were waiting to hear him speak. The gossip writers had raced to tell the evening newspapers that Eden was wearing a black fedora hat and brown doublebreasted Chesterfield. There were roars of applause as he appeared at the dinner, unruffled and debonair, the very apotheosis of the American idea of an Englishman—well turned out, quiet and reserved, firm, vaguely ascetic. The sponsoring organisation was a very powerful one, representing over five million workers, and 300 radio stations were linked to take Eden's words over the sprawling American Continent, from the Arctic to the sub-tropical zone of Florida.

It was not the most auspicious time to visit New York. The streets were covered with snow and slush, yet even goloshes, raved the gossip writers, acquired a certain elegance when worn by Mr. Eden. But the interest in the Edens was natural enough. His resignation was regarded as the crucial event of the year, and his stand for decency in international affairs had brought a whiff of hope into the fœtid atmosphere of Europe. Americans were shocked at the drift to war, and saw in Eden a young man asserting himself in a country where youth has usually been a handicap in politics.

For days Americans were regaled with the strangest titbits about the Edens. His " Oxford Accent " was greatly admired. Millions of words were written about his clothing. They were a little bewildered to find he did not carry an umbrella. At New York City he met Mayor La Guardia. Escorted by police motor cyclists—a touch of showmanship which New Yorkers always enjoy—he visited the George Washington Bridge. The *New York Times* arranged a lunch in his honour; other engagements included a visit to the World's Fair, a dinner at the Hotel St. Regis, and a play on Broadway in which Eden heard himself mentioned. Mrs. Eden, when she could get the chance, enjoyed shopping on Fifth Avenue and seeing the sights.

Eden's speech to the National Association of Manufacturers was given a tremendous reception, but the ovation, one feels, was to Mr. Eden personally. His speech was nothing special;

it said nothing that was not obvious to anyone of common sense:

"What was it twenty years ago we and you both fought to achieve? Whatever else it may have been, the world has clearly not been made safe for democracy. Other systems of government are arriving with authority from a totally different philosophy. We are conscious of the need to defend ourselves both materially and spiritually from the gathering storm.

Democracry is the university in which we learn from one another. It can never be the barracks where blind obedience is the first essential. Man was not made for the state; the state was made for him. Our conception of a modern democratic state must be based on racial and religious toleration. Each citizen must enjoy individual liberty...."

But Eden was the hero of the hour. In fact, his speech so impressed one Senator that he asked the Senate to print copies at federal expense and give them a wide circulation. And in Washington, which is more politically minded than the rest of America, Eden had embarrassing confirmation of his enormous popularity. Mrs. Roosevelt and Mr. Sumner Welles were not alone in their welcome to the Edens. The stenographers at the White House went crazy with enthusiasm, following him from room to room. The ecstatic shriek of delight from 200 typists in one room so alarmed the ex-Secretary of State for Foreign Affairs that he claimed the sanctuary of a cloakroom. In the Washington Press Club, where the Press are accustomed to lunch and dine distinguished diplomats and have the benefit of their off-the-record comments, Eden was a great success, although I am not quite sure what a correspondent meant when he wrote that "It was fortunate perhaps that Mr. Eden's speech to the National Press Club in Washington came off the reel—in other words, it was not reported."

The tour had been a personal triumph for Anthony Eden, so much so that when he got back to Southampton a few days before Christmas he carried with him over 100 press photographs. Not even Mr. Lloyd George had achieved such a personal success during his visit. In a broadcast, Mr. Eden said: "We shall never forget the kindness shown to us by all sections of the American people wherever we went..."

In fact, Senator Pitman, Chairman of the Foreign Relations

Committee, told the American Senate: " I have never known a foreigner to come to our country and be more cordially received than Captain Anthony Eden . . . "

There were some, however, who felt this adulation was carried a little too far, and that Eden's reputation rested on an unsubstantial basis. He was being praised more for what he refused to do than for what he did. Why was he popular? His looks? His achievements? Or a bit of each? Patrick Dickinson summed it up in this jolly little quatrain:

> Alas! How typically English that
> We should remember this man by his hat—
> Since he is the one politician who, it
> Is fair to say, has least of all talked through it.

SEVENTEEN

On the Brink

THE year 1939 was a preparation for war—a war which Anthony Eden, Winston Churchill and most informed people knew to be inevitable. Behind the scenes, Eden continued to work for an increased *tempo* in rearmament and for unity in the Government. His supporters and admirers could not understand why he had been so mild after his resignation; they were frankly disappointed, especially Lady Violet Bonham Carter, who had urged him to start a separate party. But Eden knew that war could not be far away. The League, as he understood only too well, was finished and perhaps he was relieved at not having to present it to the public as a practical organisation any more. Chamberlain was distressed by " venomous attacks " in the German press, and had warmly welcomed President Roosevelt's address to Congress in the U.S.A., on February 4th, of which nearly a third had been a denunciation of the dictatorships, and part had emphasised the need for rearmament against aggression. Chamberlain had learned since he administered that first stupid rebuff to Roosevelt, when Eden, hurrying back from a snatched holiday in France, had tried to undo the mischief which had been done in his absence; and Chamberlain, although still entertaining forlorn hopes of a *rapprochement* with Italy, was soon to be disabused. For the moment he reposed a naïve confidence in the Agreement he had brought back from Munich, and when reminded of Germany's broken promises would say "Ah, but Herr Hitler has given his word to *me*." Still pursuing a hope of placating Mussolini, he visited Rome with Lord Halifax and a Foreign Office contingent in February and had conversations with Mussolini, who was truculent and uncooperative, demanding recognition of General Franco and support for Italian claims against France. Chamberlain spoke apprehensively of German rearmament, but got cold comfort from his host. Chamberlain thought that a German *coup* in some other direction was being planned but the Italian dictator brushed these fears aside.

But at home, the imminence of war was something nobody really questioned. Within the last few years war had struck in so many places; no amount of talks, protests and orthodox diplomacy had been able to prevent it. Nobody believed in the League of Nations any more. In Britain Civil Defence was now being planned and spoken of as a commonplace thing—as though death from the skies was an inconvenience as much to be expected in a modern city as, say, petrol fumes from buses. By the end of January, 20 million booklets had been issued, giving details of various forms of National Service, the qualifications necessary to volunteers, the means of training and the pay.

In February the preliminary steps were taken that would enable Britain to be put on a war footing in the event of a crisis. Recruitment for the Services was speeded up, local authorities were told how to organise an air raid precautions system, and the Chancellor of the Exchequer asked the House of Commons for £580 million for defence, and got it. Experiments were made for air raid shelters, and orders for millions of steel shelters put in hand. The Ministry of Health began to organise, on paper, the evacuation of school children from cities likely to be bombed in the event of war.

Meanwhile, the Spanish Civil War was drawing to a close. By occupying Barcelona, General Franco and his forces had conquered three-quarters of the Spanish peninsula. But that was swiftly forgotten in face of another menace, which surprised the public less than it did Chamberlain. On March 10th, whilst Sir Samuel Hoare was busy telling people in Chelsea that Britain's best chance was to get friendly with the dictators, Hitler's legions were being massed on the Czechoslovak frontiers. The despatches of Sir Neville Henderson, the British Ambassador in Berlin, failed entirely to convey a balanced picture of the German menace; he stressed the peaceful references in Hitler's speeches and predicted that no attack need be expected. Within a few days of such predictions, the Germans invaded Czechoslovakia. Germany had consulted none of the signatories of the Munich Agreement, but nobody except Mr. Chamberlain had ever expected her to.

Reporting this inevitable tragedy to the House, Chamberlain made the whole thing sound much less serious than it was. The country had "disintegrated" and the arrival of the Germans was made to sound like a gracious gesture on Hitler's part. More in sorrow than in anger, he regretted the course taken as being "inconsistent with the Munich Agreement".

This speech satisfied nobody, not even the Conservative Party's supporters. Anthony Eden pressed strongly for the formation of an All-Party Government which would get resolutely to grips with the encroaching menace.

But by March 17th, Chamberlain knew that appeasement was ending. He had tried hard, perhaps in an obstinate, misguided or bigoted way, to achieve peace; he had been content to buy security at the expense of small nations, but to his practical mind it was a matter of small evils being worth enduring to avoid greater evils. But now he reminded Hitler of his promise that the Sudetenland represented his last territorial claim on Europe. " Is this the end of an old adventure or is it the beginning of a new?" he asked. "Is this the last attack upon a small state or is it to be followed by others?"

But if appeasement were ended, so too, was the League of Nations. President Benes of Czechoslovakia had telegraphed to the Secretary-General of the League of Nations invoking assistance under the League's Covenant, particularly Article 10. He telegraphed a protest to Chamberlain, Roosevelt, Daladier and Litvinoff urging them not to recognise this "international crime". But events were moving too fast. Czechoslovakia was left to her fate. Protests were made, but Germany in 1939 was not a country to be worried by such things. Without any loss to herself she had brought nearly four million people under her tutelage, gained one of the best armies in Europe, and now controlled the monster Skoda armament works and their lethal output. Chamberlain recorded this plaintive entry in his diary:

> "As soon as I had time to think I saw that it was impossible to deal with Hitler after he had thrown all his assurances to the winds..."

A German attack on Poland was now presaged by a virulent campaign of verbal attack from the German press and radio. Nobody can ever say that the Fascist dictatorships gave no notice of their intentions; verbal violence was always the precursor of physical attack except, of course, for the meaningless pleasantries exchanged between Ambassadors. Ordinary diplomacy had long since broken down.

Alarmed at the state of Britain's defences, Anthony Eden, together with Duff Cooper, Winston Churchill and thirty other Members of Parliament (all but three of them Conservatives) signed a resolution calling for the vigorous prosecution of a new foreign policy and the formation of a truly National Government by which the strength, productivity and resolution of the country could be organised and unified. This was the most urgent necessity. The trend of events had confirmed Eden in his decision, at the time of his resignation, not to rock the boat whilst it was riding a storm. To have split the Conservative Party and attacked Chamberlain personally would have seriously weakened the country. In the national interest, as these events proved, Eden had swallowed his pride.

But the Prime Minister, as much as anyone else, was now seized with the urgency of the international situation. Nobody bothered very much with the news that General Franco's legions, on March 29th and 30th, were marching in triumph through Madrid, whilst onlookers cried and cheered according to their allegiance and the future which Franco's victory implied for them. On the 29th Britain announced that the Territorial Army would be vastly increased, and on March 31st Chamberlain made a fateful statement to the House of Commons which showed how complete was the reversal of the Government's policy, and how Eden's assessment of the Fascist dictatorships was now accepted: Britain would go to the help of Poland if attacked. It was a momentous pronouncement, received with quiet understanding by the British public. Somehow any action was preferable to the continual drift and retreat in the face of threats.

In the foreign affairs debate on April 3rd, Chamberlain showed how complete was his understanding of the gravity of the situation. The guarantee to Poland was the equivalent of a cover note which is followed by a complete insurance policy.

He quoted Hitler's numerous assurances, now "thrown to the winds". The British Government would have to confer with others—not excluding Russia—on the situation. This speech, implying a rejection of past mistakes and a determination to face the facts of a grim situation, won high praise from Anthony Eden, in which he was joined by Winston Churchill, Sir Archibald Sinclair for the Liberals, and Mr. Hugh Dalton for the Socialists.

On April 7th something else happened to confirm the validity of Eden's distrust of Italy. Albania was invaded and an Italian Government installed. Following the annexation of Czechoslovakia by Germany, which gave her a front with Poland, the Memel was next wrested from Lithuania. Germany had extended her frontiers, at no great cost, so that she had a pathway into Eastern Europe, a frontier with France, and a frontier with her next victim, Poland, against whom she continued to direct the usual stream of abuse, threats and false accusations.

It was no easy matter to formulate a policy that would stem the Fascist tide. Poland had profited from Czechoslovakia's agony by grabbing the Teschen industrial district for herself; she was unfriendly towards Roumania, with whom Britain concluded a hasty pact. Neither country trusted Russia, whose influence in this coming dispute must be immense. "I must confess," wrote Chamberlain at this time, "to a profound distrust of Russia." It was a distrust not unjustified, but that did not alter the fact that in the event of a conflict Russia could throw her immense resources of manpower and materials into one camp or the other.

On April 3rd, the very day on which Hitler had issued his secret directive for the invasion of Poland to take place later in the year, Colonel Beck, Poland's Foreign Minister, arrived in London for talks. It was plain enough that an attack on Poland was coming, and that would, inevitably, involve Britain in war with Germany. Couldn't Russia be brought in on Britain's side? The negotiations with Russia were dragging; yet without Russian help, how could Britain keep her promises to Poland and Roumania? Chamberlain simply asked Russia to offer guarantees to Poland and Roumania. Russia, in reply, wanted a three-cornered pact between Russia, France and Britain, a proposal which Mr. Eden and others urged should be accepted. Sir Winston Churchill puts it pungently in *The Second World War*: " If, for instance, Mr. Chamberlain on receipt of the Russian offer had replied, ' Yes. Let us band together and break Hitler's neck ' or words to that effect, Parliament would have approved, Stalin would have understood, and history might have taken a different course. At least, it could not have taken a worse."

At this point Anthony Eden offered to go to Russia. Although not a Minister, he was the only Britisher who had had any personal contact with Stalin who had taken a liking to him at their meeting in 1935. Mr. Lloyd George, Mr. Winston Churchill and Anthony Eden pressed Chamberlain hard to come to an understanding with Russia; but it was useless.

In April when compulsory military service was introduced, Eden decided to polish up on his own military training. He joined up as a Major with the London Rangers, a Motor Battalion of the King's Royal Rifle Corps, the famous regiment with which he had served with distinction in the first World War.

In June Eden went to France for a conference—at a time when Chamberlain had sent Mr. Strang, of the Foreign Office to Moscow In July, Eden was in camp at Beaulieu, as Second-in-Command of the 2nd Battalion, the Rangers. Holiday makers, surprised to see him there, stopped him for autographs, which he never refused.

In camp Eden showed his gift for unobtrusive leadership. An international figure, he submitted in spirit and in the letter to military discipline, and was scrupulously considerate of his Commanding Officer, Lt.-Col. R. L. Bennett, who found him a hard-working and conscientious officer and a good scrounger when it came to getting equipment for the unit. Eden knew how to get on to the War Office and hustle up the delivery of equipment for which they had been waiting for months.

One August morning in Beaulieu Lt.-Col. Bennett woke up to hear a babble of voices, including Eden's outside his tent. " I never did trust those darned Slavs," said Phillip Caley, the adjutant. Bennett pulled aside the flaps of his tent and asked what it was all about. A group of half-dressed men, including Eden, were poring over the newspaper headlines:

RUSSIA SIGNS PACT WITH GERMANY. Eden must have wondered what would have happened if Chamberlain had listened to him, and let him go to Moscow to negotiate a Mutual Defence Pact between Britain, France and Russia. Now it was too late, and the outbreak of war could only be a matter of time.

The German-Soviet Pact of August 21st was followed four days later by Britain's formal announcement of a Pact with Poland. Six days later Germany invaded Poland. Sitting in the House of Commons, still as a back-bencher, Eden heard his old chief, Neville Chamberlain, inform the Members that an ultimatum had been delivered to Germany to withdraw her troops. He heard Chamberlain echoing almost the very words he himself had used when he resigned;

" ... we have no quarrel with the German people, except that they allow themselves to be governed by a Nazi Goverment. As long as that Government exists and pursues the methods it has so persistently followed during the last two years, there will be no peace in Europe. We shall merely pass from one crisis to another ... "

There were terrifying delays—delays which exasperated a suspicious House of Commons. The French Government begged for time to evacuate their women and children and mobilise their army, Mussolini had tried to confuse the issue by offering to mediate. But on Sunday morning of the 3rd September, at 11.15 a.m., Eden and a group of friends, including Mr. Robert Boothby, M.P., heard the Premier announce that Britain was at war with Germany. As he finished, Eden walked over to the window and looked out, in a brown study. " I am wondering," he told Boothby, " if there is anything more I could have done to prevent this." He had been ahead of his time, too young, too uncompromising, too clear-headed and too honest at a time when the country did not want to face facts. Now the facts faced them. The tragedy he had tried so hard to avert had come about.

EIGHTEEN

Into Office

AS this crisis had developed Mr. Winston Churchill had been advising Chamberlain on the formation of a wartime Cabinet. On the day before war was declared, he had chided the Premier: "Aren't we a very old team? I make out that the six you mentioned to me yesterday aggregate 386 years or an average of over sixty-four! Only one year short of the Old Age Pension! If however you added Sinclair (49) and Eden (42) the average comes down to fifty-seven and a half." Apart from this, Eden, said Churchill, would add to the unity of the Government by bringing with him the influence " of the section of Conservatives who are associated with him." In other words, the younger, more progressive Conservatives.

Chamberlain took Churchill's advice, and in his re-formed Government made Churchill First Lord of the Admiralty and Eden Secretary of State for the Dominions. Eden is a man who knows how to take disappointment, and if he felt any he did not show it. He was anxious to be used as the country thought best. His skill could have been used elsewhere, but the appointment was an important and useful one. Somebody had to keep the Dominions in the picture. Like most families, the English-speaking family is most united in a crisis. From Australia, New Zealand, Canada and South Africa came messages of support for Britain, followed by declarations of war against Germany. Similar messages came from India and the Colonies. Perhaps the message from Mr. R. G. Menzies, Prime Minister of Australia, best expressed the feeling throughout the Commonwealth: " There is unity in the Empire ranks—one King, one flag, one cause."

Within a week Mr. Eden was able to speak by radio with the whole of the Empire, and to say with truth that the Empire was united. "A week has passed," he said, " since this country found itself at war with Nazi Germany, and to-day we are a united people more closely knit one to another in our common resolve than at any time in our history." He outlined, clearly and chronologically, the events that had led to war, made inevitable by Hitler's " cynical dissimulation." " Flouting all the lessons of history, ignoring or deriding even their own country's experience of British character, they preferred yet once more the path of lawlessness, the path of misery and bloodshed, the path of anarchy and want . . . by Herr Hitler's own decision our new civilisation must be built through a world at war. We would have wished it otherwise. But our new civilisation will be built just the same, for some forces are bigger than men, and in that new civilisation will be found liberty and opportunity and hope for all."

Poland, attacked simultaneously by Germany and Russia, was soon crushed; now she was a colony and a reservoir of cheap or slave labour. Now her Jewish population was doomed to slaughter. In Britain the coasts were being hastily fortified, land mines laid, barbed wire entanglements erected, the Air Raid Precautions organisation streamlined. The system of twelve Regional Commissioners, each to have complete autonomy in the event of an invasion, was ready for action.

The " phoney war " was on. Germany was too busy digesting her latest prize to launch an attack yet on France or Britain. But the defence of France was a matter of urgency, and soon Dominions' representatives came to Europe and were taken by Mr. Eden to France, where they took part in Armistice Day ceremonies. They were received by the Commander-in-Chief and the Duke of Gloucester at General Headquarters and gave their reports on the state of public opinion and the preparations being made for war in the Dominions. Later they visited the Maginot Line, the vast underground fortress which had taken France years to build at the cost of millions of pounds, and which was thought to be an insuperable obstacle to an invading army.

Eden and his party had lunch in the depths of the earth below the Maginot fortifications, and he received, with the others, a special Maginot Medal with the words " *On ne passe pas* " and a representation of one of the Maginot heavy guns. And on November 20th Eden broadcast in French to the French people. He had been impressed by their "quiet determination." He was talking to an Ally, of course, and the praise for the French was laid on rather heavily and with much exaggeration:

> France has made great sacrifices, financial and material, in order to complete her Maginot Line. To-day freedom-loving peoples everywhere acknowledge with deep gratitude the debt which they owe to *these impregnable defences* (my italics). Thus, not for the first time in human history, France has placed all civilisation in her debt.

Eden has published volumes of his speeches, which do not claim to be complete. In wartime, of course, speeches are made to impress one's friends and depress one's enemies, whilst considerations of security prevent them being a reflection of one's real intentions. But one speech omitted from Eden's published books shows—to his credit, let me add, for he has never claimed to be infallible—how convincing nonsense can be made to sound once speech-making has become a professional habit. Broadcasting on October 25th, he proved that even the most well-meaning prophet can be wildly wrong. He referred to the consultations between the Dominions and continued:

> "The aggressor's early advantage is spent. The road to the East is blocked by Russia or barred by Turkey. In the west every week that passes adds to the strength of the free democracies. With fast gathering momentum we swing into our stride. German attacks by air upon our fleet or upon our merchantmen have failed utterly in their purpose. By comparison with the last war the submarine has proved to be an indecisive weapon . . . a much-heralded offensive in the west still hangs fire . . ."

All these statements were to be disproved within a matter of months. The Maginot defences, which he described as "impregnable" proved useless. The offensive which hung fire did, when it started, send the European nations down like ninepins. German submarines, planes and mines began to decimate Britain's merchant fleet. And the road to the East was not blocked by Russia. However, it was only meant to be a "pep" talk, of the sort necessary in wartime. It was a speech directed as much against Hitler and Goebbels, his propaganda chief, as to anyone else; it was intended to emphasise that Britain did not stand alone.

As organiser and co-ordinator of the Empire effort, Eden proved an excellent choice. He worked hard and long at the Dominions Office, and was seldom back in his house in Fitzhardinge Street, until nearly midnight. One pleasant duty was to welcome the contingents of Empire troops that began to arrive, including the first contingents of Canadians who came in December. And yet in the House of Commons in December, Eden had time to deliver an interesting speech on social reconstruction after the war, which shows a side of him with which the public was—and is—unfamiliar. His preoccupation with international affairs implies an understanding of them, which most people consider makes him ill-informed or unqualified in home affairs. His speech on post-war reconstruction shows how misconceived that is; not only does it show an improvement in style, but it shows how well Eden understood that war inevitably brings social changes in its wake.

In February, 1940, Eden flew to the Middle East and visited camps and aerodromes in Egypt, to greet Australian, New Zealand and Indian troops. From the Canadians in particular he received a tremendous ovation. As he watched the Anzacs coming through the Suez Canal, the Australians singing at the tops of their voices, Eden was profoundly moved. He welcomed the men with little speeches which were short and sincere.

But soon the " phoney war " was to end. The unnatural lull, the tension of being at war and yet not at war, ended. Germany swept through Belgium and Holland, Denmark and Norway. The failure of the British campaign in Norway was to divert Eden's efforts into other channels. Chamberlain, too tired and disillusioned to make a suitable leader at this moment of crisis, resigned. Mr. Winston Churchill was made Prime Minister, and formed a government in which he made Anthony Eden, Secretary of State for War—a tremendous responsibility for a man of forty-five, but one for which Eden with his flair for administration, his love of action, tremendous appetite for hard work and his understanding of the army and the men in it, would appear to be well suited.

In fact, Eden did not remain more than seven months at the War Office. It was, of course, a very onerous appointment, and involved widespread and increasing obligations all over the world at a time when Britain's war effort was only just getting into its stride. One of his first jobs was to broadcast an appeal for an anti-invasion force manned by volunteers whose age and health would disqualify them from regular military service. The swift collapse of Holland had pointed the need for a determined civilian population which would not leave all the fighting to professional soldiers. Eden, who has never had the common touch, suggested the rather dreary title of " Local Defence Volunteers ", but Churchill, the lover of good plain English words, saw the error of that. " The word ' local ' is uninspiring . . . I think ' Home Guard ' would be better " he told Eden in an official minute. And Home Guard the new force became.

It was a painful period for Eden. The weary pace of Civil Service departments unwilling or unable to adapt their routine to the demands of war; rivalries between departments; industrial bottlenecks; shortages of men, materials and equipment and the vexed question of priorities. Whether Eden had that degree of ruthless push needed in a War Minister I rather doubt; he is tough, and knows well enough how to get his way. But his anxiety to be polite and his natural sense of caution must at times have been irritating to his sponsor whose minutes, reproduced in considerable detail in Churchill's wartime memoirs, show quite often a trace of acerbity. Churchill had always admired Eden, and still did. They met from day to day and often dined and lunched together. But Churchill, in those grim days, would not let the most valued friendship stand in the way of getting things done. France had fallen, and Britain stood alone. It was no time for mincing words, and every minute of the day—and frequently at night—a note marked ACTION THIS DAY, a telegram or a minatory phone call would arrive. " Never," records Churchill, " has a great nation been so naked before her foes."

Eden had to endure a strange ordeal on the evening of May 26th. The British Garrison at Calais were fighting with their backs to the wall, and there was some talk in France of Calais being evacuated. Churchill had to make the difficult decision, with Eden, not to relieve the Garrison and to tell them to fight on to the end, so that the enemy's armoured forces might be diverted and the Dunkirk evacuation carried out. This involved Eden's own regiment. Their sacrifice was necessary to enable the evacuation of 300,000 Allied troops. So the decision not to relieve the Garrison being taken, Eden read and approved the message from Churchill to Brigadier Nicholson:

> Every hour you continue to exist is of the greatest help to the B.E.F. Government has therefore decided you must continue to fight. Have greatest possible admiration for your splendid stand. Evacuation will not (repeat not) take place and craft required for above purpose are to return to Dover. . . . "

It was a message of death for many gallant men, but there was no help for it.

While the Germans had been closing in on Paris, Eden had visited France with Churchill. They saw together the chief characters in that swift-moving tragedy, Reynaud and Marshal Petain, and tried hard to imbue them with some spirit of fight. But Petain was completely defeatist and Churchill, with a huge sigh, suggested that they catch the next plane home. It was on this visit that Eden met a Frenchman who was later to rouse France from her defeatism and inertia—General de Gaulle, who became leader of the Free French Forces.

It is plain from Churchill's memoirs that Eden was under constant bombardment from Churchill. There was the danger of German attack or landing forces by parachute; there was the slow *tempo* in the Middle East (" I really think that you, Lloyd and Amery ought to be able to lift our affairs in the East and Middle East out of the catalepsy by which they are smitten "); he demanded information on the progress of the Home Guard; he grumbled at the misuse of troops on the building of fortifications—work which should be done by civilians whilst the soldiers were drilling and training. And why were troops without transport when pleasure buses were driving up and down Brighton front? Why was the 3rd Division spread along the coast instead of being concentrated in one spot, ready for deployment to a point of attack?

In some respects Eden was too genteel, too incapable of infusing the necessary minimum of emotion into his appeals and

A thoughtful study of Lady Eden by Cecil Beaton, taken recently in her London home.

Photo: Mirrorpic

Mrs. Beatrice Eden photographed in her New York flat.

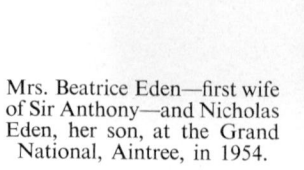

Mrs. Beatrice Eden—first wife of Sir Anthony—and Nicholas Eden, her son, at the Grand National, Aintree, in 1954.

Photo: Planet News

pronouncements to rally or rouse men. He is a leader, but he is incapable, given no following, of rallying support. The impudence, the verve, the humour and the extravert humanity —the direct appeal as from one human being to another— simply aren't there. Eden was also weak in putting over the basic idea of Commandos to the Army and in insisting that an initiative be taken. Churchill had made his ideas quite plain in a memorandum to him: " The defeat of France was accomplished by an incredibly small number of highly equipped *élite*, while the dull mass of the German army came on behind."

But the Army was obstructive. The old guard disliked the idea of " free-lance soldiers," whose almost anarchistic independence, in the military sense, seemed too unconventional and not in keeping with orthodox militarism. Eden could not put over the idea of these small, swift-striking units and his orders were ignored. " Perhaps you will explain to me," wrote Churchill on the September 8th, " what has happened to prevent your decision from being made effective. In my experience of Service departments, which is a long one, there is always a danger that anything contrary to Services' prejudices will be obstructed and delayed by officers of the second grade in the machine. The way to deal with this is to make signal examples of one or two."

Eden's knowledge of Middle Eastern affairs, always a speciality of his, was of great value to the country and to Churchill—who, in this matter, found his judgment questioned by his protégé, an experience he did not relish overmuch. In July Eden had been made Chairman of a Committee of Ministers whose task it was to advise on the conduct of the war in the Middle East. Eden's job was like that of a chef ordered to make a hundred puddings with only six currants. With the threat of invasion still in the air, and day and night air raids on Britain as an obvious " softening up " process, men and materials could only be deployed where they would be most effective. But he sent two tank battalions for General Wavell to use against the Italians in North Africa, where vast Italian motorised forces were being assembled for an attack on Egypt.

Churchill, however, needed personal contact with the men on the spot, and sent Eden to Egypt to report on the general situation. It was as well he did. Eden arrived in Cairo on October 15th and was soon consulting with Wavell and Maitland Wilson. They were storing up their strength for an offensive, whereas Churchill thought there was slackness and a defensive spirit. And when Mussolini invaded Greece on October 28th, Churchill bombarded Eden with telegrams—which Eden resisted—urging that forces should be sent to defend Crete. Eden knew that the desert Army commanders were planning an offensive, and was naturally disinclined to hint at this in a telegram to Churchill. He asked permission to return, and arrived on November 8th, where he disclosed the plan to the Prime Minister and his Service chiefs. " We were all delighted," says Churchill, " I purred like six cats." Eden, over twenty years his junior, did not mind standing up to Churchill. Had he weakened before the barrage of peremptory telegrams the desert forces would have been seriously weakened and the success of the Middle East campaign jeopardised.

Even so, one gets the impression that, much as Churchill admired Eden, he was not too keen on his being at the War Office. He needed too much chivvying, and his orders were sometimes ignored or delayed. He had done a good job in the Middle East, and on that note, Churchill thought, he had better be transferred to the Foreign Office. Lord Halifax, then Foreign Minister, was sent as Ambassador to Washington. Speaking of this transfer in *The Second World War*, the war-Premier pays a glowing tribute to Eden, " On all the great issues of the past four years I had . . . dwelt in close agreement with Anthony Eden . . . we had been united in thought and sentiment on the outbreak of war and as colleagues during its progress. The greater part of Eden's public life had been devoted to the study of foreign affairs . . . we thought alike, even without consultation, on a very great number of practical issues as they arose from day to day. I looked forward to an agreeable and harmonious comradeship between the Prime Minister and the Foreign Secretary, and this hope was certainly fulfilled during the four and a half years of war and policy which lay before us. Eden was sorry to leave the War Office, in all the stresses and excitements of which he was absorbed; but he returned to the Foreign Office like a man going home."

NINETEEN

Man Friday to Churchill

TWO days before Christmas, Eden said good-bye to his War Office staff and moved into the Foreign Office. Churchill had been wise to send him there. In total war, relations with foreign countries are part of an intricate game of chess which only a skilled player can understand. Widely travelled, a good linguist, pleasant without being weak, conscientious and with an inexhaustible appetite for work, Eden was just the man. A very close bond had developed between them. Eden was Man Friday to Churchill, whose gruff commands concealed affection, as a father addressing a son whom he does not wish to spoil.

Eden was sorry to leave the War Office, but his skill was needed to woo the neutrals, satisfy our allies and outwit our enemies. Soon the British invasion of Italian Eritrea began; the Australians entered Tobruk; reports reaching London showed that a German attack on Greece and Yugoslavia was in the offing. The Blitz on London and the English industrial centres was reaching its crescendo, with over 1,500 killed and 2,000 seriously injured in the month of January, 1941, alone.

Anthony and his wife Beatrice literally lived on top of the job—a flat in the Foreign Office originally built for Lord Halifax, with an office, two small bedrooms, a large sitting-room and two bathrooms. There were telephones fitted with scramblers, and direct lines to the Prime Minister and important Service departments. The Ministry of Works had furnished it in French style, and Mrs. Eden made it look a little more cheerful with flowers and pictures. In practice, of course, they were not always in residence together. Anthony had an incredible amount of travelling to do—visits abroad, interviews with personalities, journeys out of town, meetings which lasted far into the night. Once, to the irritation of all concerned, the

Prime Minister made his headquarters in a railway carriage and insisted on being visited in this awkwardly-placed headquarters! And Beatrice was far too active and restless to content herself with mere domesticity. At the Y.M.C.A. headquarters she took over a mobile tea canteen presented by the Allied Relief Fund for services with the troops, and operated it on alternate weeks. She often took it to the south coast towns, serving out tea in all weathers and often during air raids. She was completely fearless, and her good humour and friendly helpfulness commended her to everyone.

On February 4th, 1941, Eden had the pleasant task of assuring the House of Commons that Haile Selassie was recognised by the British as Emperor of Abyssinia. A few days later a note from the Greek Government spoke of its determination to resist German aggression. Italy had invaded Greece in October, British troops had been sent to Crete and Britain had told Greece that she would transfer troops from Libya. The Greeks were dubious, thinking that Britain could not send enough men to keep the Germans out, but that their presence might provoke Germany into assisting Italy's campaign. Churchill felt that some token assistance must be made, if only to encourage Yugoslavia, also marked down for German attack.

Eden, with the Chief of the Imperial General Staff, made his third visit to the Middle East to see what help Wavell could spare. He saw the military leaders on the spot, and found time to look in on his old regiment, the King's Royal Rifle Corps, at Mena; the men had been through the gruelling desert battle, including the taking of Benghazi, and when Eden saw them, had completed a distance of 764 miles in actual marching. He visited Ankara to sound the Turks on their attitude, saw and met President General Inonu with his Foreign Minister and the C.I.G.S. and returned to London in time to hear that there had been a rising in Belgrade as a protest against Prince Paul of Yugoslavia's pro-German activities—he had visited Hitler—and the country's freedom was being given away.

Once more Eden flew to Athens, at the end of March with the C.I.G.S.—who then went on to Belgrade, where pro-British elements had seized power. But on April 6th German troops invaded both Greece and Yugoslavia and by the end of the month the British had left Greece. Eden had hoped for an alliance between Greece, Turkey and Yugoslavia, but Turkey insisted on neutrality. Wavell had been forced to hold up his advance in Africa in order to send men to Greece—a move which weakened him without preventing the occupation of Greece. This decision was criticised, but Eden defended the decision. " I believe that had we not gone to her help, we could not have raised our heads again." But he had told Greece during his visits what help could be forthcoming; there were limits to it, since the collapse of France had deprived the Allies of three main armies in the Middle East—the French forces at Jibuti, Syria and Tunis. The British, said Eden, had been showered by flowers when they arrive in Greece, and when they left.

In March, John G. Winant, a sensitive, shrewd and kindly man arrived in London as American Ambassador. Of him Eden said: "He cares much for his work, little for party politics, not at all for himself." The two men had much in common, and an instant friendship sprang up between them which was of lasting benefit to Anglo-American relations. Britain's struggle had been misrepresented in the United States as an imperialist game of chess, a series of manœuvres to consolidate the British Empire. Eden understood Roosevelt's wish for Europe, that nationalism should take second place to humanity, and was at pains to prove to Winant—who could now see for himself the nature of Britain's struggle, and the morale of the people—that idealism was not an American monopoly.

Speaking at the Mansion House on May 29th, 1941, Eden made specific references to the American President, who had decreed a state of unlimited national emergency in the U.S.A., and praised Roosevelt's historic words: " We do not accept, and will not permit, this Nazi shape of things to come." Understanding only too well America's emotional antagonism to what is vaguely called " imperialism ", Eden seized on the President's reference to the fact that national independence must depend upon the freedom of the seas. " This freedom," said Eden, " has been maintained in the past by the British and American Navies, and both countries have fought on many occasions to preserve it . . . " Britannia ruled the waves, with some assistance from America.

But his speeches now showed far more polish and directness than they had ever done. Eden worked like a demon, and action gave fluency and vitality to his spoken thoughts, although some of his speeches read as though they have been delivered from Olympian heights; it is a mental defect of somebody who had never been in an unprivileged position, has never known the indignity of poverty and has been too genteel ever to let himself go—in public. Yet when one considers the pressure of work on the Foreign Office in wartime—the endless consultations and conferences, the mountains of minutes, the constant journeys and the distractions of the air raids—one admires Eden's immense grasp of detail. Eden is a super non-shirker. He may bite off more than he can chew sometimes, but he has never refused to bite.

Hitler had spoken of a New Order, a dictatorship that would last for a thousand years. Eden answered this by talking of the need for social change after the war, and Britain's intention to play its part in removing from the post-war world freedom from want and fear. There would be economic co-operation in Europe, not excluding Germany. This was a skilful speech, showing considerable understanding of the American psychology.

" Social security must be the first object of our policy after the war, and social security will be our policy abroad no less than at home ... the free nations of America, the Dominions and ourselves ... have the will and the intention to evolve a post-war order which seeks no selfish national advantage ... " These words, banner-headlined across the face of America, were an effective answer to the still-powerful Isolationists.

Many tributes have been paid to Eden, but that of Mr. John G. Winant is especially interesting, based as it is on years of personal friendship with him. He has said:

> Many people liked Eden because he was good-looking, well-dressed and a Britisher who frankly liked the United States. I found him a hard-working, unafraid Englishman who had spent his life in the service of his country. He was one of the best-trained diplomats I have ever met. He had no use for shoddy politics, whether at home or abroad. His views and his judgment on public affairs were based on knowledge and on a high sense of duty ... no one I know carried a heavier load in the war.

Churchill's relationship with Eden he compared with that of Roosevelt and Harry Hopkins. Most great men know that all who cross their doorstep want something; Eden wanted nothing for himself. Like Hopkins, he had the courage to tell the truth whether it was wanted or unwanted to the man under whom he served.

Eden was never away from his work, day or night. His home was the gaunt Foreign Office building, with its bomb-blasted windows stuffed with sacking or paper.

"The Foreign Secretary's personal office," writes Mr. Winant in his account, "was on the north-eastern corner of the building. It was a spacious room, cold in winter, but light and cheery, well-furnished and easily adapted for conference use. He and his wife occupied a small apartment which had been an office on the top floor of the Foreign Office. Twice it was blasted by bomb explosions and the windows blown in. Luckily there was no one in at either time.

"We had an odd informal relationship, based not only on personal friendship but also on our regard for each other's country and for our own. We both got satisfaction in working together for measures and actions that were of mutual advantage to both countries."

Later during the war Winant would spend week-ends at the Eden's country home, Binderton House, near Chichester, which Beatrice had discovered through an advertisement. It was the ideal country retreat for a man so physically and mentally pressed that occasionally, at least, he must relax or break. Built during the Charles I period, it is a pleasant brick and stone house of two stories standing in lovely parkland. Anthony had furnished a study for himself in quiet and tasteful style, the walls lined with well-bound books and his famous collection of volumes on Persia, one of his special subjects. One magnificent set of volumes was a gift from the Aga Khan. It was the first country house Eden had ever owned, and he loved it. The furniture was mostly antique, and scattered through the house were some of his favourite pictures, including dozens of water colours by his artist father, Sir William Eden. There was even a picture of his own—a water colour sketch of the countryside near Arles in France.

In this environment, nobody would have recognised the Foreign Minister. With the facility of a chameleon he could change his personality as soon as he arrived. Off would come the immaculate clothes—he can't help being a human clotheshanger, with his slim waist, broad shoulders and long legs, and has always dressed well because it is expected with his grade of job—and on would go some old flannels and a well-worn, loose sports jacket. It was a relaxed atmosphere. All who saw Eden in this, his personal environment, could hardly reconcile him with the expert diplomat, the maker of speeches, the castigator of dictators. They liked having guests, a few at a time. Sometimes Lord and Lady Cranborne perhaps, his old friend and ex-P.P.S., Mr. J. P. L. Thomas, or Ernest Bevin, for whom Eden had the most profound admiration. "Ernest is marvellous," Eden once said of the ex-docker, "he sets about a problem quite differently from the way I would, and he's always right."

It was quite a large house, run by Mrs. Eden, two maids and one evacuee. As the two maids had been in the employ of the Edens for over twenty years, there was a family atmosphere about the place which visitors enjoyed very much.

Guests would usually help with the gardening, and sometimes they would pick fruit and vegetables to go with the meals. Or they would play with "Alabama", a poodle given to Anthony by Averil Harriman. Anthony's main pleasures were browsing in his study, gardening—at which he is an expert—and going for country walks.

Winant enjoyed his week-ends at Binderton. He felt keenly and personally the tragedy that had engulfed Europe, and hated violence so much that eventually grief was to wear him out and he was to die by his own hand—being too sensitive and kindly to feel at home in a world of violence. With this make-up, the tranquil beauty of Sussex was exactly what he needed for relaxation, and in Eden he found a kindred spirit. He records, nostalgically, in his diary:

> "... we used to go down occasionally on a Sunday to his country house in Sussex.... I have never known anyone who cared more about flowers or vegetables or fruit trees, or wind blowing across wheatfields or the green pastures which marked out the Sussex Downs. We used to get our fun weeding the garden. We would put our despatch boxes at either end, and when we had completed a row we would do penance by reading messages and writing out the necessary replies. Then we would start again

our menial task, each in some unconscious fashion trying to find some sense of lasting values in the good earth."

Both men, of course, took their work with them. The red leather despatch boxes with the Royal monogram arrived in an endless stream, and Eden was constantly in touch with his office and with Service departments through his " scrambler " telephone. Once a guest sat on one which had been left in an easy chair, and jumped up at the thought of treating State equipment so indifferently.

On duty, Eden has his reserve. In his own home he is relaxed. His great passion was for growing roses, and he would often exchange cuttings with his friends the Cranbornes.

On the whole, however, a snatched week-end at Binderton was a luxury which Eden never enjoyed as often as his inclination might have dictated or his health demanded. But nobody ever heard him grumble.

The tempo of the war grew more furious every month, and the flow of work was relentless. By April air raid deaths in Britain had reached over 6,000 for a single month, yet morale was good. He was absorbed with the planning of the Conference of Allies, held at St. James' Palace as a counterblast to Hitler's proclamation of a " New Order " in Europe. He had to answer some ill-mannered sneers from General Franco, who was pro-German.

On June 22nd, Germany invaded Russia, as Eden had confidently expected. Now the whole aspect of the war was changed; the nightmare of the German High Command had become, thanks to Hitler's insistence, a reality—a front in both the East and West. This momentous development brought a declaration from Mr. Churchill, on the same day, that Britain would help Russia, and Sir Stafford Cripps and a military mission arrived in Moscow five days later. On July 12th the Anglo-Russian Agreement for mutual assistance, and guaranteeing that neither party would seek a separate peace with Germany was signed. Eden was realistic in addressing the House of Commons on Russia: " This country has probably fewer Communists than any nation in Europe. We have always hated the creed, but that is not the issue. Russia has been invaded, wantonly, treacherously, without warning . . . the Russians to-day are fighting for their soil. They are fighting the man who seeks to dominate the world. This is also our sole task."

Eden conferred with Maisky, the Russian Ambassador, and arranged with him to visit Moscow in the winter. Battles of mammoth proportions were being fought on Russian soil; Leningrad was resisting with the heroism of desperation; the Russians were withdrawing from Orel, Briansk and Odessa. Kharkov had fallen, then Rostov.

Just before the Japanese attacked Pearl Harbour on December 7th, 1941, and declared war on the United States and Britain, a few days before the Russians took the offensive on the whole of the Eastern Front, Anthony Eden went to Russia to confer with Stalin, leaving Scapa Flow by the northern route to Murmansk in H.M.S. *Kent* and spending a week in Moscow. Escorted by the Royal Navy, the ice-laden ship heaved its way through heavy seas until it rounded the North Cape and hugged the Murmansk coast. It was snowing hard when Eden landed to be greeted by Russian soldiers lined up in sheepskin coats, flanked by officers carrying the Union Jack and the Hammer and Sickle. He travelled to Moscow by train, to find on arrival that there were 58 degrees of frost, conferred with Stalin and Molotov, drove down the Moscow-Leningrad road, where corpses, blackened trees and shattered homes showed how recent had been the fighting there. In the ditches he saw piles of frozen German corpses, and he spoke to young German boys, shivering in their inadequate clothes in the bitter cold, who had been recently conscripted into the German Army.

As Eden talked to Stalin, the Germans were only 35 miles away, and their conversations were frequently interrupted by air raids. Eden had kept his visit a close secret—to the great irritation of Press correspondents, who referred to him as " the invisible man " and " you know who "—and one can imagine his thoughts as, stepping out on to the blacked-out station, he found himself suddenly in the glare of batteries of brilliant arc lights. Eden stayed at the National Hotel, near to the Kremlin, and bore himself bravely at a seven-hour Kremlin banquet where speeches and vodka were both inexhaustible. Eden, who is not a spirit drinker, was forced to drink great quantities of vodka in the interest of goodwill— his hosts were all hard drinkers.

Stalin was friendly but astonished Eden with the sweeping nature of his demands—complete recognition of Soviet conquests and guarantees that the territories seized by Russia in Poland and the Baltic states would remain hers after the war. Such commitments Eden was not, of course, in a position to make. It was agreed that equipment, planes and arms should be sent to Russia with all possible speed, but Stalin's insistence on the opening of a second front in Europe before the Allies were ready had, of course, to be resisted.

Eden had a safe if uncomfortable journey home. As a gesture of goodwill he brought with him a Soviet Trade Union delegation. Eden was able to report to the Cabinet that despite their immense losses, the Russians were inspired with a spirit of implacable resistance and offensive, hardened by the unparalleled atrocities which the invaders left in their trail.

On January 4th, 1942, Eden broadcast on his visit to Russia, but it was, necessarily, a superficial speech intended to serve the purposes of the moment; it could not give the inner history of his meeting with Stalin, who had demanded the post-war recognition of Russia's conquest of the Baltic States, of part of Poland and Finland, as the price of Anglo-Russian co-operation. This situation called for firmness, patience, and skill on Eden's part, since in the ensuing months he had to balance the need for co-operation with Russia with the equally obvious need for keeping American goodwill. America was alarmed at what appeared to be the prospect of Britain agreeing to Stalin's proposal; it would have put the seal of approval on Russian aggression in the Baltic and elsewhere, have discouraged small countries and undermined the prospects of post-war peace. And endorsement of Communist aggression would have been valuable propaganda for the German cause.

Eden did not need telling this. He had refused appeasement before, but this was a different matter. The German attack on Russia was a turning point in the Allied fortunes, diverting to the Eastern front forces which could have been used in the West. Strategically, Anglo-Russian co-operation was essential, as Churchill and Eden had been quick to see.

Throughout these negotiations with Russia Eden kept his friend Winant closely informed; they would read each other's despatches and memoranda during their week-ends together, and I doubt if a *rapprochement* has ever been so close in the history of diplomacy. They trusted each other so much that they did not bother with the elaborate *aides memoires* so beloved of diplomats. Eden steered a middle course between Russian suspicion and American apprehension, and when Molotov, the Russian Foreign Minister, visited Britain in May, 1942, Eden negotiated a Treaty of Alliance for twenty years, in which no territorial agreement was made. This was a considerable achievement, possible only because Eden had kept his head. The Treaty was signed on May 26th. Mr. Cordell Hull, Roosevelt's Foreign Minister, says: " I was enormously relieved." " It was a great relief to me," is Mr. Churchill's comment. So, I imagine, must it have been to Eden. As a retriever of hopeless situations he had proved himself again. The weight of work at the Foreign Office at this time was staggering. Now, total war meant what it said—everything was happening everywhere at once. One needed a mind like a far-ranging telescope, focusing at will on one spot after another and comprehending instantly what one saw; Eden had to understand the resolution of the Pan-American Conference on a rupture of relations between the South American States and the Axis powers; to follow the swiftly-changing scene in Russia; to keep abreast of Japanese moves in Java, Batavia, Mandalay; to contact General Giraud, who had escaped to Switzerland from France; to deal with the leaders of the exiled governments in London, including President Benes of Czechoslovakia and the unsmiling, intractable but courageous General de Gaulle, leader of the Free French. It is impossible to imagine a job more onerous, more diffuse and in most ways so disheartening. Eden was often exhausted, and sometimes irritable. But never once did he say, " No. It is too much. Do it yourself." Eden spoke from the heart when he told the workers at Merthyr Tydfil: " We should take for our motto . . . the lines from Burns:

> Wha does the utmost that he can,
> Will whyles do mair.

" The stage of war compasses the earth," Eden told them, " It is so vast that the human mind can scarcely comprehend it." He spoke movingly of the Greeks left to die in the streets, of the long-drawn out agony of Poland, Norway, Greece and Holland. And he told them: " Here in Merthyr you knew poverty, you knew unemployment, you knew the bitter feeling of despair which comes of the knowledge that one is not wanted. We cannot go back to that."

Mr. Winston Churchill, who had unloaded staggering burdens on the back of the young man he had always trusted, saw his confidence had been rewarded a hundredfold. He knew, as nobody else could, that Eden's diffidence and self-discipline were not symptoms of nervousness or inaction. In fact, when Churchill decided to visit President Roosevelt in June, 1942, he took the unusual step of advising the King as to a successor to the Premiership:

" In the case of my death on this journey I am about to undertake, I avail myself of Your Majesty's gracious permission to advise you that you should entrust the formation of a new Government to Mr. Anthony Eden, the Secretary of State for Foreign Affairs, who is in my mind the outstanding Minister in the largest political party in the House of Commons and in the National Government over which I have the honour to preside, and who, I am sure, will be found capable of conducting Your Majesty's affairs with the resolution, experience and capacity which these grievous times require."

Was any politician ever recommended in terms more glowing, more dignified and all-embracing? Churchill had no time for people who could not get things done, least of all in wartime. Eden, at the age of 45, had assumed the mantle of greatness.

TWENTY

Travel and Talk

IN November Eden was made Leader of the House of Commons—an additional responsibility which he accepted cheerfully, if unwisely. He already had his hands full as Foreign Secretary, with duties in no way comparable to a peace-time appointment. Eden took the closest interest in strategy; and his work—the whole complex of relationships with governments, international affairs and the balance of power was bound inextricably with the carnage then raging all over the world. For example, a Foreign Office communiqué —which he must have seen and approved—issued on June 12th, after the signing of the Pact with Russia, had somewhat rashly spoken of hopes for a " Second Front " in 1942. Thereafter Stalin, obstinately ignoring the fact that Britain was already carrying a considerable burden, and had been fighting Germany at a time when Russia had held aloof and indifferent, pressed continually for the opening of a Second Front in Europe. At their 1941 meeting Eden had held out no hope of an early offensive; how this incautious phrase crept into the June communiqué is a matter for speculation.

Stalin became increasingly bitter on the subject, but Churchill knew that an invasion that went off at half-cock would simply waste Allied lives, leave the French Underground Movement (which would rise in support) open to savage reprisals, and provide valuable propaganda for the enemy.

And a new complication had entered Eden's life. In August, 1941, the Atlantic Charter had been formulated, emphasising the need for co-operation between nations after the war, and for the abrogation of selfishness and the rule by force. In the House of Commons on December 1st and 2nd, 1942, Eden spoke of the measures necessary for post-war recovery. He hoped Britain would never again turn its back on Europe. He did not add, as it would have been tactless to do, that he also hoped that Europe would never turn its back on Britain.

Later Eden spoke movingly of the appalling decimation and maltreatment of Europe's Jewish population. The organised inhumanity of it shocked him profoundly. It is also certain that had Britain fallen to Germany, Anthony Eden would have been one of the first men to be shot. He was almost top on the German list of people marked out for arrest. But the tide of war had already begun to turn. Dr. Goebbels, Hitler's brilliant but perverted propagandist, could do no more than fulminate in his private diary, on December 19th:

> Eden delivered a speech in the House of Commons on the Jewish problem and answered planted questions. Rothschild, the "venerable M.P." as the English call him, took the floor and delivered a flood of sob-stuff bemoaning the fate of the Polish Jews. All members of Parliament rose from their seats as a silent tribute to Jewry. . . . the perfumed British Foreign Minister, Eden, cuts a good figure amongst these characters from the synagogue. His whole education and his entire bearing can be characterised as thoroughly Jewish.

In January, 1943, Anthony Eden, in fulfilment of a promise made to Parliament, published a White Paper, prepared by a committee of experts, on the reform of the Foreign Office. The pre-war fiasco, when he had been Foreign Minister, of interference from the Treasury, and of vital reports from abroad being pigeon-holed and never reaching the people who should have seen them, was not likely to occur again. It was proposed to amalgamate immediately the Foreign Office, Diplomatic Service, the Commercial Diplomatic Service and the Consular Service, and to separate this unified Ministry from the home Civil Service. But in the excitement of war, this important reform passed almost unnoticed. Eden had laboured hard and long to achieve it.

On February 10th, Marjorie, Countess of Warwick, Anthony's sister, died at University College hospital at the age of 56. After the death of the fifth Earl in 1928 she was Mayor of Warwick from 1929 to 1930 and 1931. Before the war she had lived in the South of France, and when France collapsed she lost literally everything except the suitcase she had brought with her when visiting London in connection with work for French refugees.

In March, Eden went to Washington to confer with Roosevelt on operational matters, military co-operation, and post-war policy. He stayed at the White House from March 12th to March 30th and had conversations with General Marshall and leading American politicians. Roosevelt was more preoccupied with what would happen to the world when the war was over than Churchill could afford to be. "Unhappily," Churchill told Eden, who had reported that America was sponsoring the idea of a Four-Power bloc consisting of the United States, Britain, Russia and China—"unhappily the war has prior claims on your time and mine." Roosevelt was toying with the idealistic but impracticable idea of scrapping all colonial territories, irrespective of the acute financial and social problems this would create, or the danger that small states left to their own devices would automatically become prey to other "imperialisms," however named. At times it sounded as though Roosevelt wished to disband the British Commonwealth. "I've tried to make it clear to Winston—and the others—that, while we're their Allies and in it to victory by their side, they must never get the idea that we're in it just to help them hang on to the archaic, mediæval Empire ideas. . . ."

Over dinner at the White House, Eden discussed innumerable problems. There was Russia's manifest intention of keeping what she had seized unless made to relinquish it by force. The Poles, too, were being difficult. Eden described how the British Government had offered them a cruiser and how General Sikorsky insisted on naming it *The Lemburg*, a city over whose sovereignty Russia and Poland were bound to dispute. This would inevitably irritate the Russians at a time when their co-operation was essential. The hatred of the Poles for the Russians, who were as responsible as the Germans for the miseries that afflicted Poland, created many problems for Eden after the Anglo-Russian Pact. According to Harry Hopkins, who was present at meetings between Eden and Roosevelt, the latter "urged the British to give up Hong Kong as a gesture of goodwill." Eden remarked, dryly, that America had not made any such gesture herself.

During this visit Eden visited Annapolis, in Maryland, of which an ancestor of his, Robert Eden, had been Governor, Eden on this occasion proved that he has a certain streak of showmanship. He was careful to stress his aristocratic connections and his association with America. "A few miles away," he said, " in the City Hall at Baltimore, now hang the pictures of the Calvert family from whom I am proud to be descended. I am even prouder of the fact that one of the Calverts, the third Lord Baltimore, was the prime mover in the great Act of 1649, by which the settlers were assured full freedom to worship God according to their conscience. That was nearly three hundred years ago, but our times have given a new significance to the event . . . " Then off he went into his own special type of rhetoric: " Let me now for a moment look back to our experience in this war and see if we may gain from it guidance for the future . . . the greatest of all peace aims is to ensure that never again shall unscrupulous leaders be able to carry their peoples into war . . . we must prosecute the war to a final victory . . . to-day more than ever war is one and indivisible."

But the speech was a resounding success. The Maryland Legislature passed a resolution registering its admiration for " our valiant British Ally in her mortal conflict with the Axis powers, a respect firmly based upon the known qualities of the British people. . . . "

Eden's visit to America was closely followed by the Germans. Exchanges of pleasantries between countries, even in peacetime, are never without purpose. Goebbels records in his diary, at this stage, that Eden's visit to America " seems not to have been as successful as we had at first assumed." But there must have been a leakage somewhere, for Goebbels reports, with perfect accuracy, " . . . I received secret reports from the Research Institute indicating that Roosevelt intends to meet Stalin somewhere."

At Ottawa, in April, Eden addressed both houses of the Canadian Parliament. He paid a handsome and deserved tribute to Canadian efforts in the war, and went on to a subject then novel to them—the United Nations. This permitted him to indulge in those platitudes reminiscent of his pre-war references to the League of Nations. " Co-operation which is born of stern necessity and forged by experience has the best chance to survive into the years of peace . . . in this sphere of international endeavour the British Commonwealth has its specific contribution to make . . . " Making speeches is, undoubtedly, one of Eden's weaknesses. He suffers in making them, and is irritable and moody when he is drafting them, but he insists on making them on the least provocation.

In May, whilst Churchill was in Washington with his Service chiefs, Eden addressed the Conservative Party Conference, where his prestige now was sky-high. As Churchill's friend, confidant, adjutant, agent and admirer his status was near to that of the Prime Minister; his status, not his popularity. Sir Winston Churchill, of course, is well known for his unswerving loyalties, especially to friends; such mutual respect and friendship is a good thing.

Shortly after the Conservative Conference, Eden allowed himself a rare luxury—an informal evening at the Queensbury All Services Club. He was invited to dance by an A.T.S. girl (it did not happen in reverse) and his acceptance was followed by an encore. This trivial incident was deemed worthy of a newspaper paragraph at the time; it is an indication of the reputation Eden had gained for himself, of a person who never unbent.

In June occurred an incident which might have ended Eden's career. The closest security precautions invariably attended every move by Churchill and Eden. Their presence in particular places might be announced, but arrivals and departures were usually secret. Mr. Churchill had been to Washington and returned via North Africa, where he was joined by Eden. The German secret service knew Churchill was in Africa and were anxious to kill the British war leader if they could. Had they succeeded, Eden would have gone too, for they returned together by plane via Gibraltar.

Mr. Churchill, in *The Second World War* says:

" Eden and I flew home together by Gibraltar. As my presence in North Africa had been fully reported, the Germans were exceptionally vigilant, and this led to a tragedy which much distressed me. The regular commercial aircraft was about to start from the Lisbon airfield when a thick-set man smoking a cigar walked up and was thought to be a passenger on it. The German agents there signalled that I was on board. Although these passenger planes had plied unmolested between Portugal and England, a German plane was instantly ordered out, and the defenceless aircraft was instantly shot down. Thirteen passengers perished, among them the well-known British actor, Leslie Howard. . . ."

The Lisbon plane mystery is almost a book in itself. Somebody will write it one day. Mr. Churchill mentions Leslie Howard by name, but not his double, a Mr. Chenhalls, who in many respects bore a remarkable resemblance to Mr. Churchill. Was Mr. Chenhalls a decoy, intended to fool the German secret service? He was on Treasury business. Mr. Churchill is convinced that the Germans thought he was on that plane and says that his likeness "*was thought to be*" a passenger on it. In fact there is no element of doubt about it.

Whether by intention or not, Mr. Chenhalls did mislead the enemy, and attention was diverted from the real plane in which Mr. Churchill and Mr. Eden were travelling.

When he got back, Mr. Churchill strongly recommended Mr. Eden to be Viceroy of India in succession to Lord Linlithgow. It was an appointment to warm the heart of the most ambitious man—in status, in comforts, in remuneration. Eden thought well and hard about it, then rejected the chance. It proves that even then, he was looking far ahead, and possibilities of more spectacular promotion were not far from his mind. Had he become Viceroy of India, he would almost certainly have been made a peer; and a peerage would have precluded him from becoming Prime Minister.

The *tempo* of war had almost reached its *crescendo*. Massive R.A.F. raids on Germany; spectacular gains by the Russian forces, including the surrender of the German 6th Army at Stalingrad; a link-up between British officers and Yugoslav partisans; the fall of Mussolini and Italy's surrender. Eden played an important part in the negotiations for the surrender of Italy, which brought her forces over to the Allied side. "Don't miss the bus" was Churchill's comment, when Eden told him of an approach he had received from an emissary of Marshal Badoglio's. Eden did not, though, perhaps in his anxiety to catch it, he used the telephone more freely than he should have done. Goebbels records having tapped and monitored a telephone conversation between Churchill and Eden in which the latter complained that the Italian Crown Prince was creating difficulties for the English.

Mr. Eden at this time had little opportunity of following the ordinary routine of the Foreign Office; almost the rest of

1943 was taken up with conferences—one in Quebec, for the co-ordination of British and American war plans and to discover how Russia's plans might be fitted in to a definite pattern. Then a trip to Moscow, which Churchill urged on Eden as Anglo-Russian relations could hardly be worse. Stalin had sent a communication to Churchill which was so offensive that Churchill had refused to accept it. Stalin was resentful that the British had not opened what he vaguely called a " second front " (the British were in action on innumerable fronts at the time), and unappreciative of the considerable stream of equipment sent to Russia by convoys which frequently suffered severe losses.

Eden, having met Stalin before, was the man to smooth it out. He explained that the cruisers and destroyers accompanying the Arctic convoys left Britain weak in other areas, such as the Atlantic. Stalin, unaccustomed to talk of naval matters, listened attentively, then came back to his favourite topic—a second front in France. Stalin was irked because he had thought the British were saying that the convoys were not an obligation but an act of charity. Eden's explanation cleared the air. He had discussions with Stalin, Molotov, Mr. Cordell Hull and Mr. Harriman, the American Ambassador, and cleverly compromised by inviting Molotov to be chairman. They confirmed that a second front was fixed for Spring, 1944; discussed post-war problems, and the question of war criminals. Cordell Hull's approach was emotional: " If I had my way I would take Hitler and Mussolini and Tojo and their accomplices and bring them before a drumhead court martial. And at sunrise on the following day there would occur an historic incident." This was just the talk to enthuse the Russians, but Eden insisted on a proper trial for criminals. Summary justice was capable of too many abuses.

During these conferences, which took place in the marble and gilt Spiridonovka Palace, Molotov interrupted the session to announce the Soviet Army's capture of Dnepropetrovsk. Eden had a more difficult task to do than talking to Mr. Stalin; Mr. Cordell Hull kept pressing him with Mr. Roosevelt's idea of the abandonment of all colonies; there was an element of patronage in the statement that trusteeship of such territories would be a means of inducing colonial powers to develop the colonies for the good of the dependent peoples. Eden would not discuss this question, except to tell Hull that the British Government did not agree with Roosevelt's views.

On the last day of the conference, October 30th, a magnificent banquet was given at the Kremlin, with all the extravagance which is possible when taxpayers have no machinery by which they can grumble at public expenditure. There were endless toasts and after the banquet a cinema show and a concert. As Eden left, he asked the pilot of his plane to circle low over Stalingrad, so that he could see for himself the staggering destruction caused during its long ordeal.

In November and December, Eden attended, with Churchill, three vital conferences which were to affect the course of the war. The first, the Cairo Conference, attended by Roosevelt, Chiang Kai-shek and Churchill, was to discuss the war against Japan; another at Teheran, at which Churchill, Roosevelt and Stalin discussed grand strategy, and another conference in Cairo with the President and Foreign Secretary of Turkey. At Teheran Eden was Churchill's main assistant in the momentous discussions with the dour, determined Stalin and the shrewd Roosevelt. Eden must have been amused at the Russian secret service men detailed to protect him. A conspicuous bulge in their hip pockets proclaimed their identity.

On his way back from Teheran Eden delighted his old regiment by visiting the First Battalion of the King's Royal Rifle Corps, which paraded for him at Boufarik, in Italy. He told them that the Government was working hard so that the Army could work hard, and added that he had been giving buns " to Bruin, who was a very nice bear ".

Eden's chats with the President of Turkey were fruitless; Turkey had no intention of entering the war.

Eden, within the limitations imposed by wartime security, gave the House of Commons an outline of his travels. His final summary was a masterpiece of vagueness:

> " . . . Let me sum up my impressions of these three weeks. My Right Hon. Friend and I were greatly encouraged by the outcome of our three conferences. So I believe were all our Allied colleagues. To that extent I bring the House a message of good cheer."

That, you would have imagined, was a fairly harmless statement. But Eden insisted on qualifying it. " These events, of course, give no cause for easy optimism—far from it. If I were to do that I would give my message falsely . . . "

However, Eden, although not responsible for any policy of his own making, or any original plan of his own, had closed a widening breach between Russia and England. So far as could be possible with three major powers having different aspirations, temperaments and constitutions, he had worked hard towards some measure of Allied unity. He had travelled hundreds of thousands of miles in a single year. His resilience and tirelessness surprised his staff. He was not always a man you could warm to, but he was one you had to respect. He was seeing more history in the making than anyone else of his age.

TWENTY-ONE

On to Victory

THE tide of war had turned in favour of the Allies, but there was still to be much bloodshed, intrigue, bickering and disillusionment before the end could come. On January 28th, 1944, Eden spoke movingly in the House of Commons of the shameful treatment of prisoners-of-war in Japanese hands; of thousands forced to live in tropical jungle conditions without shelter, food, or medical treatment. He spoke of the thousands of deaths from disease, and warned Japan that their torturing and maltreatment of prisoners would be held to their account. He also warned Generalissimo Franco of Spain that the Spanish " Blue Legion " fighting with the Germans was a violation of neutrality; diplomatic protests proved ineffective, but an oil embargo hit Spain where it hurt.

Tremendous Royal Air Force raids on Germany—1,000 tons of bombs were dropped on Berlin on each of the first two nights of January—were now almost a nightly occurrence, and plans for a major offensive for the liberation of the Continent were well under way. In March Eden was speaking to the Free Church Federal Council on " Moral Principles and Foreign Affairs," and with tortuous navigational metaphors summed up his philosophy:

> " It is certainly true that unless we set certain moral principles for our guide we shall be lost. One can only navigate a ship by some fixed guide, a compass, or, more roughly, the Pole Star. But the very act of navigation, down to the hands of the man at the wheel, is a constant correction of drift. A ship, at any given moment, is hardly ever dead on her course; it is only by a multitude of approximations that she makes her landfall and is saved from disaster. But these approximations would only make confusion worse confounded unless they were designed to hold and keep one right line . . ."

Everyone knew that preparations for D-day were in the air. Germany was being pounded mercilessly from the air; she had suffered staggering losses in Russia. The vast amphibious operation for landing Allied troops in France had been fixed for June, but although hundreds knew of this date, its secret was kept. As a precaution against leakage, Eden had to take the unusual step, on April 17th, of withdrawing the privileges from diplomatic Ambassadors and Envoys. They were told that they could neither receive nor send any telegram that was not in plain language (as distinct from code) and that no diplomatic bags might pass in or out that had not been submitted for censorship. Nor, until further notice, might diplomats or their staffs either leave Britain or come to it.

In May Eden distinguished himself by his fine handling of the Dominion Prime Ministers' Conference, which was primarily one between the Ministers of the four main Dominions, Canada, Australia, New Zealand and South Africa. The unification of foreign policies, the securing of their agreement to the broad strategic war plan and the discussions on post-war policy were vital at that stage, as the end of the war could be foreseen. In a House of Commons debate on May 24th, which was a sort of eve-of-invasion survey of foreign affairs, Eden praised Mr. Churchill: " . . . it is invaluable to be able to look at the problems we have to face in company with a man like the Prime Minister. It is then that his experience is more valuable still." A new Government had been formed in Italy. He had some friendly words for Franco for not hindering the Allied invasion of North Africa. He thought the situation in Greece, where different sections had been warring with each other, was getting better—actually it got worse. The French Committee of National Liberation was playing a part in the struggle against Hitler which entitled it to a fourth place in the Grand Alliance. (America had not recognised the Committee as the Government of France. General de Gaulle had, in fact, created considerable difficulties with both the British and Americans with his dour and dictatorial ways, but this was a closely kept secret at the time.)

General de Gaulle, Eden told the House, had been invited to London from Algiers to " clear up differences ".

Eden's work behind the scenes was immense, for at any

moment, in innumerable countries, there would be a need for provisional government following their liberation by Allied forces. Constitutional and civil administration would have to continue, yet the machinery must change hands, for the existing administrations included so many who had collaborated with the enemy. Discussions with the exiled Governments on the procedure to be followed greatly added to Eden's burden of work.

In June, a few weeks after the Allies had entered Rome, Eden told a horrified House of Commons of the cold-blooded shooting by the Germans of 47 prisoners—Royal Air Force, Dominion and Allied Air Forces. The Germans had claimed that the men were shot whilst trying to escape, but investigations showed it to have been a massacre. Amidst cheers from the House, Eden promised that the culprits would be tracked down and punished when Germany had been defeated.

Next, Mr. Eden had the unpleasant job of arguing with General de Gaulle, who was livid with rage at not having been informed of the date of the impending liberation of France. But de Gaulle had quarrelled so bitterly with General Giraud, and was regarded as so unpredictable by Washington, that the security risk simply could not be taken. The lives of millions of people were involved in that mammoth Allied operation, and the tantrums of de Gaulle had to take second place. Furthermore, as Eden had reason to know, de Gaulle's security forces could not be trusted. Eden remembered how, in January, 1941, British officials of Scotland Yard arrested the French Admiral Muselier on allegations of treachery and espionage brought by members of de Gaulle's entourage. The evidence —documents from German-occupied France—was found to be forged. The whole thing was a plot by a number of men in de Gaulle's security forces. Admiral Muselier was released with a letter of apology and regret from Mr. Eden, and was later received by Mr. Churchill and the King. Eden could not placate de Gaulle, but then, nobody could.

Soon, on June 6th, D-day arrived and a week later, as a last desperate act by the Germans, flying bombs were loosed against Britain.

Eden had played a very important part in the formulation of this complicated campaign. In all the conferences that had preceded it he had been able to think in military terms as well as from the standpoint of foreign affairs. He was in and out of his office in the Foreign Office from dawn to dusk, and even in his flat was still telephoning, reading despatches and preparing reports and memoranda. It was soon obvious that the initiative lay with the Allies; there was success in Normandy and Italy, and in Burma, especially, the position was improving rapidly. Eden followed the campaign in South-East with more than impersonal interest, for his eldest son, Simon, was now an R.A.F. pilot-sergeant fighting in Burma.

On July 27th Eden reported to Parliament on the disputes between various Greek factions, which jeopardised the liberation of Greece. There had been fighting between two rival organisations of guerrillas in Greece, E.L.A.S. and E.A.M. There had also been mutinies in the Greek Navy and Army based in Greece. M. Papandreou, leader of the Republican Socialist Party, had escaped from Greece and made his way to Cairo to urge national unity on the contending factions. He had been entrusted by the King of Greece with the task of forming a Government, and had tried to bring opponents together. Eden had done all he could to press on them the need for unity in face of the enemy, and reported that the British Government was giving Papandreou full support.

On August 23rd, 1944, Paris was liberated, and on September 10th Eden went once more to Quebec with Mr. Churchill to confer with President Roosevelt.

In August Eden, for the first time, was made Acting Prime Minister in the temporary absence of Churchill who was in Italy, and of Major Attlee, Deputy Prime Minister. He made a tour of the battlefields in France, and on September 14th, joined Mr. Churchill who, together with his Chiefs of Staff, was discussing with Mr. Roosevelt the plans for the conclusion of the war in Europe and the defeat of Japan. Edward R. Stettinius, who attended, says in his memoirs that Henry Morgenthau, Secretary of the United States Treasury, had persuaded the Prime Minister and the President to initial a drastic programme for Germany. Anthony Eden, he says, had a heated discussion with the Prime Minister over the initialling of the Agreement—which the President decided, later, not to accept. The details are past history, but it is interesting to know that Eden stood his ground with Churchill. There is evidence that he never hesitated to do so when any real principle was involved. He was to challenge Churchill later on United Nations procedure, and if Eden's advice had been followed, the whole story of the United Nations would not be so unhappily analogous to that of the pre-war League of Nations.

By September 18th, when Eden returned to England the outposts of the Siegfried Line had been reached and the invasion of Germany, so long prayed for by the inhabitants of enslaved Europe, was at last in sight. Airborne landings had begun in Holland, and the Russians had reached the outskirts of Finland. He had time to give Bristol Conservatives a speech, then accompanied Mr. Churchill on his visit to Moscow. He attended many conferences in Cairo, Athens (where he was given the Freedom) and Rome. In Athens he saw that the people would starve unless relief was speedily forthcoming, and unless they stopped their bitter political squabbling. In Moscow Eden found that one of the moral principles for which the war was fought would have to be forsaken. Russia had formed a "Lublin" Government in opposition to the London Poles, whose *émigré* Government was set up after the joint invasion of their country by Russia and Germany early in the war. Russia had no intention of leaving that part of Poland she had seized, and was hostile to the London Poles who, for obvious reasons of patriotism, were bitterly antagonistic to the invaders of their country. At this Moscow Conference Molotov presented the tame Russianised Poles who were to rule Poland under Russian sponsorship. It was hopeless to argue further, but Eden thought very little of the Poles presented to him.

On November 10th Eden went with Mr. Churchill to Paris at the invitation of General de Gaulle for the Armistice Day celebration of the liberation of France. Amidst the scenes of wild enthusiasm and the splendid processions the quiet and serene figure of Anthony Eden stood out, and whenever he was seen the cheers were loud and prolonged. It was a highly emotional scene, at which Churchill himself was in tears. All differences were forgotten, and de Gaulle, at a banquet, praised Churchill and Eden in the warmest terms. Eden, for his part, hoped that at last France might find unity. As Mr.

Churchill put it: " Happily you have at this moment an uncontested chief. I have from time to time had some lively discussions with him, but I am sure you ought to rally round your chief and do your utmost to have France united and indivisible." Eden's description of this historic event, given to the House of Commons three days later, was a somewhat colourless effort, but the physical strain of so much travelling was beginning to tell on him. There was also the added nervous tension of trying to reconcile Allies who were opposed to each other. Opposing temperaments do not mix easily, even in war-time. The Americans, for example, were backing Count Sforza as Foreign Minister of Italy, whereas the British favoured Signor Bonimi; Edward Stettinnius, Roosevelt's new Secretary of State, made a public announcement which was in effect a hint to Britain to stop meddling in Italian affairs—which brought an angry cable from Mr. Churchill to President Roosevelt. But a grimmer situation was developing, destined to shake Anglo-American relations even more. Communist partisans had crowded into Athens and on December 3rd civil war broke out. British troops on the spot had to fire to preserve order, for as Churchill pointed out, the British troops in Greece, with the consent of the Americans and Allies, could not stand idly by and " leave Athens to anarchy and misery, followed by tyranny established on murder."

The point was, however, that the partisans had been fighting the Germans, and the whole episode was a sad sequel to victory.

Mrs. Beatrice Eden, meanwhile, had taken over the running of the All Services Canteen in the Grand Hotel, Paris, and was not spending overmuch time in London. Nor, come to that, was Anthony Eden himself. But on November 21st they were seen together at the His Majesty's Theatre in London— Beatrice had flown over for the occasion, and dressed in the red and grey uniform with a SHAEF flash on her grey beret. The occasion was an entertainment organised by the All Services Club to entertain 1,200 wounded men of the Allied Services. It was a crowded, glittering occasion, with the Duchess of Kent, King Peter and the Queen of Yugoslavia present, and as the floodlight settled on Mr. and Mrs. Eden there were loud cheers. They looked such a happy couple. But in fact they were drifting apart, and had been doing so for a long time. Their tastes had never been very similar, and now their war work demanding the bulk of their time, left them less and less time together. Even Christmas Day was one they could not spend together. Anthony Eden was on another of his trips—this time to Greece with Mr. Churchill. It was urgently necessary, for public opinion in Britain was increasingly hostile to the action of British troops in suppressing an anti-monarchical party.

Eden and Churchill arrived in the thick of the fighting, and after consultation with Field-Marshal Alexander, Mr. Harold MacMillan, Resident Minister of the Central Mediterranean, the British Ambassador to Greece and the Greek Prime Minister, convened a conference to which representatives of all parties were invited. Churchill spoke to them directly, assuring them that Britain had no territorial ambitions at all but was simply anxious to see an end of tyranny in Greece. The result of this conference was that King George of the Hellenes made way for Archbishop Damaskinos, who was appointed Regent. M. Papandreou resigned. As Eden and Churchill flew home to Britain, fighting continued, but British forces were, within a few days, able to restore order.

No Foreign Minister could have had so many problems, and held the peace between so many contestants, as Anthony Eden in 1944. Pressure from Russia; a good deal of well-intentioned interference by America—such as the printing of French money despite the fact that neither the French Government nor the British would guarantee it, whilst the U.S.A. would not recognise the French National Liberation Committee; the hatred of the Poles for the Russians, and *vice versa*. American criticism of British action in Italy, Belgium and Greece; the intransigence of General de Gaulle, who refused to let his officers accompany the landing force; the anxiety of preventing a leakage through diplomatic channels of the projected Normandy landings—all these things were a severe strain.

But time was to confirm his judgment, for if British forces had not acted swiftly against the Communist terrorists, the iron curtain would have slammed down on Greece as it did on so many other countries. Once again, Eden had not hesitated to court unpopularity in the cause of what he considered right. " I am sure that it was our action, unpopular and difficult as it was, hard as it was to explain to our American friends I admit, that prevented a massacre in Athens. That is my absolute conviction," Eden told the House of Commons.

TWENTY-TWO

Yalta and After

THE year 1945 opened with the end of the war confidently predicted within a matter of months. Except for the illness of his wife Beatrice, who was suffering from pneumonia at the Allied Expeditionary Club in Paris, of which she was British Director, Anthony's newest preoccupation was the historic Yalta Conference—a meeting of the " Big Three ", Churchill, Roosevelt and Stalin. The preparatory work was considerable, and fell largely upon Eden's shoulders. There were so many issues, on almost all of which each had different opinions, such as reparations, the definition of post-war frontiers, the type of government to be set up in the liberated countries, the disarmament and occupation of Germany and post-war co-operation between the great powers, especially through the medium of the United Nations Organisation.

Sir Winston Churchill's memoirs make it plain that he pressed Roosevelt for a preliminary meeting at Malta. Roosevelt was a sick man, and an obstinate one. He could not spare Mr. Stettinius, his Foreign Secretary, for the preliminary conference of Foreign Secretaries, but sent his friend and emissary Harry Hopkins to England to see Churchill and Eden before their departure for Malta. Eden was worried about the American insistence that any decision by the World Security Council must be endorsed unanimously. This would mean that if the majority of the member states decided on a course of action with the object of stopping aggression, any one member who either refused to vote or voted against the proposal could prevent its being made effective. Eden, with painful memories of the impotence of the pre-war League of Nations, doubted if this would be an effective safeguard for peace, and said so. Sir Stafford Cripps had submitted to Churchill a memorandum arguing that the Soviet proposal for complete unanimity was in the best interests of Britain.

Eden went first to Malta, in company with Sir Alexander Cadogan, Mr. Winston Churchill and his daughter Sarah. In the lovely and battered island—or rather off the island, as too many buildings had been destroyed by bombs to enable the parties to stay at hotels—Eden and Churchill met Edward Stettinius, whose public strictures on English conduct in Italy had so infuriated Churchill. Stettinius was emissary of a man who was often more worried about British imperialism than about Russian ambitions, of which ominous indications had been given by her attitude to Poland, which she invaded in 1939. But Roosevelt had strange ideas about Stalin. He once told the Polish leader, Mikolajczyk: " Stalin is a realist, and we mustn't forget, when we judge Russian actions, that the Soviet regime has had only two years of experience in international relations. *But of one thing I am certain, Stalin is not an Imperialist.*"

Stettinius tells an amusing story of how Eden, as he walked off H.M.S. *Sirius*, was recognised by the shipyard workers and given a great ovation. On return to the ship one of the British N.C.O.'s did not recognise him, and asked a bugler, who had just piped him aboard, who that was. The bugler remarked that the man was the Foreign Secretary. The non-commissioned officer remarked: " You're crazy. He's too bloody British to be a foreign secretary."

The conversations between Stettinius and Eden show that the latter had a shrewd presage of Russian intentions. " Eden wondered whether the Russians might give assurances to Britain and the United States of really free elections in Poland. He realised, he added, that this would be asking ' rather a lot.' I am not sure what prompted this remark." Events since then have no doubt answered Mr. Stettinius's question. With the arrival of Roosevelt all was harmony.

In conversation with Roosevelt, however, Churchill stated that he was confident about winning the General Election in Britain four months hence. " I remembered this prediction the following May," writes Stettinius, " when Mr. Eden told me that there was a distinct possibility that the Conservative Party might be defeated. He remarked to me at the time that

Photo: Kemsley Picture Service

"Welcome, Your Majesty." Sir Anthony Eden, K.G., gives a courtly bow of greeting to Queen Soraya of Persia when she arrives with her husband the Shah for a dinner in their honour given in the London house of the Foreign Minister and Lady Eden (1955).

Eden with M. Mendes-France, the French Prime Minister, and Mr. John Foster Dulles, U.S. Secretary of State, at the Paris talks in July, 1954.

Photo: Planet News

Photo: Central Press

In Winston's shoes. A picture of Sir Anthony Eden with Sir Winston Churchill, taken outside 10, Downing Street a day before Sir Winston retired, recommending Eden as his successor.

Where Britain's Prime Minister forgets his cares. Sir Anthony Eden is a country lover. He likes to spend week-ends at Rosebower Cottage at Broadchalke, near Salisbury. It belongs to Lady Eden, who bought it some years ago for £3,000.

Photo: Kemsley Picture Service

I might be seeing Ernest Bevin at the next Foreign Minister's Conference." It is clear from this—as of course from so many other things—that Eden was not His Master's Voice, and that his independence of thought was not stifled by working with as strong a personality as Mr. Winston Churchill. It also shows that Eden was even more in touch with popular opinion than his chief, who took a Conservative victory at the next General Election completely for granted.

There followed a dinner on the United States cruiser, *Quincy*, attended by President Roosevelt, Mr. Winston Churchill, Anthony Eden and Edward Stettinius, who together discussed a general plan for the whole war and the issues arising from it. The war in the Pacific, the campaigns in South-East Asia, General Eisenhower's plan for bringing his forces to the Rhine and beyond—these and innumerable other problems were explored in tremendous detail. Between the two Governments there were no fewer than 700 advisers and experts in the party.

After the dinner Eden and Churchill flew by Royal Air Force plane to Yalta, in the Crimea, the rest of both parties also making the fourteen hundred miles journey by plane across the Mediterranean, the Ægean and the Black Sea. On the journey to Malta, fifteen members of Mr. Churchill's mission had lost their lives when the plane carrying them crashed near Pantelleria. The accident cast a cloud over the conference, but against the larger tragedy of the world war, which this fateful conference was to discuss, it had to be forgotten.

Seldom can Eden have arrived at any conference in which more elaborate precautions and preparations had been taken. As his plane touched down at Saki airfield, on the west coast of the Crimean Peninsula, he was welcomed by massed bands, corps of Soviet and American photographers, and after a greeting from Molotov, Russia's Foreign Minister, he was taken into one of three refreshment tents to make free with Russian tea, vodka and a whole galaxy of cold dishes. Guards with tommy-guns were stationed at intervals of every twenty feet.

The senior members of the British delegation, including Eden, were housed in a beautiful villa built for a former Russian Ambassador to Britain in the nineteenth century. Its gardens and courtyards, its fantastic architecture and riot of subtropical plants—and its site, for it commanded a magnificent view of the snow-capped Crimean mountains—gave the proceedings an appropriate touch of drama. There were Russian sentries everywhere, some of them Amazonic looking women. Every imaginable comfort was laid on for the members of the mission, and once somebody remarked that there was no lemon peel for the drinks a lemon-tree appeared as if by magic, growing in the hall.

At this conference were taken the decisions that decided the future conduct of the war and the balance of power in the postwar world. Germany was to be dismembered and occupied by military forces of the United States, Britain, France and Russia. Germany was to be disarmed and war criminals tried and punished. And a conference of 47 nations was to be held at San Francisco " to prepare a Charter for a General International Organisation for the maintenance of peace and security." The Big Three would co-operate in solving the economic and political problems of the liberated peoples. And Russia had her way with Poland, keeping what she had seized by force. During the eight days of discussion, the subject of Poland had come up at almost every session. Eden knew that the Lublin Poles were a puppet government created by the Soviet Union; but his misgivings were not shared by the Americans. Chester Wilmot in his *Struggle for Europe* says that developments in Europe had " led Roosevelt and some of his intimates to assume that the future threat to world peace and the independence of small nations would come not from Russia or international Communism, but from the old colonial powers, and particularly Britain. This peculiar aberration can be explained only if it is remembered that at this time Roosevelt did not believe that Stalin cherished any imperialistic ambitions."

What happened at Yalta has been described from many points of view. Inaccurate accounts have been published in America. But, as Eden pointed out frequently during the conference, the interpreting arrangements were cumbersome, whilst everyone made his own notes. There were no combined and agreed accounts, issued as an official record. Thus the British, Russian and American records may well vary. But Eden, as all accounts show, did not give way on the Polish issue without a struggle; and he did refuse to agree to Molotov's figure for German reparations to Russia—a sum so excessive that its effect would have been to ruin Germany economically, and to make it a hotbed of despair in which political tyranny might once again take root and flourish.

Although the agreement about Poland provided for the formation of a Polish Government of National Unity and the holding of free elections, Members of Parliament were restive and critical when Eden reported to them on his return. Already a point of principle had been sacrificed. The Germans would be punished for aggression; the Russians, guilty of it themselves before they fought Germany in self-defence, were to profit by their invasion of Poland. Eden, as we know, had tried to prevent it (but failed, as did everyone else at Yalta; the Russians, after all, were already in Poland, and neither America nor Britain could afford to start a new war to get her out), but once a policy has been decided, good or bad, Eden finds words to support it. He sometimes overdoes his defence of policies which have been agreed. When Members of Parliament were apprehensive of Russian intentions, and felt that Poland had been deserted, Eden chided them for their suspicion. "As I listened to some of the speeches I could not help feeling that some of my Hon. Friends, in talking about Poland, had not only Poland in mind but the fear that Russia, flushed with the magnificent triumph of her armies, was also dreaming of European domination." This, he said, was the favourite theme of German propaganda, implying that critics of the Yalta agreement were victims of it. " Can anyone doubt," he demanded, "that if we had had, in 1939, the unity between Russia, and this country and the United States that we had cemented at Yalta, there would not have been this present war? Can anyone doubt that so long as we hold that unity we can establish peace for twenty-five or fifty years? "

There were several who did doubt. The concessions to Russia over Poland looked more like yielding to force than unity. The ink was hardly dry on the documents before Stalin was using strong arm methods to impose his rule on countries in Eastern Europe.

On April 12th President Roosevelt died, and preparations were put in hand for a State funeral which Eden was invited to attend. Meanwhile, he was polishing up his Turkish—he is a fine Turkish scholar—with Dr. Ali Riza at the Turkish People's House in Fitzhardinge Street, near his pre-war home. He was also appointed Hon. Air Commodore of the 500 County of Kent Squadron, Royal Air Force, for he had always been interested in flying and has probably done more of it than any other politician.

Eden was greatly moved by the death of Roosevelt, whose warm-hearted support of Britain during her years of danger, and whose idealism appealed so much to Eden's sensitive nature. Although the Foreign Minister thought that Roosevelt underestimated the ruthless nature of Russian Communism, he had always shown the greatest personal regard for him. In most communications between Roosevelt and Churchill, Eden was usually referred to as "Anthony" and not "Foreign Minister".

Eden went to the United States to attend the funeral of President Roosevelt at Washington, and then went on to San Francisco for the conference of Allied Nations on the formation of a new world organisation—the United Nations. The British Delegation, headed by Mr. Eden, included Major Attlee, the Deputy Prime Minister, and Lord Halifax, and were housed in the luxurious Hotel Mark Hopkins.

Events were moving swiftly in Europe as the Conference talked. On April 28th, Mussolini was dragged to the shores of Lake Como, together with his mistress Clara Petacci, where both were shot and then hung up ignominiously in the Piazzale Loreto in Milan. Hitler had committed suicide with his mistress, Eva Braun, whom he married in the air-raid shelter of his Chancellery in Berlin. The German Army surrendered unconditionally in Italy on May 2nd, and on the 8th Britain celebrated V.E. Day (Victory in Europe Day) with a mixture of rejoicing and sad relief.

In San Francisco VE celebrations were delayed until the 11th. Eden snatched a few hours for dinner and a dance with a group of friends, choosing the Peacock Court at the Mark Hopkins so that he could stay within call. For over two hours he danced with two of San Francisco's most attractive young women, Mrs. James Flood, a 27-years-old blonde and Mrs. Richard Osborne, a 26-years-old brunette. He was more relaxed and gay than he had been for years, but even amidst these celebrations his sense of formality did not quite desert him; he was the only man in a black dinner jacket. And of course, when the band played a rhumba, he smilingly refused to dance. Quite properly, I think. A photograph of a Foreign Minister of Britain, dancing the rhumba, after the most devastating and tragic war in history, would not have seemed very appropriate.

Both Eden and Churchill were worried at the darkening scene in Europe. In getting the Nazis out of Europe, the Allies had let Russia in. The Allies, as agreed, would have to withdraw to their zones of occupation. Over half a dozen countries, including most of Austria, would be under Russian control. After the funeral of President Roosevelt, Eden had met President Truman and confided his misgivings to him. He told Stettinius, too, that something had happened in Moscow since the Yalta Conference. The Russians were putting their own picked men into the Government of Poland, where the promise of free elections was being obviously ignored. Eden wondered what basis for unity there could be for the new United Nations Organisation if, at this early stage, Russia was to be unco-operative.

When Eden returned to Britain on May 17th, 1945, he was feeling unwell. Years of overwork, with irregular meals, constant change of climate, thousands of miles of travelling by air, sea and land—not to mention the excessive nervous strain of dealing patiently with difficult men like General Sikorski or General de Gaulle—had begun to take their toll. Actually Eden is a remarkably resilient man with enormous reserves of stamina; but there is another side of him, which is revealed when he has a "throwing-things-about" mood. Once a Foreign Office colleague, tired of his petulance and sharp speech, refused point-blank to work with him; but he reversed his decision when the Foreign Secretary came to his room and said: "I'm sorry. I'm afraid I'm the *prima donna* they say I am." Such incipient flashes of temper are not the signs of an intolerant or domineering nature—Eden is the least intolerant of men; they are symptoms of exhaustion in a man who has always demanded the utmost from himself, and is so conscientious that if anything goes wrong his first instinct is to blame himself.

Eden was never a man to flinch from trial. Nor was he

ever disposed to let others know of his private sorrows. At this time he had many cares and sorrows all at once.

Major Attlee had decided that the war-time Coalition must end, and it was announced that the present Parliament would be dissolved on June 15th.

A few days after his return, however, Eden was found to have a duodenal ulcer and on his doctors' orders was confined to bed for six weeks. This meant that he would be unable to campaign personally, but his wife Beatrice addressed election meetings on his behalf and conducted his campaign for him. Eden was still immensely popular in his constituency.

On June 17th, too, his mother Sybil Lady Eden, died at her home, Park House, Windlestone, at the age of 78. It was a cruel irony that Anthony should have been ill and unable to travel as her life drew to its close. He was devoted to her, and through the years had kept her abreast of his activities, interests and hopes with the simple humility of a son who knows what he owes to his mother. She had been the brightest spot in a difficult childhood. She had been his greatest confidante throughout childhood, boyhood and adolescence. And her faith in him had never faltered. " My son will be Foreign Minister again," she said firmly, at the time of his resignation, " you'll see." Until the last she had busied herself in charitable work, the National Society for the Prevention of Cruelty to Children; the Royal Society for the Prevention of Cruelty to Animals.

On June 27th Eden broadcast to the nation from his sickbed at Binderton. It was a long survey of foreign affairs and Conservative policy, interspersed with digs at the Socialists which were too gentlemanly and gentle to have any effect. But it was a reasonable and sensible speech infinitely to be preferred to Mr. Churchill's florid, scare-mongering speech which implied that if the Socialists got in Britain's authority would have to be maintained by " Gestapo " methods. Socialists like Ernest Bevin and Major Attlee had served him loyally thoughout the war. Mr. Churchill's speech did much to lose the 1945 election for the Conservatives; he counted so much on his popularity as a war leader that instead of presenting a constructive programme to the electorate he confined himself largely to abuse of his Socialist opponents.

On July 5th, as Anthony lay ill, the General Election took place. Two days later another piece of sad news. Simon, his elder son, serving as a sergeant-navigator in Burma, had been posted missing. " Edenny " as he was known to his friends, was 21 at the time of his death—a high-spirited, promising lad with a ready humour and his father's habit of facing up to life without further argument. When war broke out he was a rosy-cheeked schoolboy with slightly protruding teeth, studying at Eton, absorbed in history and his stamp collection. He had joined the Eton Junior Training Corps, graduated from the Air Observers' School at Edmonton and went to Canada for training at Regina, Saskatchewan. When the Japanese war was over he had planned to go back to Oxford, explore the Rocky Mountains, visit Ottawa and then join the Diplomatic Service. Later Anthony Eden received confirmation of his son's death. The plane with which he was travelling was on a supply mission to a forward area in monsoon weather when it crashed into a mountain.

By July 16th, when the General Election had taken place and the slips were safely in their sealed ballot boxes, Eden felt well enough to accompany Mr. Churchill to the " Big Three " conference between Churchill, President Truman and Generalissimo Stalin at Potsdam. It was a conference that resolved very little. Russia's seizure of a large part of Poland was now a *fait accompli*. Further, Russia had authorised Poland to take over German territory as far as the rivers Oder and Neisse, and the Red Army were helping to expel the seven million Germans there. Irrespective of agreements reached at Yalta, Stalin had " settled " these problems in his own peculiar way.

After eight days of abortive argument, mostly with the Russians, Mr. Churchill and Eden flew back to London to hear the result of the General Election. Churchill was astonished and dismayed to find the Conservatives beaten at the polls. Eden was not surprised; he had throughout kept an open mind. The Conservative Central Office had relied too much on Churchill's reputation as a war leader; admiration of the man did not imply admiration of the leader of the Conservative Party, whose pre-war muddling could still be remembered. The Socialists had muddled too in the pre-war years, but were not in authority. For many the second World War seemed a natural climax to years of Tory mismanagement; a gross over-simplification, of course, but there it was. After years of office Anthony Eden, who was returned by his constituents with a good majority, was out of office and a member of His Majesty's Opposition.

TWENTY-THREE

Opposition—Again

AT the Potsdam Conference, Mr. Stimson, who accompanied President Truman, came over to Churchill with a scrap of paper. It read " Babies satisfactorily born." This odd message meant that an atomic bomb had been exploded in the Mexican desert. A terrifying new weapon had been invented, destructive beyond the imaginings of the most insane tyrant.

On August 6th, 1945, the first atomic bomb was dropped on Hiroshima in Japan. On August 8th, with a nice sense of timing, Russia declared war on Japan—to get the credit of being an Ally without the expense of any effort, for Japan was beaten. On August 9th an atomic bomb was dropped on Nagasaki. The next day Japan surrendered.

The Conservative Party was a minority in the House of Commons, and after four and a half years as Foreign Secretary, Eden now found himself Deputy Leader of His Majesty's Opposition in the absence of Mr. Winston Churchill. His first speech from the Opposition front bench congratulated Mr. Ernest Bevin, the new Foreign Minister, on " the vigour and eloquence of his maiden speech." Mr. Eden hoped—and found his hopes fulfilled—that Britain's foreign policy would be kept free of party politics.

As a deliberate policy, Eden spoke as much as possible on home affairs as well as on foreign affairs. Since Mr. Churchill had been grooming Eden as his successor, it was necessary that he should establish a reputation as expert on affairs in general, and not a specialist on some single aspect of government. But on controversial issues he could never get airborne. It cannot be held against him; he belongs to the dying race of gentlemen and disdains the more vulgar, though more successful demagogic tricks. His habitual delivery is one of avuncular admonition: " ... these objectives which I have set out will, I think, be generally endorsed by most of you. ... "; " ... but I want to speak to you also of the other principal task of this new Parliament. ... to make and keep the peace in Europe "; " I want to say a word or two about an important matter ... the radio campaign which has been going on against Greece from Sofia, Belgrade and, I think, Moscow. ... ".

But if his delivery was uninspired, the facts were sound and he could speak with the moral authority of one who had given the best part of his life to public service.

In October, 1945, Eden was given the Freedom of Durham. He also had to find paid work, for the parliamentary salary would not enable him to maintain his two homes in London and Binderton. He was given his first directorship of a public company with the Westminster Bank—a remarkable thing, an almost unprecedented thing, for a politician of Eden's stature to have reached the age of 48 before taking a commercial directorship. He has never sought to exploit his popularity commercially. The chairman was Mr. Rupert Beckett, brother of Anthony's father-in-law, whose family bank was absorbed by the Westminster Bank.

During the first three months of 1946 Eden led the Opposition in debates on the coal industry, trade unions, national insurance and various domestic issues. Into all these speeches he put enormous effort; it is one of the faults, as well as one of the merits, of his speeches. In March 1946, realising that the Labour Party was claiming a monopoly of interest in social progress, he re-stated Conservative principles, making it clear that his Party had a practical programme—as distinct from simply being anti-Socialist, as Conservative propaganda had implied during the General Election. He complained that excessive taxation was freezing enterprise; that prudence and hard work were treated as offences; that profit had been misrepresented as something shameful. He attended many by-elections and mass meetings.

Eden attended the Victory Parade in London in June, visitied Bermuda as a member of the United Kingdom delegation of the Empire Parliamentary Association, made a goodwill tour of the U.S.A. and Canada (where his friend Mr. McKenzie King called him " No. 1 Goodwill visitor,") and was back by August to resume the Opposition. Perhaps because he was better in health, his speeches assumed a little more punch, especially when he attacked the nationalisation of large industries.

In a speech at Watford on September 23rd, Eden expressed the general misgivings of people everywhere at the imperialistic expansion of Soviet Russia. " What makes it so particularly tragic," he said, " is that little more than a year ago the armed forces of these same nations were dying together on a common battlefield. Are all the revelations of Nuremburg and Belsen, and other camps of horror, where whole populations were murdered, already forgotten? " The Peace Conference which had met in Paris a few weeks earlier had seen a sharp division between the Slav bloc of nations and the United Nations.

At Christmas, 1946, just before the Labour Government were transferring the coal mines to State ownership—a measure which Eden had attacked vigorously a few months previously—Anthony and Beatrice Eden, accompanied by their son Nicholas, who had just finished his spell at Eton, sailed in the *Queen Elizabeth* for the United States. It was to be their last journey as a trio. For years they had been outwardly united. In fact, Mrs. Eden was bored, bored with politics and all its works. To both Anthony and Beatrice the loss of their elder son was a terrible blow. For years Beatrice had been a " politician's widow ". They had been seeing less and less of each other as his journeys abroad became more protracted and frequent. Nicholas, who loved both impartially, tried to reconcile them, for the rift could hardly pass unnoticed. Beatrice had been a loyal helpmate through the years. She admired him, and has said that she still does. When the *Queen Elizabeth* berthed in New York harbour, Mrs. Eden the First said good-bye. After nearly a quarter of a century of marriage, their partnership was ended.

From America Eden visited the Barbadoes, Trinidad and Brazil, where the British Ambassador gave a reception in his honour at which most of the Diplomatic Corps were present. He addressed the Brazilian Chamber of Deputies, and was cheered wherever he went in Rio de Janeiro.

On his return, he indicted the Government for the creation of " giant state monopolies " and criticised flagging coal production. In June he spoke to the House of Commons on the increase of terrorism in Europe and the expansion of Soviet dominion. In October he accepted his fourth directorship, this time to the board of the £3,792,000 Board of the Phœnix Assurance Company—his other directorships at this time being of the Westminster Bank, its subsidiary the Westminster Foreign Bank and the £3,750,000 Rio Tinto group. He worked quite hard at these jobs but being out of office was an unaccustomed ordeal to him. He did not fit in very easily into the hurly burly of commercial life.

In September his speeches were published under the title *Freedom and Order*—a title almost certainly of his own choosing. It has the authentic Eden ring about it. One critic said that he thought it impossible to say so much and say so little. The *Sunday Times* critic said: " It is unlikely that Mr. Eden will be remembered as a great orator, but none of his speeches lacks outstanding and distinctive qualities. He is above all civilised . . . " The last compliment I would certainly accept, but I am not so sure of the former. Most people would find the speeches heavy going.

By the beginning of January 1948 Eden was in Persia, arriving by air from Baghdad. There were parties for him at the British Embassy, the Anglo-Persian Institute and the Persian Press Club. Everywhere in his travels he was received in semi-state, despite the fact that he was temporarily out of office. The Embassy party was attended by the entire diplomatic corps and by Persian Foreign Office officials. He toured the oil-producing areas of Persian Khuzistan and Abadan, speaking Persian fluently with all the Persians he met.

At Bahrein, a fortnight later, he was entertained to lunch by the Sheikh at Manama Palace, where a guard of honour of state troops was posted. Mr. Eden has always been popular amongst the Arabs and was given a royal welcome in all senses. Sheikhs of the ruling family and leading members of the American and British colonies paid tribute to him, and as he left the Sheikh presented him with an ancient sword in a gold and pearl-encrusted scabbard and a set of Arab robes.

On this trip Anthony Eden was accompanied by his son Nicholas, who was all that was left of his personal family life. He had relied more and more on his companionship since his wife deserted him, and shared many tastes in common—a love of travel, of strange sights and sounds, of tennis and gin rummy. From Bahrein the pair went on to Saudi Arabia to spend an unforgettable holiday as the guests of King Ibn Saud at his summer palace at Ryadh. They squatted in Arab fashion at a banquet which included 12 whole sheep, two baby camels and immense quantities of sour milk. Nicholas played football with one of the King's sons, who proudly displayed trophies brought recently from America—a cinema projector, without any films to show on it; a billiards table and a fine collection of " pin-up " photographs.

As he left, Mr. Eden was given a gold watch and a jewelled dagger as a present from the King. He asked the King what he would like, and managed to keep a straight face when Ibn Saud told him—he asked for a sporting gun, which cost Eden 200 guineas when he got back to London. But at least this time he could keep his present. He was no longer a public servant. At a previous meeting with the King both he and Mr. Churchill were presented with a casket of jewels—which the Treasury promptly claimed as " official presents " and the property of the British Government. In return they gave the King a Rolls Royce; there had been some comfort in the thought that they could reclaim this cost on expenses.

These contacts were to prove of immense value, especially in unravelling the Persian Oil dispute later on.

Back in Europe, Eden next led a British Parliamentary Delegation to Belgium, and on his return, he entered a London nursing home for an operation for appendicitis. In the meantime, America was pouring money into Europe under its Marshall Aid Scheme, British railways had been nationalised, Russia tightened her grip on the satellite countries with the exception of Yugoslavia, which, although it had a Communist regime, had the temerity to defy Russia and was dismissed from the Cominform; Czechoslovakia had been brought into the Soviet orbit by a *coup d'état* backed by the Red Army, and Jan Masaryk, the warm-hearted, lovable, liberal Foreign Minister of Czechoslovakia, had in despair taken his life by throwing himself from a window of Cernin Palace, though some Czechoslovaks believe that he was murdered. Eden was sick when the news was broken to him. He knew Jan Masaryk well and had seen him constantly during the war years. With joy in his heart, Eden had risen in the House of Commons, early in the war, to announce the Government's repudiation of the Munich Agreement. Eden had counselled caution to President Benes when the latter announced his intention, during 1943, of going to Moscow and negotiating a Soviet-Czechoslovak Alliance. He knew that Russia's post-war plans were a mystery. But Benes, looking for allies, thought: the Poles and Hungarians dislike us and we them; we hate the Germans and cannot trust them; Austria is too small and too weak to count; Britain and France are too far away and let us down at Munich anyway—what can a small nation do to secure itself? There is only Russia. But eventually he found himself treated no better than Hitler behaved to the Austrian Chancellor at Berchtesgaden. " I thank you from the bottom of my heart," was Masaryk's tribute to Eden on returning to Czechoslovakia after his years of exile in London. Eden was out of office, but Masaryk was no fair weather friend.

Eden's speeches on home affairs hardly bear re-reading. His efforts at opposition are too self-conscious, the minatory note an obvious strain. One trouble, I imagine, is that Eden always has too much to do. Overwork seems to be an obsession with him, though one that springs from a strong and highly creditable sense of duty. But a heavy intake of mental stodge over the years had given him, quite frequently, mental indigestion. He is not incapable of making a moving speech, or speaking from the heart, and there are occasions, such as his first speech as Foreign Minister when the Labour Government was defeated later on, when his very restraint has a certain drama about it. But in general he is no good at Opposition. Even quotations, allusions and metaphors seem to be laboured and fail to enliven the body of his speeches, as he clearly intends. Sir Winston Churchill has given Anthony many lessons on speech-making. He had told him to wave his notes in his hand and refer to them openly, instead of peeping furtively at them, as though ashamed of needing them; he had recommended his special magnifying spectacles, which enable Sir Winston to read the text of his speeches from a distance of five feet; he has told him how good it is to growl at the audience. But all these devices are part of Churchill's temperament, and are not easily transmitted. They would not suit Eden's make-up.

Eden's speeches have been published in book form, and in their bulk and variety they are a tribute to his industry if not his imagination. They reflect the care and caution that go to everything he does. Few men try harder than Mr. Eden to try and get first-hand knowledge of so many varied problems. And his judgment on some things has been prophetic. An article in *Collier's Magazine* published in 1948 alleges that Eden warned Roosevelt as far back as 1943 that Russia would be the world's greatest post-war problem.

In September 1948 Eden denounced India's invasion of Hyderbad state as " a flagrant and inexcusable breach of their own agreement." The outlook in Burma was bleak. There was anti-British intrigue in Siam. He told the Conservative Conference at Llandudno in October that he took " a very sombre view" of the international situation—a statement which was probably true, but by that time most people in the world were taking a sombre view of it. He enjoined a foreign policy based on (1) Unity within the British Commonwealth and Empire; (2) Unity of the Western nations; (3) Anglo-American unity. There was sound sense in his warning that a negative approach to politics could not rally support—the one lesson that emerged from the defeat of the Conservatives at the last election. " I hate Communism," he said, " for its materialism and for its intolerance, because tolerance and not material gain are surely the hallmark of civilisation. But it is not enough to say that we hate Communism. We have to recognise that those who hold the creed hold it with a fervour that is almost a religion. If we are to defeat them we must therefore believe just as fervently in our faith and in ourselves."

* * *

In 1949 Anthony Eden left on a tour of the British Commonwealth accompanied by Commander Noble, Member of Parliament for Chelsea and unofficial Parliamentary Private Secretary to Eden. Twenty-five years ago he had made a similar journey as representative of his father-in-law's newspaper, the *Yorkshire Post*.

But a quarter of a century is a long time. Eden had risen to real stature, and even if he is not good at expressing it, his affection for the Empire is a real thing. He is one of the few politicians to-day who still use the word Empire instead of the more timid and fashionable euphemisms.

Eden did a round-the-world tour of 40,000 miles in 70 days, visiting Canada, New Zealand and Australia and returning not via Ceylon, Aden and Gibraltar as he had before, but this time via Malaya, India and Pakistan. In Wellington, New Zealand, and at Auckland, named after an ancestor of his, Eden was given a warm civic welcome. Through the paddy fields of Malaya, bazaars and palaces in India, town halls, universities, farms he made contacts, formal and informal.

His heart must have been warmed at the receptions he was given everywhere. At Wellington, New Zealand, more than 3,000 assembled to hear him speak on the need for international law. At a state dinner in Parliament House, Brisbane, on February 21st Eden was interrupted with cheering and applause nine times from a crowd of nearly four thousand people. Asked to look in at the University of British Columbia he was astonished to find 6,000 students assembled to hear him. Everywhere Eden went his quiet assurance and dignified demeanour made friends for Britain. Once, in Sydney, he had swum out to a raft and was joined by two husky Australians who did not recognise him. They talked about their hopes for the future, what they thought of Australia, and how their parents had emigrated from the home country, which they longed one day to see. The ex-Foreign Secretary did not reveal his identity, thinking it would spoil their pleasure. At last it dawned on them who he was and soon they were as friendly and relaxed as though they had known each other for years.

"The strongest impression of my whole tour," Anthony Eden said, on his return, in a broadcast, "was of our underlying unity.... Isn't it that in a world so much at odds, where there is stress and strain, and some bad temper too, this British family of ours has a special message to give? We are not bound together by any precise code of rules or by any elaborate constitution. We have our kinship and devoted loyalty to our

Sovereign. But for the rest the bonds are not those of script or law. They are natural friendships and affinities. . . ."

"We come home", he concluded, "more than ever convinced of the constructive contribution which the British family of nations can make to the peace of the world."

Mr. Eden was loudly cheered when he entered the House of Commons after his world tour. There is no questioning the fact that he has travelled the world more than any other living statesman—more, probably, than Sir Winston Churchill. And his visit on this occasion was of the greatest value in showing the scattered units of the Commonwealth that British politicians care about their problems and take the trouble to be informed about them.

One day in June, however, at a gala and fête held at Warwick Castle, Eden had another warning that he taxes himself too hard physically. He collapsed twice whilst addressing a United Nations Association meeting. In July, braving heavy rain, hundreds of his constituents assembled at Stoneleigh Abbey to celebrate his 25 years of representation in Parliament for the Warwick and Leamington Division. A reporter who attended his first electioneering campaign in this constituency in 1923 told me the other day: " I was flabbergasted when he was elected. His speeches were the dullest, the driest and the dreariest I have ever heard in my life. I suffered agonies reporting them. I gave him no future at all." But no constituency has ever had a more conscientious Member of Parliament. A message from Mr. Churchill was read: "Warwick and Leamington have won material distinction by their choice and by their steadfastness. Anthony and I have been colleagues and comrades, hand and heart, in some of the most formidable events, as the war, and we now work together to win for our country the prosperity and progress which are her due."

The *Birmingham Post*, in one of the most moving tributes ever paid to Eden, said on this occasion: " Leamington has had, for twenty-five years, the sort of member it wanted; a tolerant, broad-minded man who never allowed political differences to affect his relations with any of his constituents. . . ."

Later in the year came an outstanding example of this—the sort of thing he does so often, and keeps to himself. On

Christmas Eve of 1949 Eden was told that a family were due to be evicted on Christmas Day from a shack in a field at Lowsonford, Warwickshire. Immediately he telephoned to his agent, Mr. John Devine, asking him to seek out the owner of the field, to secure an extension for the family, and report back to him. Contacting the owner was not easy, but eventually Mr. Devine was able to assure Mr. Eden that the family would not be turned out, and that the owner had agreed to give the family another month's grace. This information could only be given very late at night, but Anthony Eden refused to go to bed until he was positively assured that the threat to evict the family on Christmas Day had been lifted. It is this type of sheer decency, or chivalry, which makes Eden, once accepted as a friend, a friend for life. His occasional flashes of temper are easily forgiven, because he is plainly an idealist who does not spare himself; if he cannot translate his feelings into terms which awaken a glowing response in others, it would be harsh to hold it against him. Good oratory is rare, but integrity of such a high order is rarer still.

* * *

In February, 1950 the Labour Government was returned with a narrow majority and Eden was back in Parliament again as an Opposition Member, polling 27,353 votes against his Socialist opponent's 18,400, an increase in his majority of 189 votes. Soon he was asking pertinent questions about Egypt's interference with shipping in the Suez Canal, a development to which a country which has links with a scattered Empire cannot be indifferent. He criticised the Government's decision to recognise Communist China as " fortunate neither in its timing nor in its method ".

In April Eden, his son Nicholas (an almost inseparable companion since Beatrice Eden decided to stay in America), Commander Alan Noble and Mrs. Noble, went to Cannes to stay at the villa of Lt.-Col. Alan Palmer, an expert on Balkan affairs who organised the partisans in Albania in 1943. Eden spent most of his time reading, mostly the works of Arthur Koestler and Andre Gide. He played a certain amount of tennis but did little bathing. The fact is that, in the emotional sense, he was marking time. He had instituted divorce proceedings against Beatrice Eden and was waiting to end a long chapter in his life.

On June 8th, 1950, Eden won a divorce decree by testifying that his wife deserted him in 1947 to live in the United States. The hearing before Mr. Justice Hodson took only five minutes. The evidence was that Mrs. Eden, who was not represented at the hearing, accompanied Eden on his visit to the United States at the end of 1946 and refused to return. Mr. Eden was the only witness, and when the decree *nisi* was granted, he hurried from the court, ignoring the importunities of reporters and refusing all comment.

In New York, Mrs. Beatrice Eden was besieged in her New York flat by reporters. To none of them did she say anything which could embarrass her husband, whose career she had no wish to jeopardise—she had helped him to make it. The London *Daily Mirror* quoted her as saying: " I was never fitted to be a politician's wife "—which could be taken as a hint that she did not consider him entirely responsible for the break up in their marriage. " I am good friends with Mr. Eden," she was quoted as saying, " and admire him tremendously as a politician." In all her interviews Mrs. Eden wished Anthony every success, and there is no doubt at all that she meant it. She was living with a friend in a small flat full of her paintings— like her former husband she is an enthusiastic and talented artist, and later in the year she held an exhibition of her landscapes and still life paintings, in oils.

Later in 1950 Mrs. Eden flew to Britain to see Nicholas, then doing his National Service with his father's old regiment, the 60th Rifles, and stationed at Winchester. She denied that she had any plans for re-marrying, although some thought she might be contemplating engagement to Dr. Robert Hedges, a gynæcologist whom she had met in Bermuda in 1948, who served with the Medical Corps in Italy as a Major. Dr. Hedges, who is in his fifties, is fond of art and a good pianist, has a large private practice in New York and is attached to a large New York hospital. Marriage was rumoured when friends noticed a life-size portrait of Mrs. Eden in his flat.

Eden's main contribution during 1950 was his attention to foreign affairs. In June he asked the Government " in the interests of peace and full employment " to take part in the discussions of the Schuman plan for economic co-operation in Europe. In July he paid tribute to "sense of world responsibility" which the United Nations commanded, and to America's leadership in world affairs. He warned the House in September that "Russia for years has not fulfilled either the letter or the spirit of negotiations and terms into which she freely entered on her own account. He criticised Britain's defence position, especially the strength of Royal Air Force fighter units, and called for better equipment of Auxiliary Air Squadrons. As Honorary Air Commodore of the County of Kent Royal Auxiliary Air Force Squadron he keeps himself abreast of the latest developments in aviation, visiting the squadron regularly and going on flights with the men.

He found time, before 1950 closed, to visit Austria as the guest of the British Minister, meeting the President, Chancellor and Foreign Minister, to attend the proceedings of the Royal Institute of International Affairs, of which he was President, and to travel to Canada to receive an honorary degree from McGill University. These honorary degrees, a conventional practice by which institutions honour men of distinction, are almost an index of a man's rise in international esteem. By this criterion Anthony Eden was doing well. He now possessed honorary degrees from the Universities of Oxford, Durham, Cambridge, Sheffield, Belfast, Birmingham and Leeds, besides sundry Freedoms of the City, of which the Freedom of Leamington, his constituency, is naturally the one he values most.

* * *

The year 1951 was unremarkable except for the October Election which put the Conservatives back in power and brought Eden back into Parliament for his third term of office. In January he was writing well-paid though somewhat unreadable articles, which could have been detected by their style even had he not signed them: "These are stern and critical times..." begins one feature in a Sunday newspaper whose circulation has been built on crime and sex. The solemn features of the ex Foreign Secretary looked oddly juxtaposed with the misdemeanours of unfrocked parsons and the aberrations of Teddy boys.

Later in January Eden visited the British Army of the Rhine

in Germany, looked in on his son Lieutenant Nicholas Eden, who was serving with the 60th Rifles, near Paderborn and was due to finish his National Service in September.

In February Eden opened a debate on foreign affairs in the House of Commons, emphasised the need for co-operation with Germany and added that " the whole course of international experience taught us that we best served peace by warning any would-be aggressors of the consequences of their acts before they made them." Later he warned an audience in Glasgow that " . . . the Soviet Union, never, in fact, disarmed after the war in any way comparable with the Western Powers. Her forces are still on a scale which has no parallel in history for any nation in time of peace." He called for a firm handling of the Persian oil dispute, on which he could speak with the authority of one who knew the area and the language. In August he was travelling again, this time to Canada and America, mixing with the members of the M.C.C. cricket team as he crossed the Atlantic in the *Empress of France*. He challenged them at tennis, which, together with swimming, is his favourite sport, and together with another passenger, Mr. Robert Carr, Conservative M.P. for Mitcham, played Mr. R. W. V. Robins and J. R. Thompson, Captain and Vice-Captain of the team, in two matches. The score was one all, and Eden demonstrated that he had not forgotten how to throw a good spinning shot.

Whilst in Canada as the guest of Mr. Vincent Massey, Eden talked to him about his son's future. Nicholas seemed disinclined to scholarship, and Anthony was anxious for his son to see something of the Empire as soon as possible. In Denver, Colorado, Eden gave a true-to-form speech on international affairs, and continued a highly successful tour in which he proved his abilities as a television personality. Almost everywhere his plane touched down he was invited to be televised. He is very photogenic, and quite at ease in front of the television camera and under the glare of the lights. Because he is a sincere person, his speeches come over far better in this medium; and his easy manner in interviews is a decided asset.

This experience was to serve Eden in good stead in the 1951 General Election. His constructive approach to current problems made a welcome contrast to the alarmist polemics of the previous election. Instead of telling listeners of the gloom and doom which must attend on a Socialist victory, he talked of practical policies in housing, agriculture and economics. He also made good use of a graph showing how the cost of living had risen—and was taken to task by Mr. Christopher Mayhew, for the Socialists, who claimed that the statistics supplied by the Conservative Central Office had been "faked".

In an election broadcast Eden showed that he was more in touch with public opinion than his critics supposed. "Britain has been pushed around too much lately," he said, "This is bad for us: bad for our friends: bad for peace." He asked that there should be no further nationalisation, for a cut in waste and extravagance in Government spending and a speed-up of housing. By a narrow majority, the Conservatives were returned. Sir Winston Churchill, still disinclined to retire and anxious to taste office again after the shock of the Conservative defeat in 1945, was Prime Minister again.

TWENTY-FOUR

Prime Minister Designate

IN the new Churchill Administration, Anthony Eden was once again Foreign Minister. Some had expected that he would also be Leader of the House of Commons, a burden which Eden was not keen to accept. The cold war with Russia; co-operation for defence amongst Western Powers as an insurance against Communist aggression; Germany's future, the machinery of the North Atlantic Treaty Organisation; war in Korea; trouble in Egypt; the Anglo-Persian Oil dispute —these, added to the daily routine of a normally busy Ministry, would take up all of his time.

Furthermore, it would have been politically inadvisable to have got embroiled in home affairs, which were far too controversial. In general, Eden had gone from strength to strength by keeping clear of controversy in home affairs. The de-nationalisation plans, pay increases for Members of Parliament and old age pensions—all these could be pitfalls for a Prime Minister Designate. Feelings ran high on all these issues and there could be no course which would not give offence to a great number of people.

Eden's first job was to attend the sixth United Nations General Assembly in Paris where his maiden speech made a profound impression. *The Times* thought it "distinguished for its calm and courteous approach to world problems. Courtesy in international affairs belongs almost to a past era. One certainly remembers no speech in this setting which has attracted more favourable or such animated comment."

This was one of those occasions on which Eden's customary restraint was a more effective weapon than demagogy. For the Soviet Union the United Nations had been simply a platform for Communist propaganda. The Russian delegate, true to form, had proved obstructive, mendacious and abusive. On this occasion Eden excelled himself. " Here we have an instrument at hand. We must use it, as the Charter says, as a centre for harmonising the actions of nations . . . it would be a tragedy if this organisation lost for any reason its universality . . . but the instrument cannot produce harmony in an atmosphere of discord and abuse . . . M. Vyshinsky's cataract of abuse did not anger me, but it saddened me, as I think it must have saddened and discouraged the millions throughout the world who read or heard of it . . . all men are fallible and peace can only rest on mutual forbearance and restraint. Should we not then do much better to proclaim a truce to name-calling and angry words?" Mr. Eden prescribed preparation, conference and agreement, starting with small issues and working to the great.

Much of that speech had not been prepared. Eden is at his worst speaking from a prepared brief. A few days later he was speaking to the House of Commons in the jargon of diplomacy: " In view of the uncertainty caused in the Sudan and elsewhere by the Egyptian Government's unilateral action in purporting to abrogate the 1936 Treaty of Alliance . . . " He meant that the present Sudanese Government was firmly in the saddle and would stay there until the country achieved self-government.

On November 19th he spoke of the widening chasm between East and West, the ferment in the Middle East, the war in Korea and the North Atlantic Treaty Organisation, which would not have existed but for Soviet intransigience. He again recommended the Schuman Plan as a means of unifying Western Europe economically, and promised support to the conception of a " European community within the constantly growing Atlantic community." He praised the United Nations forces fighting in Korea. (It was the first attempt by a world force to repel aggression, but it had become long-since, a bloody stalemate from which either contestant would have gladly withdrawn if it could have done so without loss of face. As it was, Armistice negotiations at Panmunjon dragged on interminably.)

At the North Atlantic Council in Rome a few days later, Eden spoke of the purpose of NATO. Nobody wanted rearmament; but weakness made effective negotiation impossible. " We have no aggressive aims. We seek no quarrel. We have no territorial ambitions," he added. But a European Army containing a German element would stand alongside the British and United States Armies in a common defensive front.

Next, Eden and Churchill went to confer with the French President and his Ministers on the Schuman Plan. The opening of 1952 saw Eden on the move again. He visited Washington with Mr. Churchill to see Mr. Truman; and in New York collected an honorary degree from Columbia University where he gave a long lecture on foreign affairs. " The human crisis to-day " he said, " is not primarily a material one; it is a crisis of the mind and spirit." He quoted Milton:

> But that two-handed engine at the door
> Stands ready to smite once, and smite no more.

" To-day the grim engine is Communism, which once it has seized upon a country, destroys the minds of the people and turns them into truckloads of unanimous and anonymous robots. Let us make no mistake. The Communist assault on free and democratic thought is more formidable than was its Fascist counterpart of yesterday."

Back in the Foreign Office the staff were glad to have him in charge again. Eden can be petulant and unreasonable. He fusses too much. But as an administrator he is first-class. A few days after he had returned to office, somebody asked him for a directive respecting a certain country. Back came the minute, a cursory note written on it in red ink—which by tradition is reserved for the Foreign Secretary. Eden's reply consisted of just six words: " Be firm; be friendly; be fair." The official looked at it. " Thank God for a directive I can understand! " he said.

On his return from America Eden sold his old home at No. 4, Chesterfield Street to the Duke of Devonshire.

He threw himself into the struggle to mitigate the hardship of the war in Korea, if it could not yet be ended. When Eden cannot get his way, he asks for something less, or gets what he wants in such a way that the giver feels that his own points have been met. This extraordinary pertinacity makes him one of the best living diplomats. It is easy to underestimate Eden. His seeming diffidence, his reasonable approach, the speeches crammed with Foreign Office jargon, euphemisms and clichés—these do him less than justice. He does not put his best wares in his shop window. When the Chinese Communists refused to exchange prisoners unless 100,000 men captured by the United Nations forces were handed over whether they wanted to return or not, Eden knew that such a transfer would be a tragedy. Thousands of Chinese and Koreans were terrified at the prospect of returning and would have committed suicide. While the haggling went on, Eden suggested that at least the sick and wounded might be exchanged as an interim measure; soon Pekin agreed to this, and a few months later, a general Armistice followed. That is typical Eden diplomacy. Never despair. If you can't get agreement on big things, try and achieve agreement on something smaller—then follow up and exploit the goodwill created in other directions.

It looks so simple—but later on, by this same technique, Anthony Eden saved the European defence system from crashing in ruins.

In March 1952, Nicholas, for whom Anthony Eden had given a coming-of-age party some months previously, gave up his studies at Oxford to go to Canada as aide-de-camp to Mr. Vincent Massey, losing any immediate prospect of an Oxford degree. Nicholas wanted to earn a living without further delay, and to see more of the world, and his father arranged the appointment with Mr. Massey, who is a friend of many years' standing.

The months before the August recess of Parliament were taken up with complex international negotiations. A Foreign Minister's job nowadays is far more than a matter of dealing with individual countries. The rocket, the aeroplane and the atom bomb have ended that. Nowadays he is almost lost in an alphabetical forest—N.A.T.O., U.N.O., E.D.C., W.H.O., and other abbreviations; a special directory of these abbreviations had had to be complied. Eden attended the ninth session of the North Atlantic Council at Lisbon; he was constantly plying between the capitals of Europe in his efforts to build up a mutual defence system between the Western Powers. In January 1952, the Foreign Ministers of France, Western Germany, Italy, Belgium, Holland and Luxembourg had agreed on the structure and common military budget of a European

Army. There were to be forty-three divisions drawn from these different nations, under the command of the North Atlantic Treaty Organisation. Britain was associated with it, but not of it, for reasons which Eden made clear to its members. Britain is not just an over-populated island but the centre of a scattered Commonwealth, with relations with, and obligations to each country in it. But as Mr. Eden explained, " the U.K. will continue to maintain on the mainland of Europe, including Germany, such armed forces as may be necessary to contribute its fair share of the forces needed for the defence of the North Atlantic area, and will continue to deploy such forces in accordance with agreed North Atlantic Treaty strategy for the defence of this area. . . . "

Eden handled this complicated transaction with enormous skill. In May the E.D.C. Treaty was signed by the six powers concerned; Eden signed on behalf of Britain a Treaty of Mutual Security between Britain and E.D.C. members; and a Declaration affirmed the faith of Britain, the United States and France in E.D.C.'s purpose—a united column of defence against aggression. Thus Britain integrated her forces with Europe's without complicating her relations with Commonwealth members.

There was the crisis in Trieste; the hostility in Egypt; the problem of Germany; the war in Korea. Then after Parliament had gone into Autumn recess, Eden forgot his preoccupation with Foreign Affairs and prepared instead for a turning point in his life.

* * *

On August 12th, 1952, the news was released that the Foreign Minister was to re-marry. His fianceé was Miss Clarissa Churchill, niece of the Prime Minister and daughter of the late Sir John Spencer-Churchill, a distinguished soldier who fought in the South African War and the first World War. Her mother was Lady Gwendeline Spencer-Churchill (daughter of the 7th Earl of Abingdon) a charming hostess who had been a beauty in her day and was a life-long friend of Lady Oxford. Immediately the attention of the world was focused on a shy, petite lady of 32 who was destined to be an important figure in British public life.

Clarissa Churchill has been variously described as "the most beautiful débutante of 1938" and "the world's most beautiful blue-stocking". With her aristocratic connections and relationship to the Prime Minister, she had easy access to all the prominent people in Britain and had met Anthony both at her uncle's house at Westerham and at the Duchess of Kent's house at Iver in Buckinghamshire. Clarissa Churchill was wholly unknown outside her own special circle of aristocrats, academics and cosmopolitans. She had so far had a mixed career. She had studied philosophy at Oxford, been presented at Court in 1938, been photographed a good deal for fashion magazines and studied at the Slade School of Art before the war.

During the war, Miss Churchill worked at the Ministry of Information on *British Ally* a newspaper intended to give Russia some idea of Britain's war effort. Later she worked at the Foreign Office where she was engaged on decoding telegrams and similar duties.

She had decided literary gifts and for a while was Features Editor on *Vogue* writing about the ballet, theatre and the arts. Her articles show a perceptive mind and cultivated tastes. Writing, however, does not come easily to her and there is no doubt that her social status counted a good deal in the magazines which printed her work. Later Miss Churchill was one of the two beautiful and fashionable women employed on publicity in Sir Alexander Korda's film company. Here, she was liaison officer between Korda and American magazines, picking up stories and material about films and film stars and describing them. She was " fair to middling " at this. Publicity is not really her line for she is not only shy, but critical. She does not suffer fools gladly and does not like people as such unless they have some special quality she admires. She finds it an effort to be polite to people who bore her.

Once, she infuriated Orson Welles by ostentatiously reading a newspaper during what he considered one of his most dramatic scenes in " The Third Man ". The fact was that she disliked him for mimicking the producer Carol Reed to cameramen and technicians. She helped publicise the " Fallen Idol " and " Anna Karenina ", but grew tired of publicity and left to join " *Contact* " magazine on the editorial staff. *Contact* was a highbrow effort with a vaguely left-wing bias. Typical subjects were, " The Psychology of the Displaced." " Blueprint for Peterlee: a Town for Miners." " Industrial reconstruction in the U.S.S.R."

At the time of her engagement Miss Churchill had a flat in Rossmore Court in Regents Park. Most of her friends were either in society or were creative in one sense or another. At the parties she gave, the conversation was apt to be highbrow. In general, she had more acquaintances than friends. Amongst her close circle of friends were Greta Garbo, Cecil Beaton, the society photographer, Nicholas Lawford, then Anthony Eden's private secretary, and Lord Norwich (formerly Mr. Duff Cooper). Apart from her flat, she had a pleasant country cottage at Broadchalke, near Salisbury, where she liked to spend week-ends.

She has a distinctive personality. Her deep voice and cool air of self-possession coupled with the vaguely mystical expression of her clear blue eyes give her an indefinable charm. When she retires into herself, however, anybody in her company is made to feel very much in the way. She dresses simply, almost starkly and looks her best, as most Englishwomen do, in evening dress. She uses slight make-up and wears little jewellery.

With Anthony Eden she has a great deal in common, an aristocratic background, a liking for golf, tennis, swimming and gardening; love of arts; a fondness for travel; a dislike of ostentation and conceit and an intelligent interest in current affairs. In the theatre, however, their tastes do not coincide. Eden likes sheer relaxation in the lighter forms of entertainment, Clarissa prefers more solid stuff such as Ibsen or Shakespeare.

From the moment the news was announced, telegrams and telephone messages of congratulation poured in. One of the first telegrams to arrive was from Mr. Eden's son Nicholas in Canada.

The next day, Miss Churchill left her flat and moved into 10, Downing Street, and on August 14th, 1952, the wedding took place at Caxton Hall, the Registry Office in Westminster. The simplicity of the arrangements were in striking contrast to Eden's wedding to Beatrice at the fashionable St. Margaret's Church, Westminster in 1923. Then, there was an elaborate church service, an Archbishop to officiate and uniformed pageboys to hold the bride's train. But even had they wished for it, a church service would have raised complications. Eden is an Anglican and generally the Church of England does not marry divorced persons so long as the divorced partner is still alive.

London looked at its best on their wedding day. The sky was blue, the sun shone, and the room where marriages are contracted was decorated far more than usual. There were banks of white roses and pink gladioli. On the mantelpiece behind the Registrar, Mr. Holiday, was a signed wedding picture of Elizabeth Taylor and Michael Wilding, and next to that a lucky elephant made of green felt. Mr. Eden was accompanied by his brother, Sir Timothy Eden. Miss Churchill was escorted by her brother, Sir John Spencer-Churchill. Others in the room were the bride's two brothers, Mr. Peregrine and Mr. John Churchill, whose wife Mrs. John Churchill was also present; the Marquess and Marchioness of Salisbury, Lady Islington (the bride's god-mother), Viscount Bracken, once Minister of Information; the Earl of Warwick one of Eden's oldest friends, and his sixteen-years-old son, Lord Brooke; Mr. Randolph Churchill, the Prime Minister's son; Mr. and Mrs. Duncan Sandys; Mr. and Mrs. Anthony Beauchamp (Sarah Churchill); Mrs. Christopher Soames and Mr. John Eden, Eden's twenty-six-years-old nephew. Sir Winston Churchill was the principal witness.

The ceremony took fifteen minutes. When it was over Mr. Eden kissed his bride, then, as they were about to leave, asked her " On which side should I stand, left or right? " Mrs. Eden was not sure and appealed to Sir Winston. " I am no expert in these matters," he said drily. The Registrar came to the rescue. " On the right, sir " he prompted.

Outside over two thousand people waited for a glimpse of the Foreign Minister and his new wife. Mounted police kept them back and women were pushed against the flanks of the police horses by the pressure of the people behind them.

There was a brief wait on the stairs, and an American journalist who was a guest at the wedding gives me this account of what happened: The reporter observing the frantic excitement of the crowd, and seeing Sir Winston Churchill was standing next to him said to the Prime Minister:

"Did they make all this fuss for your wedding?"

Sir Winston turned a withering gaze on his questioner. "I wasn't married in a place like *this*!" Then, thinking perhaps this remark could be misinterpreted, he turned sharply to the reporter: "Who are you?"

"A newspaperman."

Sir Winston bristled with all the aggressiveness of a man who knows he is in the wrong. "What are you doing here? You've no business to be here!"

"I'm a guest," explained the reporter. That silenced the Prime Minister for a minute. Then he turned on him again. "What paper do you write for—who's your publisher?"

"Oh, the *New York*——" There was an expressive silence. In a moment Sir Winston was more conciliatory. "He knew by then," my informant said, "that he couldn't bulldoze a publisher 3,000 miles away."

As the bride and bridegroom paused for a moment at the foot of the steps, a Stepney housewife Mrs. Jane Delew, ran through the police cordon and handed Mr. Eden a silver horseshoe from her own wedding cake 29 years ago.

Later, twenty guests attended the reception at 10, Downing Street, in a room decorated with flowers from the Prime Minister's house at Westerham. Then after driving from Downing Street to the cheers of the waiting crowds, Mr. and Mrs. Eden spent the first night of their honeymoon at the home of Mr. Whitney Straight, the aviation millionaire, whose house is near London Airport. A suite in the west wing was made gay with masses of roses and gladioli.

The next day they flew to Lisbon. On arrival at the hotel where they had made a reservation, the receptionist had a sample of the Eden temper; when he found that there was no bathing pool as he expected and refused to stay. They spent a quiet week's honeymoon at Uregirica, an inland beauty spot.

* * *

Whilst Mr. and Mrs. Eden were away, some acid comments on their wedding appeared in the *Church Times*.

> The marriage this week of the Foreign Secretary during the life of his former wife, who he divorced in 1950, cannot pass without

comment. Mr. Eden's private life is his own affair as much as any other man's, but high public position is bound to lend a special significance to private actions.

A generation ago, a Foreign Secretary who was likely one day to become Prime Minister would have felt compelled to choose between a career and such a marriage. It is only recently that a reigning monarch was forced to make a choice between such a re-marriage and his throne. Mr. Eden's unprecedented action this week, like the adoption by the American Democrats of a divorced man as a candidate for President, shows how far the climate of public opinion in this matter has changed for the worse since 1936 . . . the world is openly rejecting the law of Christ in this as in so much else . . . "

This direct reference to Mr. Eden's re-marriage caused some controversy in Church of England circles. The Anglican Church is the established Church of the Realm and its attitude to divorce is well known. A Prime Minister has, by virtue of some historic anachronism, the responsibility of appointing Church of England bishops. The situation of a Prime Minister appointing leaders of a Church which would have refused to marry him is certainly unusual.

Apart, however, from the false analogy drawn with King Edward VIII (who did not, as the *Church Times* put it, have to " make a choice between re-marriage and his throne "; the King had never been married before), the Anglican Church has no inflexible rule. *The Church of England Year Book* says that in the case of a person who has been divorced " the Incumbent *may* refuse to officiate, or allow the use of his church for such a marriage." May, not must. Many church-people thought the attack on Mr. Eden uncharitable, in bad taste and mistimed. The Rev. H. G. Marshall, a former Secretary of the Church of England's Men's Society said: " To make a statement like that is entirely unchristian. It is unfair to Mr. Eden and an insult to our Prime Minister." Churchmen in Eden's constituency of Leamington were strongly critical of the *Church Times*. The Vicar of Leamington expressed the view that while the Christian ideal of marriage must be preserved there must be a more charitable way of dealing with hard cases. The Modern Churchmen's Union, whose President is Sir Henry Self, chairman of the British Electricity Authority, said flatly: " There is no law of the Church of England against divorce and re-marriage . . . many clergy and most laity do not support the narrow view and regard it as contrary to Christian principles."

The *Church Times* answered its critics. " We stated simply the view of the Church on re-marriage after divorce. We were not concerned with a person but with principles. The views of correspondents both to this paper and others have been divided, but with a preponderance in favour of re-marriage after divorce. The outcry . . . has shown . . . the extent to which public opinion in this country has now abandoned the idea of Christian marriage and the sanctity of the pledged word."

In all that argument, certain facts escaped attention. Eden would certainly have discussed his divorce with the Prime Minister and sought his advice on its possible effect on his career. Eden was the innocent party in the divorce proceedings. The greater a man's responsibilities, the more essential it is that he should be absolutely happy in his domestic life, so that he can bring a clear and untroubled mind to bear on the many problems he must face.

* * *

Shadowed by Major Philip Attfield, the detective assigned to guard the Foreign Minister, Mr. and Mrs. Eden had a quiet honeymoon in Portugal and arrived back in London on August 28th to take up residence in the Foreign Office house in Carlton Gardens—a flat which she soon impressed with her personality, combining the elegance of past centuries with modern ideas of colour. The drawing room, with its combination of greens and reds, was rich in effect while avoiding any suggestion of ostentation. A few good pictures; one or two pieces of choice china; an antique table; these few things gave the apartment dignity and individuality—but the humblest of the Middle East potentates whom Eden knows so well lives in splendour compared with Britain's Foreign Minister. The panelled dining room, the Georgian silver and glistening crystal give a deceptive air of luxury. In fact Anthony Eden is a man of quite modest means—a matter of choice. It is undeniable that he has never sought wealth for its own sake, and has put public service before money making. Of that there is not the slightest question.

Mrs. Eden the Second settled in quite naturally, adapting herself to the cosmopolitan atmosphere of that strange household without any difficulty. She took up the round of political meetings, social occasions, House of Commons Sessions (which she rarely misses if her husband is going to speak) and the entertainment of distinguished visitors as though she had been accustomed to it all her life. In a sense, she had, for with her social background she has been able to move on any social level she liked. Apart from the fact that she is well educated, attractive and comes of a good family, being niece of the most popular Prime Minister Britain ever had, has always been a useful cachet.

She soon got used to the fact that her husband is never away from his work. The red leather despatch boxes were ubiquitous. Going to work or coming from it in his car, his lap was invariably covered with papers. The despatch boxes littered his study and drawing room. But she is not, like Mrs. Eden the First " bored to tears with politics." And she has quickly learned that, whilst as a private individual she could show people when she was bored with them, there are occasions when the wife of a prominent Minister cannot do so.

In September Eden decided to sell his house at Binderton, where Winant and other diplomats used to spend their week-ends, and where he relaxed between his hectic war-time journeys. Thus both the homes associated with his first marriage were disposed of. In starting a new home there is much to be said for breaking away from the scene of former domestic associations. In any case, Binderton was not necessary. The Prime Minister has first call on Chequers, the official country house provided from public funds; the Chancellor of the Exchequer has second call, and the Foreign Secretary third. But Mr. R. A. Butler usually spends his week-ends at Stanstead Hall in Essex, and has no use for Chequers. Eden, therefore, virtually had second claim on Chequers whenever he pleased.

After attending a session of the Council of Europe at Strasbourg, Anthony Eden paid an official visit to Marshal Tito, Communist dictator of Yugoslavia, the first country to break away from the Russian bloc. Eden did not take his wife. He was disinclined to " cadge a lift " for her on a Service plane. Eden is extremely careful to observe the strictest formality in the spending of public funds; inevitably a Foreign Minister must travel—that is inherent in his work, and the costs a justifiable charge—but he does not consider that the privilege extends to his wife. But he has since taken her, at his own expense, on some of his trips.

Tito organised the most extraordinary security precautions for Eden's visit. Some streets were cleared entirely and lined with troops. Windows and roofs facing the route were searched beforehand, and all windows had to be shut. Tito received Eden in the White Palace and took him on a yachting trip amongst the islands off the coast, near Dubrovnik. Yugoslavia's relations with the East and West were discussed, and the question of Trieste, a constant source of friction between Yugoslavia and Italy. The Yugoslav Communist Party official organ described Eden as " .... a statesman of extraordinary reputation esteemed in the world for his ability."

After visiting Austria, Eden came back to find his desk piled high with problems and crises. The Persians seemed bent on seizing British property; terrorism was increasing in Malaya; over 10,000 children had been abducted from Greece by Communist neighbours; a note had to be prepared for Egypt on the Sudan. In Paris, at an O.E.E.C. meeting, Eden grappled with complex financial problems concerning the recovery of Europe, Marshall Aid and economic co-operation. He handled Persia with great patience, but Mussaddiq broke off diplomatic relations with the United Kingdom in October. He received a great ovation at the Conservative Party's Annual Conference. He ignored a rather rude attack from Mrs. Barbara Castle, Labour M.P. for Blackburn; " They talk about the clash for personal power in the Labour Party—have you any idea how much Butler and Eden watch each other for the succession to dead men's shoes? " Personal attacks do not worry Eden; but an oblique attack on Sir William Strang, Permanent Under Secretary at the Foreign Office, left him absolutely incensed. An anonymous writer in a Sunday newspaper had urged Eden to get rid of Sir William, who was held responsible for pre-war appeasement despite the fact that he was a public servant, not a policy maker. " I know that if Mr. Bevin were alive to-day he would agree with me as my other predecessors would, " Eden declared, " in paying tribute to

... Sir William Strang for the services he has rendered to British foreign policy and to this country." He referred to the tradition by which public servants, who are not allowed to defend themselves, should not be attacked in this way. " If anyone wants to attack our foreign policy, they should attack the Foreign Secretary direct, who is responsible with his colleagues in the Government." That was typical Eden. An attack on himself went unnoticed, but an unjust criticism of a colleague spurred him to anger.

This moral integrity is the key to his make-up, and accounts for his immense moral authority throughout the world. Men who put honour before honours are rare in the world to-day.

TWENTY-FIVE

His Fight for Life

IN January, 1953, Eden accompanied Sir Winston Churchill to Washington for informal talks with General Eisenhower, then President Elect of the United States. In a broadcast two days later, Eden summarised Britain's foreign policy as consisting of two aims, security and solvency. The free nations would need to be strong enough to resist aggression and should develop between themselves a healthy and balanced economy. Rearmament was still necessary because Russia was still committed to a programme of world domination.

The visit in February of Mr. John Foster Dulles, the new American Secretary of State, and Mr. Stassen—they were on a lightning tour of Europe—gave Mr. Eden a chance to criticise America's policy in Formosa, the headquarters of the Chinese Nationalists. Without consulting Britain, America had ordered its fleet not to protect the coast of China which was in the hands of the Communists. This sounded like an overt approval of the Nationalist raids on Communist China—a situation which could extend the war. If these pin-pricking raids were encouraged, Communist China might be provoked into large scale military action. On February 5th, Eden was able to assure the House of Commons that an attack on China from Formosa was not contemplated.

In the meantime, Eden's health was manifestly breaking down. Even before his marriage he had been ill with jaundice and now, with a formidable programme of engagements and obligations, his energy flagged unaccountably. At the end of January, he was compelled to take a week's rest at his cottage in Wiltshire. He recovered sufficiently to explain the Anglo-Egyptian Treaty to the House of Commons on February 12th. There was general satisfaction in the House that Eden had lost so little time in reaching a settlement on the Sudan, although

Mr. Assheton, a Conservative back bencher, thought it farcical to force self-government on the Sudanese who, he said, did not want it and were quite unfitted for it.

As Stalin lay dying early in March, Eden sailed for America with Mr. R. A. Butler to discuss a wide range of problems with President Eisenhower and Mr. Dulles. News of Stalin's death reached Eden in mid-Atlantic and when the ship docked he was surrounded by newspaper reporters who went empty away. Asked what the effect of Stalin's death would be, he gave his questioner a charming smile and said, " That is a good question for you to ask, but not a wise one for me to answer."

On his return, Eden gave the House of Commons a vague and unsatisfactory description of his visit in a speech that the *Annual Register* describes as being " full of his too-familiar platitudes ". There were cries of " Have the Marines heard about this? " and " Cliché, cliché ".

Two days later, Marshal Tito arrived in Britain on a state visit during which involved security measures were taken because the visitor was unpopular with Roman Catholics, orthodox Communists, the Russians and the Italians. Tito was received by the Queen and was later entertained to dinner by Mr. and Mrs. Eden at Carlton Gardens. Nobody was allowed within 100 yards of the house without a police pass.

On April 6th, the public learned the real reason for Eden's poor show in the House of Commons. It was announced that he was ill and would need to be operated on for chronic colecystitus (inflammation of the gall bladder). A glance at his medical record shows something of the enormous strain of his work:

June, 1945	..	Duodenal ulcer. Ordered to rest.
March, 1948	..	Entered nursing home for operation for appendicitis.
June, 1949	..	Collapsed twice at a meeting.
January, 1951	..	Laid up with influenza in Germany.
June, 1952	..	Confined to bed with jaundice.
March, 1953	..	Ill with gastric influenza.

Apart from these illnesses, which were announced, Eden had suffered annual attacks of gastric influenza.

On April 12th, Eden was operated upon at the London Clinic and next day the operation, a long and difficult one, was stated to have been successful. The jaundice, however, still persisted and a second operation was necessary on April 29th, after which he went to Chequers to convalesce. Although his condition had been described as " satisfactory ", Clarissa could see that he was still very ill. Throughout May he made no progress. Visits to Turkey, Greece and Italy had to be cancelled and Sir Winston told the House of Commons that Eden's illness was due largely to overwork. Later, Eden's condition became worse. Clarissa took the situation firmly in hand and insisted that Dr. Richard Cattell, the American specialist in gall bladder complaints, should visit him at Chequers. On May 31st, it was announced that Eden would fly to Boston U.S.A. for a third operation, and would be accompanied by Mrs. Eden.

This operation was successful and Eden left the New England Baptist Hospital to convalesce at the home of a friend, Mr. John Ryan, brother of Lady Ogilvy. The house at Newport, Rhode Island was set in beautiful grounds and overlooked the Atlantic. Mr. Eden's bedroom was a restful apartment with white walls and gay chintz curtains, and the green and white dining room boasted a fine painting of the Riviera by Claude Monet, the French impressionist, one of Eden's favourite artists. In this tranquil atmosphere, his health began to mend. Instead of the usual round of conferences and meetings, he spent his time reading, strolling in the garden and watching television programmes. Still thin and worn, he flew with Mrs. Eden and his son Nicholas to Lord Warwick's villa on the French Riviera. Next, he sailed to Greece in the despatch vessel *Surprise* in which the Queen had made her Coronation review at Spithead. He visited Crete and spent many happy hours exploring the ancient palace of Knossos.

During his absence from Parliament, the *Daily Mirror* had been talking of Eden being too ill for his job and unsuited for it anyway. " Churchill ", it said, " knows how to scare the daylights out of ugly customers. Can Eden express anything more than distaste and displeasure ? "

On his return to work at the beginning of October, Eden looked wonderfully bronzed and fit. At the Conservative Party Conference in October, he was greeted with prolonged cheers as he rose to talk. " I am bound to admit ", he said, " that I would not be very upset if I never saw another Foreign Office box or telegram again." He added, "We must not by any of our actions injure the unity of N.A.T.O. No N.A.T.O, no security." There was the usual pile of problems waiting for him at the Foreign Office including the disorders in Trieste. A few weeks later, Eden left for the Big Three conference in Bermuda, a meeting between the leaders of France, Britain and the United States at which it was hoped a conference between France, Britain, United States and Russia might be arranged to settle outstanding questions. The talking marathon lasted for six days but the 200 journalists who made the journey only wasted their time. The official communiqués were no more than platitudes re-stating what had been said so often before.

* * *

The year 1954 was an important year for Anthony Eden in more ways than one. If not the busiest, it was certainly one of the most active years of his life so far as politics were concerned. Eden was primarily responsible for planning, advocating and carrying through many fateful decisions in foreign affairs. In respect of some of these, such as Britain's evacuation of the Suez Canal zone, he brought upon himself lavish praise and strong condemnation. The wisdom or otherwise of foreign policy decisions cannot be decided immediately. Anthony Eden tries to look ahead, and time alone will show whether his vision was clear and his judgment sound.

Early in January the Foreign Office staff and his friends noticed how much better he looked, and how steadily he was putting on weight after his fight for life. He had learned one useful lesson from his long illness, however. On Clarissa's insistence he agreed to spend week-ends in the country, and to forget work for at least one day a week. After their marriage she was horrified to discover how little leisure and rest Anthony permitted himself, and how he was followed by despatch boxes and telephone calls every minute of every day. She saw for herself how right the Prime Minister had been when he told the House of Commons that Mr. Eden's illness has been caused largely by overwork. After the scare of last summer she was taking no chances.

But apart from his restored vigour, friends noted another

change in Eden. Since his re-marriage he was more relaxed, more cheerful and less inclined to outbursts of temper.

On January 11th, 1954, Eden broadcast on foreign affairs in the light of recent international developments. He tried to interest his listeners in N.A.T.O., although it is an almost impossible job to interest the public in defence measures in times of peace. N.A.T.O., he said, had doubled its strength and more than doubled its effectiveness; it was the sure deterrent to aggression. If N.A.T.O. had existed before the war, there would have been no second World War. As to the Middle East, Britain's responsibilities had been related to the " changing strategic picture and political climate."

On East-West relations Eden spoke of the forthcoming Berlin Conference, which he had done so much to bring about, and which was due to commence on January 25th. Since 1951 he had striven to bring the Russians to the conference table and get their agreement on the future of Germany and Austria. Without German unity there could be no real peace for Europe; but the first essential was free elections so that a peace settlement could be discussed with a truly representative government.

The Western world owes a good deal to Anthony Eden for his firm and dignified handling of relations with Russia. In dealing with military dictatorships it is hopeless to negotiate from weakness; he remembered how Britain had dithered in face of Fascist threats in 1938. And the Russian threat was more formidable even than the German had been. In Europe alone, since 1939, the Soviet Government had annexed, from friend and foe alike, nearly 180,000 square miles of territory containing over twenty million people. She had imposed a Communist government on Eastern Germany and the Soviet zone of Berlin by strong-arm methods, and had tried to oust the Allies from Berlin by a blockade which failed. But for the air-lift, all of Berlin would have come under Russian control, and the seizure of the rest of Germany, which would have given the Communist forces a border with France, would inevitably have followed.

N.A.T.O.—a defence alliance of the Atlantic Powers, with the European Defence Council being a smaller unit within it, was the inevitable answer to this menacing threat from the East. And the manner in which countries like Czechoslovakia were swallowed up showed that there was no time to waste. Since N.A.T.O. came into existence, Russia had attacked it, claiming that a rearmed Germany would be a menace to East and West alike. But Eden, in his broadcast of January 11th, pointed out that there were already far-reaching safeguards for Russian security against Germany falling back into " aggressive habits." These were the United Nations and the Anglo-Soviet Treaty of 1943, which Britain still regarded as valid.

The conference of the Foreign Ministers of Britain, France, the United States and the U.S.S.R. opened in Berlin on January 25th and lasted until February 18th. This was the first top level meeting with the Russians since the death of Stalin, and Eden was interested to know whether the Russians would stop their sabre-rattling and co-operate in the cause of peace. If so, an agreement to hold free elections throughout Germany, including the Soviet zone of Berlin and Eastern Germany, would be a first start.

Eden submitted a carefully drafted plan known afterwards as the Eden plan. It was in five stages, and provided for (1) free elections throughout Germany; (2) arising from the elections, the establishment of an all-German National Assembly, or Parliament; (3) the drafting of a Constitution and the preparation of peace treaty negotiations; (4) the adoption of the Constitution and the formation of an all-German government responsible for negotiating a peace treaty; (5) the signature and implementation of the peace treaty.

M. Molotov, for the Russians, showed that Stalinism was not dead, and poured out the usual " cataract of abuse " with particular reference to N.A.T.O. and E.D.C. Anthony Eden answered his objections with great skill. He thought the European Defence Community was the best answer to Molotov's fears of a revival of German militarism. E.D.C. was a defence organisation; and if Germany wished to violate its pledges it would be unable to do so, since the six armies of the E.D.C. powers would be combined and under an independent, and not national, command.

The Berlin Conference did not achieve its main object, but it had one outcome. Agreement was reached that the powers should confer again at Geneva on the wars in Korea and Indo-China.

During his absence the London *Daily Mirror* reverted to its attack on Eden, " the Crown Prince who Has Been Waiting Too Long." " His toothy smile is appealing. He is tall and handsome, six foot of glamour from the iron-grey hair to the highly-polished shoe-caps. His clothes, like any tailor's dummy, are immaculate. His voice is resonant as a stage parson's. He has had a hat named after him. What else? "

Reporting to the House of Commons, later, Eden said that Russia's desire was to annexe the whole of Germany and force the United States out of Europe. He represented that the West's best chance of security lay with N.A.T.O. and the European Defence Community.

A few weeks later, sitting in an armchair at his home in Carlton Gardens, Eden was the target of a number of quick-fire questions on the Conservative party's 20-minute television programme. It was a spontaneous broadcast, in the course of which his questioners put questions received from constituents. Eden answered questions about the cost of living, slum-dwellers and housing, but told viewers that over-riding all domestic questions was the issue of peace. The risk of war was lessened by the unity of the West, and atomic power had been a deterrent to war. The television broadcast was declared a success. Eden is completely at home in this medium.

While Eden was preparing for the Geneva Conference, the Communist forces had increased their pressure on French forces in Indo-China. A war which was steadily bleeding France of her youngest men—already her casualties were over 90,000 dead and over 100,000 wounded—had reached its bitter climax in the siege of the French fortress of Dien Bien Phu. Mr. Dulles, the American Secretary of State, made a speech on March 29th in which he urged the Western Nations to warn China against continuing to support the Communist rebels in Indo-China.

Here was a very dangerous situation, and Eden had to do some hard and quick thinking. A warning to a vast Communist empire the size of China would be useless unless backed by force, and if such a warning were backed by force, it might provoke a war with China at a time when fighting men were needed in Europe to stop Russia spilling over into Western Europe. The long-drawn-out agony of Korea and Indo-China was a reminder that wars are easier to start than finish. There was anxiety at the Foreign Office lest the U.S.A. should embark on some precipitate action which might enlarge the scope of the war in Indo-China.

At this point Mr. Dulles paid a flying visit to England and Mr. Eden handled another difficult situation with great skill. He dissuaded Dulles from his rash and impracticable idea of a public slap-in-the-face for Communist China. He interested him instead in a rough plan he had formulated for a system of collective defence or security pact " to assure the peace, security and freedom " of the whole of South East Asia and the Western Pacific.

At the same time Eden was busy putting what he hoped might be the finishing touches to his plans for an European Defence Community—the political, economic and military alliance of the Western Nations, which would be backed by British forces and be in effect a localised unit of the North Atlantic Treaty Organisation, whose job is to secure peace over a larger field. Eden told the House of Commons on April 13th that an Agreement had been signed in Paris the previous day regarding co-operation between the United Kingdom and E.D.C. " Our aim," he said, " has been to confirm that British forces will be present in strength on the Continent of Europe before, and not after, any aggression begins."

In a speech in Belfast Eden referred to the coming Geneva conference and said that the hydrogen bomb was " an appalling warning " to anyone contemplating aggression. He hoped Geneva would achieve peace in the Far East.

The conference in Geneva, which started in April, looked like going on forever. Week after week went by, the discussions concerning both the campaign in Korea and the war in Indo-China. The representatives of the 16 United Nations countries which had taken part in the Korean war tried to reach agreement on Korea with the representatives from the U.S.S.R., the Chinese People's Republic and delegates from North and South Korea. The Western Powers insisted that there should be free elections, supervised by a neutral international body, before the formation of a government. The Communist delegates would not acknowledge the authority of the United Nations or agree to free elections. This part of the conference ended in failure despite day and night work by Mr. Eden and his team.

Representatives of Britain, France, the U.S.A., the U.S.S.R., China, Viet-Nam, Viet Minh, Laos and Cambodia, then discussed the war in Indo-China. Here Eden showed tremendous patience. After weeks of work it seemed that no agreement could be possible. Again and again Eden brought the conference back to realities. In May he framed five questions demanding " urgent answers "—questions which ignored points of disagreement but sought to pin down the representatives on points of agreement. For example: Are we all agreed that all troops on both sides shall be concentrated in determined areas? Are we in favour of international supervision? If so, in what form?

On another occasion Eden's understanding of Far Eastern affairs enabled him to break down Chou En-lai's resistance by proving that the invaders of Laos and Cambodia could not possibly have been " resistance movements " as they did not come to fight the French. In race and culture the forces of Viet Nam were separated by hundreds of years; they had crossed the border between Indian and Chinese cultures.

An agreement for a cease-fire was at last concluded on July 20th, 1954, and signed the next day, and Sir Winston Churchill telegraphed his congratulations to Eden for his " patient, persevering skill " at Geneva. The agreement meant an end to fighting in the three states, and the evacuation by French forces of territory gained at appalling cost of human life. Eden told the House that the most notable thing about the conference was that " the real rulers " of China took part. It was a farce not to recognise the Communist government, in China, he said, and hoped that all nations, including America, would make " a realistic approach " to China. This declaration did not go down well in America, which had never recognised the Communist Government of China. Many saw in this agreement a second Munich, a sell-out to the Communists. But Mr. Eden said that " as we form judgment on these events, it is a fair comment to make that the only alternatives to these arrangements was continued fighting, further misery and even greater sacrifices in the end."

During the Foreign Secretary's absence the *Daily Mirror*

made front-page " news " of its disapproval of Mr. Eden as a successor to Sir Winston Churchill. There was, said the *Mirror*, controversy over his divorce. The Church of England frowns on re-marriage, and the Queen as head of the Church would therefore find it difficult to choose him as Prime Minister. Hannen Swaffer had also written that High Churchmen who believe in the inviolability of marriage, and Roman Catholics, might be antagonised by the choice of Mr. Eden as Prime Minister.

It is doubtful if the controversy was ever acute. And since the *Mirror* dislikes all Tories with equal impartiality, their anxiety as to which Tory should be chosen as Prime Minister was difficult to understand. Eden himself was busy at Geneva at the time, but perhaps Mrs. Beatrice Eden, who was on a visit to England at the time, wondered if the break up in her marriage to Anthony had affected his career adversely. She had always hoped that it would not, and has never uttered any word of reproach or criticism of her former husband.

While some were saying that the Geneva conference was an ignominious defeat for the Western Powers, and others saw it as a triumph of diplomacy on Eden's part, there was general satisfaction that the Persian oil dispute had at last been settled. Throughout that unhappy controversy Eden had kept his temper with the Persians despite the most outrageous abuse and misrepresentation.

But there was no time for satisfaction. Geneva had hardly finished before a most serious crisis arose, fraught with grave consequences for Western Europe. The French National Assembly, a third of whose members were Communists, rejected the scheme for an European Defence Community (E.D.C.). Once again Europe was disunited in face of the threat of invasion from the East. Years of hard work had come to nothing.

Eden had seen this crisis coming. France feared German rearmament, and M. Mendes-France had asked the five other signatories at a conference in Brussels to modify the E.D.C. proposals to make them more acceptable to the French Assembly. They had not done so, and Mendes-France came to England to see Sir Winston Churchill and Mr. Eden at Chartwell. Before the crisis developed, Mr. and Mrs. Eden had gone to Austria for a holiday, but Clarissa was to discover that a Foreign Minister does not often get time to himself. Apart from the fact that the four-engined turbo-prop Viscount had to land with only two engines at Schwechat Airport, Vienna, they had hardly settled in to Castle Tentschach before a urgent telephone call brought Anthony back to London.

When news came that the French Assembly had rejected E.D.C., Eden had a special telephone service laid on to his Wiltshire cottage and worked day and night working out an alternative plan. His substitute plan preserved the essentials of European unity by taking the existing Brussels Treaty of 1948 (which provided for co-operation between the U.K., France, Belgium, Holland and Luxembourg), extending it to Italy and Germany; ending the occupation regime in Western Germany and admitting Germany to N.A.T.O.

With this plan in his pocket Eden made lightning visits to Brussels, Bonn, Rome and Paris within four days. His prompt initiative saved the European security system from collapsing in ruins. Western defence without Germany was clearly impossible. Eden's next problem was: how could France, which had suffered three disastrous German invasions within a century, be reconciled to German rearmament.

On his return, Eden talked with Mr. Dulles. Invitations were then issued by the British Government to the six E.D.C. powers, including Western Germany, and to Italy, Canada and the U.S.A., to attend a Nine-Power Conference in London on September 28th, 1954. Since E.D.C. had collapsed, Eden was simply using the old Brussels Treaty, which most people had forgotten, as a basis for a new treaty, by associating three other countries—Italy, Canada and the U.S.A.—with it.

At this conference, of which Mr. Eden was chairman, France was still the main obstacle to agreement, refusing to accept a scheme for the control of arms to which the rest had agreed. But on September 30th, Eden sprang a sensation on the conference by announcing that the United Kingdom would maintain an army of four divisions and a tactical air force in Europe for fifty years and undertook not to withdraw it without the consent of the majority of the Brussels Treaty Powers.

This pledge was the answer to France's misgivings, and was

a considerable concession on Britain's part to French policy. The signing of the document summarising the work of the conference took place in the state drawing room of Lancaster House on October 3rd, 1954. The nine ministers sat in a line at the table, with Eden, who signed first, in the centre. When the document was complete tension was broken at last. Waiters came in with tables, cutlery, wine, cigarettes and cold buffet. And everyone crowded round Eden to congratulate him. He had committed Britain to a completely new departure in British foreign policy; for half a century Britain's fortunes are now linked irrevocably with those of France. Mr. Eden had told the conference that for Britain it was " a very formidable step " to take. Britain was making this sacrifice to help the conference to succeed. As a result of Eden's patience, there was Western unity at last; Germany was to receive full sovereignty, to join in the defence of the West and to be admitted to N.A.T.O., and both Canada and the U.S.A. re-affirmed their faith in N.A.T.O.

This, undoubtedly, is the most important initiative Eden has taken in his career. He has staked his future on it, and Britain's as well. His prestige in international circles was now sky-high; no other statesman, it was felt, could have produced order out of that chaos. And at the Conservative conference at Blackpool a few days later, under the eye of the TV cameras and surrounded by microphones, Eden heard himself cheered to the echo by 4,000 constituency representatives. When he rose to speak at the end of the debate there was not one word of criticism of foreign policy, but sustained clapping, cheering and the singing of " For he's a jolly good fellow."

But there were a few lone prophets of doom. Mr. Aneurin Bevan predicted that " Eden's laurels will look pretty tawdry in a few weeks' time . . . " and Lord Beaverbrook, on leaving the West Indies for Canada, declared " I go in gloom and sorrow. Mr. Eden is sending to European countries 120,000 young men of Britain. Eden has succeeded in making Mendes-France the most popular man in Europe. I hope he has also succeeded in making himself the most unpopular man in England." From M. Mendes-France, Mr. Dulles and Dr. Adenauer Eden won high praise. And on October 20th Eden was received at Buckingham Palace by the Queen, who conferred upon him the honour of Knighthood and invested him with the insignia of a Knight Commander of the Most Noble Order of the Garter. Now he was The Rt. Hon. Sir Anthony Eden, K.G., P.C., M.C., M.P., with one of the most coveted honours in existence; the Garter was the reward for the effort, imagination and skill with which he had handled the whole business of European defence. Eden may be impatient in small things, but to difficult problems he brings enormous reserves of patience and hope. In fact, speaking at Leicester a few weeks later Eden epitomised his attitude to diplomacy: " Real progress in diplomacy is most often the result of perseverance. Take time, take trouble. If you negotiate with a man who is in no hurry and you are in a hurry you will lose out every time."

Two other unexpected honours came to Eden before the close of 1954. The Carnegie Foundation awarded him the Wateler Peace Prize of £2,100, and in December the *Daily Mirror*, which had attacked Eden with all its considerable resources for over a year, " made " Eden the " Politician of the Year." He had saved the Geneva Conference and stopped the war in Indo-China; he had rallied a bewildered Europe after the collapse of E.D.C.; he had saved the London Nine-Power Conference, which looked like breaking down over French fears of Germany, by his pledge to keep British troops in Europe for 50 years.

These bold acts of statesmanship had forced even his severest critics to admit that there is more to Eden than good looks and a Homburg hat. He had risen from a sickbed after a fight for life and strained himself the the last degree in the interest of world peace. He had proved himself a man of stature as distinct from status.

TWENTY-SIX

Top of the Ladder

ON January 15th, 1955, Sir Anthony Eden completed his tenth year as Foreign Secretary. In the history of the Foreign Office only four men have served in that capacity for longer periods, and none, it is safe to say, have had such a burden to carry. To oversee an organisation of nearly 4,000 men who are scattered across the face of the earth and to cope with 10,000 telegrams they send every month calls for decision, speed, clarity of thought and a systematic mind. But apart from the patience, skill and confidence needed to manage the Foreign Office's thirty-nine departments, an international outlook is needed nowadays. Foreign affairs do not only consist of day-to-day relations with other countries; to-day Britain is a member of innumerable agencies of international co-operation, such as the United Nations, whose proceedings and activities add enormously to the Foreign Secretary's flow of work. In travelling Eden has covered as much ground in a week as some of his predecessors did in a year. The after-dinner box of telegrams, which must be read and answered before 9 a.m. the next day, so that work can proceed, has been part of his daily life for years.

On February 19th Eden left for a 15,000 miles tour, a sort of diplomatic refresher course in Middle Eastern and Far Eastern affairs. At Bangkok, capital of Siam, a meeting of S.E.A.T.O. (South East Asia Treaty Organisation) was to discuss the setting up of a defence organisation for South East Asia; Eden used the opportunity of attending it as a means of making many other important calls on the way there and back. A glance at his itinerary is enough to show his enormous physical resilience and appetite for work—for not only was there the travelling to do, but constant hard work in between journeys:

Leave London	.. ..	19th February
Arrive Cairo..	.. ..	20th February
Cairo to Karachi	.. ..	21st February
Karachi to Bangkok	..	22nd February
Bangkok to Singapore	..	26th February
Singapore to Kuala Lumpur		28th February
Kuala to Delhi	.. ..	2nd March
Delhi to Baghdad	.. ..	4th March
Leave Baghdad	.. ..	5th March
Arrive London	.. ..	6th March

Everywhere Eden went he was well received. He helped Mr. Dulles to keep the Bangkok conference on its course; he had long chats with Mr. Nehru; he talked to Colonel Nasser in Cairo, establishing an improved relationship between Egypt and Britain; from both Dulles and Nehru he was able to get a clue to their policy regarding Formosa, which could be the flash point for a war between the United States and the Communist Republic of China. India can exert influence on China, whilst Britain is in close accord with the United States. Eden's visit did something to bridge the gap between China and America. He was able to show the need to avoid any premature resort to arms by either side. In such negotiations Eden has an enormous advantage. Nobody regards him as a politician who has worked his way to a temporary position of power; he is accepted as the epitome of British decency and discipline. His moral authority has enabled him, on many occasions, to bring dissentients together.

The tour was in keeping with his attitude to modern diplomacy. The Foreign Office may look a sooty, sleepy building but its occupants can hurry when they want to and Eden had certainly set an example. The leisurely ways of past Foreign Ministers such as Castlereagh or Canning are hardly suitable in a world where countries can be annihilated at the touch of a button. But although Eden returned looking fit and well, the trip did exhaust him. Shortly after his return he contracted influenza and had to postpone a projected visit to Turkey, at which he wished to discuss Middle East defence. Sir Anthony and Lady Eden spent a week at their cottage in Wiltshire before taking up work again. Sir Winston had made his plans for retirement, and must have been wondering anxiously if Eden's illness would once again jeopardise his succession.

But all went smoothly—almost too smoothly, because thanks to a newspaper strike, one of the most dramatic moments in British political history was missed by the British public. Without sure information, the thousands who would undoubtedly have gathered wherever Sir Winston Churchill appeared did not know what to do. Many were not sure that he had in fact resigned until they heard it on the radio or saw it happen, days later, in newsreel shots.

On the first floor of No. 10, Downing Street, Sir Winston Churchill entertained the Queen and the Duke of Edinburgh. Sir Winston and Sir Anthony wore full court dress, the Garter ribbon and George, and the Garter itself. A small crowd saw the door of No. 10 open and Sir Winston open the car door for the young Queen, bowing low as he did so. As a young cavalry subaltern he had served her great-great-grandmother. Now it was time for him to go, to hand over to Sir Anthony, whom he had tried, tested and groomed over the years.

The following afternoon Sir Winston, in black frock-coat, top hat and carrying a gold-tipped cane, arrived at Buckingham Palace. The Queen, said the official announcement, " has been graciously pleased to accept his resignation as Prime Minister and First Lord of the Treasury." In the House of Commons everyone waited in the hope that Sir Winston would appear and make a dramatic farewell; but this, one feels, would have been too moving an experience for him. Sir Winston did not appear.

On Wednesday, April 6th, 1955, Eden's great moment came, the climax of a lifetime of public service. He was received in audience by the Queen, accepted the office of Prime Minister, and kissed hands on his appointment. In the afternoon he appeared in the House of Commons for the first time as Prime Minister and in moving words praised the courage of his old chief—" the courage which expresses itself not only in the first enthusiastic burst of fervour but that endures also, perhaps the rarer gift of the two." Eden was succeeding one of the greatest Prime Ministers in British history, a man of robust personality, salty wit and vigorous independence; Eden, it seemed must suffer by comparison. Eden was Sir Winston's deliberate choice and he had years of empirical experience to go upon. In Eden's integrity, judgment and capacities Sir Winston has unlimited confidence. And of course, Sir Anthony must succeed him as leader of the Conservative Party too. Nominating Eden as his successor in the Tory party, Sir Winston wrote: " . . . who will, I am sure, sustain the highest interests and traditions of Britain, and uphold the cause of Tory democracy which Lord Beaconsfield proclaimed, which Lord Randolph revived and which I have tried to serve."

Sir Anthony waved cheerfully to the crowds which greeted him in Downing Street, and seemed fitter and happier than he had ever looked before. The press gave him a warm welcome, although *The Scotsman* remarked that " it would be a help if he could now develop a sense of humour." Telegrams of greetings and good wishes flooded in from all over the world. At last Eden was the supreme political leader of Britain. But for how long? The time for a new General Election was drawing near. If the Conservatives were to lose this election, Eden would miss the opportunity of a lifetime, a chance he had awaited patiently for years.

* * *

Eden, beyond doubt, was a popular choice, both as Prime Minister and leader of the Conservative Party. True, some Tories had their misgivings. They felt that Eden lacked the popular touch and might lose working class votes. But on April 21st, at Church House, Westminster, over a thousand Tory leaders, including Members of Parliament, prospective candidates and a committee representing the local Associations, gave Eden a rousing welcome and elected him leader of the Conservative Party. There was new vigour and definiteness in his delivery—perhaps the opportunity makes the man, and with authority fully in his grasp he may throw off the last semblance of diffidence and reserve. " If we hold to our faith," Eden told the meeting, " we can do that which after all is our heart's true wish to do; serve our country, our Empire and the world." It is interesting to note that he disdained the use of the word Commonwealth, so often used as a euphemism for Empire. Mr. R. A. Butler, whom many felt might have succeeded Sir Winston, paid a generous tribute to Sir Anthony: " I am perfectly clear that he has three great qualities for leadership.

The first is courage; the second is integrity; the third is flair."

For a while Sir Anthony and Lady Eden continued to live at their old residence in Carlton Gardens, although officially in possession of No. 10, Downing Street. Their furniture had to be moved, and Lady Eden spent hours planning where it was to go.

At the same time Lady Eden accompanied her husband to political meetings, and had overcome her original shyness to such an extent that she was now quite at home on a platform. She also had a vivid insight in the ensuing weeks on just how much work her husband can get through. During his election programme Eden travelled over 2,000 miles and addressed over 80,000 at forty different meetings—all within four weeks. Although it was a somewhat colourless election, Eden's meetings were marked with extraordinary enthusiasm. At Leamington, his constituency, the streets were lined with cheering crowds, and prolonged cheers and singing greeted him as he rose to speak. He recalled his first election speech there in 1923, as " an inexperienced youth ", and in a simple, relaxed way thanked them for their support. " I have never seen Eden more human, more happy and more relaxed," one spectator told me afterwards. But since his second marriage this lack of edginess has been constantly remarked upon by those who know him well.

Lady Eden accompanied her husband throughout the tour. On one day he addressed no fewer than six different meetings. In his Party political broadcast he coined the phrase " first a deterrent to prevent aggression; then disarmament to make it impossible. That is why we speak of the hydrogen bomb as a deterrent. Both parties are agreed that we should make the hydrogen bomb, just as the Socialist Government made the atom bomb. To draw back now would be to abandon our own defence and leave it to others. No great nation can do that. On the other hand, the more we can reduce international tension, the less are the chances that any bomb will ever be used."

In a speech opening the campaign at Leeds, Eden gave his ten-point programme, devoting half of his speech to foreign affairs. His programme was peace and security; attempts to bring about meetings with the leaders of the Soviet Union;

disarmament when compatible with security; the improvement of standards of living in the Commonwealth and Empire; an increased standard of living at home; the peaceful application of nuclear energy; more personal freedom for everyone; better schools and housing; the modernisation and equipment of railways and the building of new roads; and legislation to improve working conditions.

As Election Day drew nearer, Eden scored a triumph for the Conservative Party on television. In an 18-minute talk, without a script and with no prompter he talked of foreign and home affairs " like a family doctor who had a simple and reasoned explanation for the hopes, fears and ills of the nation." Cleverly, he avoided any harsh criticism of his political opponents allowing it to be inferred that their competition did not worry him. But at all his political meetings he warned his audience not be complacent.

Eden led his party with a vigour and confidence it had not known for years. There is nothing apologetic about his Toryism. He believes in it, whereas some Conservatives have given young people the impression that they embrace the creed because they are frightened of anything different. And he does not dodge awkward questions or situations. When a heckler was manhandled at one of his meetings he pleaded with the audience to leave him alone. When a deputation from the local Trades Council called on him in Leamington after a gruelling day of speech-making and travelling, he answered all their questions civilly and in detail. Several of the members were Communists, and their questions were often based on false premises. They asked about Nazi war criminals being given positions of responsibility in Germany. Immediately Eden nailed them down; *which* war criminals; *what* jobs had they been given, and *where*? Sulkily they withdrew.

The following day Sir Anthony and Lady Eden knew that they could settle in to No. 10, Downing Street and make themselves at home. Sir Anthony had retained his seat for Warwick and Leamington by a majority of over 13,000; and the Conservative Government had been returned to power, this time with a good working majority.

TWENTY-SEVEN

Eden the Man

SIR ANTHONY EDEN is one of the best known, yet least understood men in the world. Hardly anywhere would he escape recognition. Yet most people, asked to list his positive achievements, would find themselves in considerable difficulty. What decisions has he made which have yielded tangible dividends? British foreign policy, with which he was to some extent identified in the thirties, did not prevent a war; but perhaps nothing could have done that. His work during the war defies final assessment, for the fruits of many of the decisions made in concert with Sir Winston Churchill have yet to come; the legacy of the Yalta Conference, for example, is very different from what most people hoped for. Similarly with the settlement in Indo-China; it is a good thing that fighting has ceased, but half of Viet Nam is now in Communist hands. Will the Communists be content with this limited conquest, or will they, like Hitler after Munich, take the rest of the country at their own leisure? And Britain's promise to keep an Army in Europe for fifty years—only the future will show the implications of this gesture for good or ill. What is certain is that Anthony Eden has seen enough of dictators and dictatorships to know the uselessness of negotiating from weakness. After years of work, it looks as though the North Atlantic Treaty Organisation and the other pacts negotiated as an insurance against Communist aggression in the West have achieved at least a temporary immunity. And there are signs that Russia realises that her technique of conquest by internal intrigue has been studied and understood by her potential victims.

But for the moment, Eden's achievements cannot be assessed. What of Eden the man? At 58 he is still handsome, still lithe and athletic, resilient and energetic. He has a gargantuan appetite for work, and he is backed by a long record of empirical knowledge. Most of the capitals of the world are as familiar to him as London. He knows more international personalities than any other living statesman, and he converses fluently in many languages. He speaks in Persian to the Shah of Persia, in Arabic to King Ibn Saud, in French to M. Mendes-France.

Politics have monopolised almost all his life ever since his youth. Gardening, swimming, golf, gin-rummy, reading, tennis, country walks and visits to art galleries take up what little spare time he has. He dislikes small talk, cocktail parties and night clubs.

It is Eden's psychic make-up which is so elusive. What makes him tick? Those who knew him well in his early days describe him as a dull, colourless man with no humour and a flair for making long, vague speeches; clearly that estimate is incomplete. There are many dull men in the world, but they do not become Prime Minister. What has raised him to such eminence? Application; patience; an understanding of the rather dreary mechanics of government, conferences, international parleys and general administration; a sense of thoroughness and detail; an ability to mix well; a knowledge of constitutional and Parliamentary procedure; courage; sincerity.

His application showed itself early in life, when for instance, he chose Oriental Studies as a subject at Oxford, and gained a First. Patience he has shown on numberless occasions; for years he was Sir Winston Churchill's understudy, a job which could never have been an easy one. Indeed, some of the most handsome tributes to Eden have come from his political opponents. Mr. Richard Crossman, one of his fiercest critics, said of Eden's negotiations over Indo-China: " . . . the result of his courage and patience is the Geneva Agreement, the most hopeful thing which has happened since World War II." And *The Times* remarked, after the Geneva conference: " Mr. Eden and M. Mendes-France have averted one of the most acute dangers of a great war that the world has faced since 1946."

Of his courage, Eden gave ample proof in the first World War. Even in those days his Commanding Officer, Major Foljambe (later killed in action) recognised in Eden, then only 18, a lad " with a great future before him."

After Eden had rescued the Western security scheme, Mr. Walter Lippmann declared " Mr. Eden has achieved a brilliant success." Similar praise came from President Eisenhower, Mr. John Foster Dulles, M. Mendes-France and others. Even M. Molotov has praised Eden's " genuine and sustained effort."

The very qualities which make Eden achieve these things are those which are least spectacular from a dramatic point of view. Caution is not as exciting as caprice; a man attracts more attention if he raves instead of reasons; keeping the peace is quite as hard, but rather more thankless, than winning a war. Nor does he always lack spontaneity; his lightning tour of European capitals after the collapse of E.D.C. was a snap decision made solely by himself.

On the debit side, he is without rhetoric. He scores best in the serious exposition of serious topics. He has little sense of humour. He is at ease in company, but I would not say that he is especially gregarious; he is with people but not of them. There is about him an intellectual insularity, coupled, one feels, with a suspicion that anything that is not serious and solemn cannot be worth while. He is given to flashes of temper, although overwork or emotional strain could have accounted for much of that. But I would say that he is incapable of any mean act; there is nothing petty about him, and when he has lost his temper he has been quick to apologise.

What makes him lose his temper? I look at my catalogue of incidents. (1) He is gambling at Cannes in 1938, trying out a special system; he leaves the table and asks a woman in the party to play his hand; she doesn't comprehend the system and bungles it; result—an angry scene. (2) A hostess, hoping to land one of her male friends a job, invites the Foreign Secretary with the express hope that her protégé will meet with approval. Her protégé drinks too much before Eden arrives, and in order to appear well informed, criticises the " poor progress " being made by the Allies at Caen. White with anger, Eden trounces the foolish youth for denigrating brave men whilst flourishing a cocktail glass. (3) When he is in opposition, an appointment is made with him at the House of Commons for him to meet some Italian visitors who are on a tour of Britain. A representative of the Government department which was organising the programme arrived on time, but the visitors did not. The goverment employee got the full measure of Eden's wrath. (4) Eden arrives in Portugal on honeymoon and refuses to accept the hotel reservation because there is no swimming pool.

But what is the common theme? He was angry at (1) stupidity; (2) selfish conceit; (3) inefficieney and (4) a broken promise. However, there is not always a good reason for his irritability, except that he feels that way.

Lord Norwich thought Eden " sensitive." John Winant, American Ambassador during the war years, found him " simple, truthful and courageous." Mussolini thought him " the best-dressed fool in Europe." Mr. Woodrow Wyatt, a parliamentary opponent, thinks that " under that polished exterior is a quality of mysticism which induces him to rely on intuition more than on hard facts." Sir Gerald Barry has described Eden as " a man who speaks with the authority of moral conviction." His neighbours, his Party colleagues and those who have worked with him are unanimous about his integrity and sincerity.

Eden, I feel, has not yet reached the climax of his career. So far, even in authority, he has always been overshadowed by others, although they were far from getting their own way with him all the time. Now he has risen to full stature and authority. Of course, any man succeeding Sir Winston Churchill must suffer by comparison. Sir Anthony lacks Sir Winston's verve, colour, robust humour and sense of the dramatic, nor does Eden relax easily. He tends to overwork, and not to delegate as much as he might; this physical strain, which has often taxed his health dangerously, could account for the anæmic quality of some of his speeches. On the other hand, since Eden is a patient negotiator, he often avoids direct references which might offend the very people from whom he seeks co-operation; and a good poker player should not reveal his hand too soon, Perhaps authority will develop these other qualities in him. After all, Eden has proved himself thoughout the years not simply as a man of reserve but a man with reserves. He can easily be under-estimated, and does not seem to mind if he is. For example, the imagination, drive and daring which he displayed during the E.D.C. crisis in 1954 were certainly not evident in 1923; " I never heard such dreary speeches in my life," I was told by a reporter who covered that election. "Would you have considered it feasible that in time Captain Eden could have become Prime Minister?" I asked. "Feasible!" answered my informant, "I'd have said it was impossible. And I would have been wrong."

Is he a showman? Is his dandyism a sign of vanity? I think that his mother's comment on this trait of his holds good still; it was to get on in his job. The Foreign Office expect its employees to be smart. "In order to choose my perfect diplomatist," said Mr. Frank Ashton-Gwatkin, former Assistant Under-Secretary at the Foreign Office, in the course of a lecture to Syracuse University in 1949, "... I would look first at his personal appearance. He need not be an Apollo. But he has to represent Great Britain, and the undersized, crablike, scruffy type simply will not do. These are not articles for export."

"Eden," Randolph Churchill has said, "has been notably successful in keeping his private life private." Churchill revels in contact with all and sundry. Eden tries to like it, and is more at ease than he used to be, but he is certainly more remote. I would not call him "inhibited" as some critics have done. Restrained would be a better word—and his restraint, it is worth remembering, has enabled him to produce order out of chaos when a bull-in-a-china-shop approach would have been disastrous.

Eden is English. In his passion for fair play and integrity he has achieved for himself a moral authority amongst nations of totally different creeds and politics which must be almost unique. For people all over the world he typifies the ideal Englishman. I think he keeps alive ideals which have been gravely jeopardised by two world wars. He works for international peace, but is realistic enough to know that twisting the lion's tail is a game which must stop. Britain has given the world much, and has yet much to give.

One day another biography may have to be written of Sir Anthony Eden. Undiscovered aspects of his elusive personality may yet be revealed, whilst his diplomatic achievements can be better assessed when put to the test of time. Sir Anthony Eden has not reached the climax of his career. He has started a new one.

BIBLIOGRAPHY

The following works have been consulted in the course of compiling this biography, and the author wishes to express his thanks to the authors and publishers concerned:—

The Annual Registers; Longmans, Green & Co.
A Letter from Grosvenor Square; J. G. Winant. Hodder & Stoughton, 1947.
British Prime Ministers; Allan Wingate, 1953.
British Politics Since 1900; D. C. Somervell. Dakers, 1950.
Ciano's Diary, 1937-8; Methuen, 1952.
Ciano's Diplomatic Papers; Odhams, 1948.
Days For Decision; Anthony Eden. Faber & Faber, 1949.
Europe Since 1914 in its World Setting; F. Lee Benns. Indiana University.
Europe in Decay; L. B. Namier. Macmillan, 1950.
Foreign Affairs; Anthony Eden. Faber & Faber, 1939.
Freedom & Order; Anthony Eden. Faber & Faber, 1947.
The Goebbels Diaries; Hamish Hamilton, 1948.
History of *The Times*.
Hitler: a Study in Tyranny; Alan Bullock (Odhams).
Hansard.
The Life of Neville Chamberlain; Keith Feiling. Macmillan, 1946.
The Memoirs of Cordell Hull; Hodder & Stoughton, 1948.
Memoirs of Dr. Edouard Benes; Allen & Unwin, 1954.
Munich: Prologue to Tragedy; J. W. Wheeler-Bennett. Macmillan.
Nine Troubled Years; Viscount Templewood. Collins, 1954.
Old Men Forget; Duff Cooper. Hart-Davis, 1953.
Orders of the Day; Earl Winterton. Cassell, 1953.
Places in the Sun; Anthony Eden. John Murray, 1926.
The Reign of King George V; D. C. Somervell. Faber & Faber, 1935.
Roosevelt and the Russians; Edward R. Stettinius. Cape, 1950.
The Second World War; Sir Winston Churchill. Cassell, 1948.
Stanley Baldwin; G. M. Young. Hart-Davis, 1925.

BIBLIOGRAPHY

The State of the Poor; William Morton Eden. B. & J. White, 1797.

The Semi-Attached Couple; Emily Eden. Mathews & Marrot, Ltd., 1927.

Step by Step; Sir Winston Churchill. Macmillan, 1942.

The Struggle for Europe; Chester Wilmot. Collins, 1952.

Survey of International Affairs.

Two Frenchmen; Laval and De Gaulle. D. Thomson. Cresset Press, 1951.

The Thirties; Malcolm Muggeridge. Hamish Hamilton, 1940.

Tribulations of a Baronet; Sir Timothy Eden. Macmillan, 1933.

White House Papers of Harry L. Hopkins; Eyre & Spottiswoode, 1949.

INDEX

ABYSSINIA, 133, 135, 138, 139, 140, 141, 146, 150 151 152, 153, 154, 157, 160, 162, 175, 180, 183–4–5, 190–1, 195, 198, 206.
Adenauer, Dr., 304.
Admiralty, Lord of, 16, 17, 135
Afghanistan, 17
Aga Khan, 231
Air Convention, 124
Air Pact, 148
A.R.P., 220
Albania, 20, 216, 274
Alexander, King of Yugoslavia, 118
Alexander, Field-Marshal, 253
Ali, Rizi, Dr., 260
Allies, Conference of, 233
Amery, 148, 224
Anglo-Egyptian Treaties, 157, 293
Anglo-French Convention, 87
Anglo-German Naval Agreement, 135–6
Anglo-Italian Agreement, 196, 205
Anglo-Russian Agreement, 233, 298
Annual Register, 294
Arabic Language, 44, 313
Arcos Raid, 81
Arundel, Earl of, 12
Ashby, Mrs. Corbett, 100
Ashton-Gwatkin, Frank, 316
Assheton, Mr., 294
Atlantic Charter, 238
Atom Bomb, 265, 282
Attfield, Major Philip, 289
Attlee, Major Clement, 113, 115, 148, 153, 166, 167, 198, 250, 260, 262
Aukland, George, Earl of, 14, 17, 19
Aukland, N.Z., 17
Australia, 69, 71, 148, 219, 222, 272
Austria, 83, 113, 117, 124, 126, 136, 168, 173, 176, 182, 186–7–8, 190, 194, 198, 200, 204, 206, 276, 291, 297, 303
Austrian Requiem by Dr. Schuschnigg, 176
Axis, 135, 185, 241
Azana, President, 156

BADOGLIO, MARSHAL, 243
Baldwin, Stanley, Lord, 54, 59, 65–6 –7, 71, 77, 85, 88, 90, 92, 94, 98, 121, 134, 142, 150, 166, 168, 169, 170

Barry, Sir Gerald, 315
Barthou, 117–8
Batey, John, 45
Baxter, Beverley, 43
Beauchamp, Anthony, 286
Beaverbrook, Lord, 72, 163, 394
Beaton, Cecil, 285
Beck, Colonel, 129, 216
Beckett, Sir Gervase, 37, 48, 203
Beckett, Beatrice (*see* Eden)
Beckett, Lady, 37
Beckett, Rupert, 266
Belgium, 67, 158–9, 222, 253, 269, 282, 303
Benes, Dr., 129, 205, 207, 214, 236, 270
Bengal, 19
Bennett, Lt.-Col. R. L., 217
Berlin, 15, 113, 125, 126, 195, 247
Berlin Conference, 297–8
Berliner Tageblatt, 185
Betjeman, John, 46
Bevan, Aneurin, 304
Bevin, Ernest, 232, 257, 262, 265, 291
Bhutan, 19
Binderton House, nr. Chichester, 231, 262, 266, 290
Birkenhead, Lord, 66
Birmingham Post, 273
Bishop Auckland, 22
Bismarck, 205
Blanche, 29
Blatchford, John, 46
Bolivia, 118, 134
Bonfield, Margaret, 93
Bonham-Carter, Lady Violet, 200, 212
Bonomi, Signor, 252
Boothby, Robert, 218
Boris, King of Bulgaria, 145
Bova-Scoppa, Renato, 175
Bracken, Viscount, 286
British Ally, 284
Broadstairs, 19
Broke, Lord Willoughby de, 54
Brooke, Lord, 48, 51
Bruning, 102
Brussels Conference, 182
Brussels Treaty, 303
Bulgaria, 83
Bullitt, 127
Burma, 19, 250, 263, 271
Butler, R. A., 290–1, 294, 309

319

CADOGAN, SIR ALEXANDER, 185, 256
Cairo Conference, 245
Caley, Philip, 217
Cambodia, 301
Campbell, Lady, 18
Canada, 70, 219, 221, 241, 248, 263, 266, 272, 276–7, 282, 285, 303–4
Carlton Club, 123
Carlton Gardens, 289, 294, 299, 310
Carol, King of Rumania, 145
Carpenter, Boyd, 54
Carr, Robert, 277
Castle, Mrs. Barbara, 291
Cattell, Dr. Richard, 295
Cecil, Lord, 82
Chamberlain, Sir Austen, 66, 74, 77, 81–93, 150, 182
Chamberlain, Lady, 182–3, 197
Chamberlain, Neville, 88, 94, 139, 141, 151, 169, 170–1–2–3–4–5–6–7–8 –9, 180–1–2–3–4–5–6, 189 190–1, 194–5–6, 198–9, 200–1–2, 205–6–7–8 212, 214–5–6–7–8–9, 222
Chamberlain, Mrs. N., 202
Charles II, King of England, 11, 12
Chequers, 290, 295
Chenhalls, Mr., 243
Chesterfield St., No. 4, 281
Chiang Kai-Shek, 245
Chilston, Lord, 127, 129
China, 23, 79, 97, 99, 102, 134, 171, 173, 179, 206, 274, 282, 293, 299, 300–1, 397
Chaco Commission, 118
Chou En Lai, 301
Christ Church College, Oxford, 12, 15, 34, 43
Christies', 19
Church of England Year Book, 288
The *Church Times*, 287
Churchill, Clarissa (*see* Eden)
Churchill, Ernest Lee, 34
Churchill, John, 286
Churchill, Peregrine, 286
Churchill, Randolph, 286, 316
Churchill, Sarah (Mrs. Anthony Beauchamp), 256, 286
Churchill, Winston, 1, 23, 66, 75–6, 92–3, 106, 117, 121, 145, 156, 169, 193, 199, 205, 208, 212, 215–6–7, 219, 222–3–4–5–6–7, 231, 233, 235– 6–7–8, 240, 242–3, 245, 248–9, 250– 1–2–3, 256–7, 269–1–2–3, 265, 269, 270, 272–3, 278–9, 281, 286, 293, 295–6, 301–2, 307–8–9, 312–3, 315
Ciano, Count, 160, 162, 173–4–5–6, 180, 182–3, 186, 189, 191, 205
Civil Defence, 213
Cole, Percy, 49
Collective Security, 27, 83, 109, 126, 130, 147, 150–1, 163–4, 167–8, 176, 179, 186
Colliers' Magazine, 271
Commandos, 225
Committee of Eighteen, 146
Communists, 71, 78, 100, 102, 108, 126, 156, 161, 166-7, 204, 233, 235, 252, 258, 269, 271, 274, 279, 281, 291, 294, 299, 300, 311–2
Concentration Camps, 186, 204
Conference of Mayors, 88, 98
Conservative Party, 23, 65–6, 73, 91, 94, 140, 164, 168, 206, 214–5, 219, 242, 256, 262–3, 265, 271, 276, 278, 291, 295, 299, 304, 307–8–9, 310, 315
Conservative Party Central Office, 45, 189, 263, 278
Conversion Loans, 92
Cook, A. J., 91
Cooper, Duff (later Lord Norwich), 199, 215, 285, 315
Copenhagen, 15
Council of Action 203
Cranbourne Lord, 196–7, 201, 232–3
Cranbourne, Lady, 232
Cripps, Sir Stafford, 114–5, 233, 255
Curzon, Lord, 63, 66
Czechoslovakia, 67, 128–9, 133, 204–5, 207–8, 213–4, 216, 236, 269, 270, 297

" DAILY EXPRESS," The, 72, 195
Daily Herald, 195
Daily Mail, 72, 75
Daily Mirror, 275, 295, 299, 301–2, 305
Daily Telegraph, 195
Dalton, Hugh, 216
Damaskinos, Archbishop, 253
Das Kapital by Karl Marx, 16
Dawes Report, 59, 63
Daladier, 105, 116, 214
Delbos, 175
Delew, Mrs. Jane, 287
Denmark, 222
Devine, John, 274
Devonshire, Duke of, 281
Dewhurst, Prof. R. Paget, 44
Dickenson, Patrick, 211
Diplomatic Twilight by Sir Walford Selby, 178
Disarmament, 60, 82, 98, 102, 105, 108–9, 112, 114, 118, 120, 126
Dolfuss, Dr. 117
Dost Mahommed, 17
Doumergue, President, 117
Dulles, John Foster, 293–4, 299, 300, 303–4, 307, 314
Dunkirk, 224

320

EASTERN PACT, 126, 128–9
Eden, Sir Anthony, Descent 11, Birth 22, Childhood 26, On cruelty to animals 32, Religious education 33–4, Volunteered for Army 37, At the Front 40, Military Cross 41, At Oxford 43, Lecture on Cezanne 44, Finals 44, First election 45, Married 48, Elected to Parliament 55, Takes seat 57, Maiden speech 59–60, First parliamentary appointment 68, Birth of son 69, World tour 70, To the Foreign Office 74, Under-Secretary for Foreign Affairs 95, Lord Privy Seal 111, Visit to Hitler 115, Off duty 123, in Berlin 125–6, in Moscow 127–8, Breakdown 130, Minister without Portfolio 131, Foreign Minister 142, Resignation 192, in U.S.A. 208–9–10–11, Joined up 217, Secretary for the Dominions 219, Secretary for War 222, Chairman of the Committee of Ministers 225, Return to the Foreign Office 226, Meets Stalin 234, Leader of the House of Commons 237–8, Reform of the Foreign Office 239, in U.S.A. 240–1, Attempt on life 242, Deputy Prime Minister 250, Hon. Air Commodore 260, At Roosevelt's funeral 260, Duodenal ulcer 262, in Opposition 265, Made Director of Westminster Bank 266, Parted from Mrs. B. Eden 267, Appendicitis 269, Collapses 273, Divorced 275, Honorary Degrees 276, Foreign Secretary again 279, Engaged 283, Married 283, Cronic Colecystitus 294, Knighthood and Order of the Garter 305, Wateler Peace Prize 305, Prime Minister 308, Speeches 100, 109, 118, 120, 131, 157, 161, 164, 166, 179, 186, 201, 206, 208–9, 210, 219, 220–1, 223, 229, 235–6, 241–2, 247, 262, 267, 271–2, 277, 280–1, 292–3, 295, 300, 310
Speeches in the House of Commons 59, 62, 74, 80, 85, 92, 96, 100, 105, 115, 137, 146, 149, 151, 162, 171, 196, 222, 228, 238–9, 245, 247–8–9, 252, 254, 259, 265–6, 268, 277, 280, 294, 300
Letters 36, 39, 41, 192, 202
Election Address 49
Press Article, 73
Clothes 35, 111, 120, 126, 143, 165, 209, 232, 299, 305

Eden, Sir Ashley, 19

Eden, Beatrice (*née* Beckett), 48, 69, 85, 89, 194, 122, 123, 127, 130, 143, 149, 154 166 183, 192, 197, 202, 203, 208–9 227–8 232, 252-3, 255, 262, 267, 274–5, 285, 290, 302
Eden, Lady Clarissa (*née* Churchill) 283–4–5–6–7–8–9, 290, 294–5–6, 302 307, 310–1
Eden, Eleanor, 13
Eden, Eleanor (Lady Hobart), 14
Eden, Emily, 13–4, 17–8
Eden, Major the Hon. Evelyn, 48
Eden, Fanny, 14, 19
Eden, Sir Frederick Morton, 16
Eden, George, 16
Eden, Sir John, 12, 15
Eden, John, 22, 39
Eden, John, 286
Eden, Lena, 19
Eden, Marjorie, Countess of Warwick 22, 48, 239
Eden, Morton, Lord Henley, 15
Eden, Nicholas, 122, 192, 203, 267–8, 274–5, 277, 282, 285, 295
Eden, Sir Robert, 1st Baronet of West Auckland, 12
Eden, Sir Robert, 15, 240
Eden, Simon Gascoign, 69, 122, 203, 250, 263
Eden, Lady Sybil, 22, 24, 31, 33, 42, 45, 104, 123, 143, 155, 262
Eden, Sir Timothy, 22–3, 28, 30, 34, 42, 103, 123, 286
Eden, William, 12
Eden, Sir William, Bt., 4th Baronet of Maryland and Baronet of West Auckland, 20
Eden, Sir William, 5th Baronet, 21–2, 34–5, 38, 122, 231
Eden, County of, New Zealand, 17
Eden Farm, Beckenham, 14
Eden Lodge, Kensington Gore, 19
Edinburgh, Duke of, 308
E.D.C., 282, 298–9, 300, 302–3, 305, 314–5
Edward VIII, King of England, 90, 145, 159, 288
Egypt, 23, 82, 92, 202, 222, 225, 274, 279, 280, 283, 291, 292, 307
Eisenhower, General Dwight, 257, 293–4, 314
Elizabeth II, Queen of England, 294, 302, 394, 308
Ellenborough, Lord, 17
Empire Settlement, 80
Empress of France, S.S., 277
Entente Cordiale, 81
Eton College, 12, 30, 34, 42, 263
Extra Territorial Privileges, 92

FARINACCI, SIGNOR, 189
Fascism, 89, 102, 108, 113, 117, 120, 132, 157, 161, 166-7-8, 173 177, 183, 185, 189, 191, 199, 215, 281
Faversham, Earl of, 37
Finland, 235, 251
Fitzhardinge St., No. 17, 111, 192, 203, 222, 260
Flandin, M., 124, 145
Foljambe, Major, 40, 313
Foreign Office, White Paper on the reform of, 239
Four Power Pact, 107, 112
France, 20, 67, 76, 81-2, 87, 93, 99, 100, 105, 107-8-9, 112, 118, 124, 128, 130, 135-6, 139, 148-9, 157-8-9, 163, 167, 175, 177, 183-4-5, 187-8, 194, 198, 200, 203, 205, 207, 212, 216, 218, 220-1, 223, 225, 229, 236, 238-9, 244, 248-9, 250-1-2-3, 258, 270, 281-2, 295, 298-9, 301-2-3, 305
Franco, General, 156, 161, 164-5 174, 181, 205, 212-3, 215, 233, 247-8
Freedom and Order, the Collected Speeches of Sir Anthony Eden, 268
Free Trade, 1, 59
Freemasons, 187

GALLAGHER, WILLIAM, 166
Garbo, Greta, 285
Gaulle, General de, 224, 248, 251 253, 261
Gayda, Signor, 185
General Strike, 66, 75-6, 81, 108
Geneva, 74, 82, 98, 105, 111, 123, 127, 135, 142 150, 172, 302
Geneva Conference, 299, 300-2, 305
Geneva Protocol, 83-4-5, 98
George V, King of England, 59, 94, 131, 139, 142-3, 145
George VI, King of England, 165, 237, 249
George, King of the Hellenes, 250, 253
George, Lloyd, 74, 152, 180, 200, 210, 217
Germany, 63, 67, 74, 83, 86-7, 93, 99, 100-1-2, 104-5, 108, 112-3, 117, 121-2, 124-5, 128, 130-1, 134, 138, 145, 149, 156, 158-9, 160-1-2, 165, 168-9, 170, 172-3, 175, 180-1-2-3-4-5-6-7-8, 194, 198, 200-1, 205, 208, 212-3-4-5-6, 218-9, 220-1-2, 224, 228, 230, 233-4-5, 238, 240-1, 243, 248-9, 250-1-2, 255, 258-9, 263, 270, 277, 279, 281-2-3, 297-8, 302-3-4-5, 311

Giraud, General, 236, 249
Gloucester, Duke of, 220
Goebbels, Dr., 117, 221, 239, 241, 243
Goering, General, 162, 199, 204
Gold Standard, 66, 104
Golding, Louis, 43
Graham, Mr., 24
Grandi, Count, 148, 157, 171, 173-4, 177, 186, 189, 190-1
Granville, Earl of, 145
Greece, 226-7-8-9, 236-7, 248-9, 250, 253-4, 265, 291, 295
Greenwood, Arthur, 152
Greville, the Hon. Louis, 51
Grey, Sir Edward. 172
Grigson, Geoffrey, 70

HAILE SELASSIE, 150, 152-3, 158, 160 195, 228
Hailsham, Viscount, 100
Halifax, Lord, 181-2, 184, 193, 197, 212, 226-7, 260
Hansard, 92
Harriman, Avril, 232, 244
Harrop, Sergeant W. H., 40
Hedges, Dr. Robert, 275
Henderson, Arthur, 108
Henderson, Sir Neville, 213
Herkomer, 29
Herriot, M., 63
Hess, Rudolph, 117
Hicks, Sir William Joynson, 66, 68
Hitler, Adolph, 38, 58, 100, 107-8-9, 112, 115, 117, 119, 121, 124-5-6, 135, 141, 145, 148-9, 154, 158, 160, 162, 168-9, 174, 176, 178, 180-1-2, 184, 187-8, 194, 196, 200, 204-5, 207, 213-4, 216, 220-1, 228, 230, 233, 244, 248, 260, 270, 312
Hoare, Sir Samuel (later Lord Templewood), 59, 60, 132, 134, 138, 140-1-2, 150, 164, 167, 170, 173, 213
Hoare-Laval Pact, 140-1, 145, 171, 198, 200
Hobson, Captain, 17
Hodson, Mr. Justice, 275
Holiday, Mr., 286
Holland, 140, 222-3, 237, 251, 282, 303
Hopkins, Harry, 231, 240, 255
Howard, Leslie, 242-3
Hull, Cordell, 236, 244-5
A Hundred Commoners by James Johnston, 95
Hungary, 83, 118, 120, 270
Hunger March, 94
Hyderabad, 271

IBN SAUD, King of Saudi-Arabia, 269, 313
Imperial Press Conference, 69
India, 14, 17–8, 23, 92, 219, 222, 271–2, 301
India, Viceroy of, 243
India, Gov.-Gen. of, 16–7, 132
Indian Civil Service, 19
Indo-China, 298–9, 300, 305, 312–3
Industrial Revolution, 19
Inonu, General, 228
"An Instrument Dealer at his Booth in the Open Air" by Carel Fabricius, 20
International Peace Society, 108
International Transfer Committee, 63
Iran, 105
Iraq, 71–2
Islington, Lady, 286
Ismet Bey, 127
Italy, 20, 68, 73, 82, 87, 93, 100, 102, 104, 113, 130, 133, 135–6, 138–9, 140, 145–6, 150–1–2, 156, 160, 162, 168–9, 171, 173–4–5, 180, 183–4–5–6–7–8, 190–1, 194, 196, 198, 200–1, 205–6–7, 212, 216, 225, 228, 243, 245, 248, 250, 252–3, 275, 282, 291, 294–5, 303, 314.
Crown Prince of Italy, 243

JAPAN, 23, 82, 97, 99, 107, 128, 145, 171, 173, 179, 182, 234, 236, 247, 250, 265
Jewish People, 108, 122, 186–7, 204, 208, 220, 239
Jones, Morgan, 100

KEITEL, 207
Kellog, Mr., 86
Kellog Pact, 86
Kemal, Mustapha, 61
Kent, Duchess of, 252, 284
Kent, H.M.S., 234
King, Mackenzie, 266
Kitchener, Lord, 166
Knox, William, 15
Korda, Sir Alexander, 284
Korea, 279, 280–1–2–3, 298–9, 300

LABOUR PARTY, 91, 95, 108, 130, 137, 153, 266, 270, 274, 291
La Guardia, Mayor, 209
Lansbury, George, 126
Laos, 301
La Rochelle, 44
Laval, Pierre, 121, 124, 126, 136, 139, 140–1, 149, 171
Lawford, Nicholas, 285

League of Nations, 27, 64, 67, 71, 74, 76, 84, 86, 92, 96–7, 99, 104–5, 107–8, 111–2–3–4, 118, 121–2, 127, 131–2–3–4–5, 138–9, 140–1, 145–6, 148, 150–1–2–3–4–5, 157–8, 161–2–3, 167, 172, 175–6, 178–9, 180, 185, 193–4–5, 200–1, 205–6, 208, 212–3–4, 241, 251, 255
Lees-Smith, 146
Liberal Party, 23, 57, 91, 94–5, 137–8, 153, 216
Lindsay, Sir Ronald, 184
Linlithgow, Lord, 243
Lippmann, Walter, 314
Lithuania, 216
Litvinoff, Maxim, 64, 127, 214
Lloyd, Mr., 224
Locarno Treaty, 68, 71, 74, 85–6, 98, 105, 112, 148–9, 200
Locker-Lampson, Commdr. Godfrey, 68, 77, 81
Locks of St. James' St., 111
London Clinic, 294
Londonderry, Marquis of, 45
Luxembourg, 282, 303

MACMILLAN, HAROLD, 253
Maginot Line, 149, 220–1
Maisky, Ivan, 127, 157, 234
Malaya, 272, 291
Manchester Guardian, 195
Marshall, General, 240
Marshall Aid Scheme, 269, 291
Marx, Carl, 16
Maryland, U.S.A., 15, 240
Masaryk, Jan, 129, 269, 270
Massey, Vincent, 277, 282
Maxton, James, 92, 108
Mayhew, Christopher, 278
McDonald, Ramsay, 59, 63, 67, 74, 91, 93–4–5, 97, 99, 105, 108, 124, 130–1, 140,
Means Test, 94, 102
Mediterranean, 20, 150, 153, 158, 160, 162, 164, 170, 172, 174-5, 180, 183, 186
Melbourne, 69
Mendes-France, M., 302, 304, 313–4
Menzies, R. G., 219
Mesopotamia, 44
Middle Temple, 12
Mikolajczyk, 253
Military Cross, 41
Mint, Master of, 16
Molotov, Mr., 127, 234, 236, 244, 257–8, 298, 314
Monet, Claude, 295
Moore, George, 27
Morgenthau, Henry, 250

Moscow, 126, 218, 234, 244, 251, 266, 270
Moscow Conference, 251
Mosley, Sir Oswald, 94, 108
Mulberry Walk, No. 1, 56, 68, 86, 111
Munich Agreement, 207, 212, 214, 270
Munich: Prologue to Tragedy by John W. Wheeler-Bennett, 116
Muselier, Admiral, 249
Mussaddiq, 291
Mussolini, Benito, 100, 105, 108, 112, 115, 117, 121, 133–4, 136, 138–9, 140–1, 146, 150, 152, 154, 158, 160, 162, 168, 170–1–2, 174, 176–7, 180, 185, 188, 190–1, 194–5, 200, 204–5, 212, 218, 226, 243–4, 260

NAPIER, SIR WILLIAM, 17
Nasser, Colonel, 307
National Industrial Council, 76
National Labour Party, 95
National Unemployed Workers' Movement, 102
National Zeitung, 199
Naval Conference, 148
Nazi, 119, 122, 182, 186–7–8, 205, 218, 261, 311
Nehru, Mr., 307
Neurath, von, 117, 145
News Chronicle, 195
New York, 123, 209, 275, 281
New York Times, 209
New Zealand, 17, 69, 70–1, 219, 222, 248, 272
Nicholls, George, 51
Nichols, Beverley, 43
Nicholson, Brigadier, 224
Nine-Power Conference, 179
Nine Troubled Years by Lord Templewood, 169
Noble, Commander, 271, 274
Non-Aggression Pact, 148
Non-Intervention Committee of, 156, 162–3, 165, 171, 175, 181
North Atlantic Treaty, 279, 280, 282-3, 296–7–8–9, 300, 303–4, 312
North Africa, 225, 242, 248
North-West Provinces, 17
Norway, 222, 237
Norwich, Lord (*see* Cooper, Duff)

OGILVY, LADY, 195
Oxford, Lady, 283

PAKISTAN, 272
Palestine, 92
Palmer, Lt.-Col. Alan, 274

Pan-American Conference, 236
Panmunjon, 280
Papandrou, M., 250, 253
Paraguay, 118, 134
Paris Peace Conference, 83
Paul, Prince of Yugoslavia, 228
Peace Ballot, 137
Persia, 44, 268, 277, 279, 291, 302, 313
Perth, Lord, 186, 189, 205
Petain, Marshal, 224
Peter, King of Yugoslavia, 252
Philip, Prince of Hesse, 204
Pilsudski, 129
Phoenix Assurance Co., 268
Pitman, Senator, 210
Pitt, William, 14
Places in the Sun, by Sir Anthony Eden, 71
Plebiscite in the Saar, 120–1, 124
Ploegsteert, 40
Plumer, Lord, 42
Poland, 67, 129, 133, 215–6, 218, 220, 235, 237, 239, 240, 251, 253, 256, 258–9, 263, 270
Pollock, Sir Ernest, 46
The Pope, 117
Portraits of People and Places in India by Emily Eden, 18
Portugal, 242, 287, 289, 315
Potsdam Conference, 263, 265
Principles of Penal Law by William Eden, 12
Protection of Home Industry, 55, 59, 66

QUEBEC, 244, 250
Queen Elizabeth, S.S., 267
Quincy, H.M.S., 257

" RATTLESNAKE," THE, 17
Reading, Lord, 97
Rearmament, 96, 105, 110, 126, 130, 158, 161, 163, 168, 176, 200, 212, 280, 293, 302
Reed, Sir Carol, 284
Regima Fascista, 189
Regional Commissioners, 220
Reminiscences of a Whipper-In by Jack Bevans, 24
Reynaud, M., 224
Ribbentrop, Herr von, 135, 157
Rio Tinto Group, 268
Robins, R. W. V., 277
" The Rokeby Venus " by Velasquez, 20
Roman Catholics, 187, 294, 302
Rome Agreement, 124

Roosevelt, Franklyn Delano, 179, 184, 212, 214, 229, 231, 237, 240–1, 244–5, 250, 252, 255–6–7–8–9, 260–1, 271
Roosevelt, Mrs. Eleanor, 210
Rosebery, Lord, 144
Rothermere, Lord, 97
R.S.P.C.A., 155, 262
Roumania, 216
Runciman, Lord, 207
Ryan, John, 295

SAAR, 119, 121–2
St. Margaret's Church, Westminster, 48
Salisbury, Marquis and Marchioness, 286
Samuel, Sir Herbert, 67, 94
Sandroy School, Chobham, Surrey, 34
Sandys, Duncan, 286
Santal Rising, 19
Saudi Arabia, 269
Scalata, Senator, 176
Scarbrough, Lord, 43
Schuman Plan, 276, 280–1
Schuschnigg, Dr., 176, 187–8, 204
Scotsman, The, 309
The Second World War by Sir Winston Churchill, 217, 226, 242
The Second World War by M. Stoyadinovich, 181
Second Front, 235, 238, 248–9
Selby, Sir Walford, 178
Self, Sir Henry, 288
The Semi-Detatched Couple by Emily Eden, 18
The Semi-Detached Villa by Emily Eden, 18
Sergeant, 29
Seyss-Inquart, 188
Sforza, Count, 252
Sikkim, 19
Sikorski, General, 240, 261
Simon, Sir John, 97–8–9, 105, 108, 112–3, 121, 124–5–6, 130, 132, 135, 153, 167, 170, 173
Sinclair, Sir Archibald, 153, 216, 219
Sirus, H.M.S., 256
Smith, Adam, 16
Smith, Gipsy, 58
Snowden, Philip, 94
Soames, Christopher, 286
Socialists, 57, 87, 94, 114, 117, 122, 187, 197, 204, 208, 216, 262, 264, 274, 278, 310
South Africa, 219, 248
S.E.A.T.O., 306

Spain, 20, 100, 155, 160, 162, 165–6, 172–3, 175, 180, 185–6–7, 189, 190–1, 195–6, 198, 205–6, 213, 247
The Spectator, 132
Spencer, Lord, 2
Spencer-Churchill, Sir John, 283
Spencer-Churchill, Lady Gwendoline, 283
Spencer-Churchill, Sir John, 286
Spennymoor Division of Durham, 45
Stalin, Joseph, 127, 217, 234–5, 238, 241, 244–5, 255–6, 258–9, 263, 294
Stalingrad, 243, 245
The Star, 195
Starhemberg, Prince, 145
Stassen, Harold, 293
The State of the Poor by Sir Frederick Morton Eden, 16
Stettinius, Edward R., 250, 252, 255–6–7, 261
Stimson, 265
Straight, Witney, 287
Stoyadinovich, M., 181
Strang, Sir William, 127, 292
Stresa Agreement, 187–8–9, 190, 194, 204
Stresa Conference, 130
Stresemann, 102, 109
Struggle for Europe by Chester Wilmot, 258
Sunday Times, 268
Suvich, Signor, 126
Swaffer, Hannen, 302
Swan, J. M., 29
Switzerland, 142, 175, 236
Sykes, Sir Mark, 44

TEHERAN CONFERENCE, 245
Templewood, Lord (*see* Hoare, Sir Samuel)
Thomas, J. H., 79, 93, 99
Thomas, J. P. L., 192, 232
The Times, 65, 91, 136, 148, 279, 313
Tito, Marshal, 290–1, 294
Tojo, 244
Trades Disputes Act, 81
T.U.C., 75
Treaty of Alliance with the U.S.S.R., 236, 238, 240
Treaty of Versailles, 125–6, 135
The Tribulations of a Baronet by Sir Timothy Eden, 23, 124
Truman, Harry, 261, 263, 265, 281
Turkey, 61, 72, 163, 221, 228–9, 245, 259, 295

"UP THE COUNTRY," by Emily Eden, 18

United Nations, 241, 251, 255, 260–1, 267, 273, 276, 279, 280, 282, 293, 300, 306
U.S.A., 20, 23, 67, 76, 82, 87, 93, 98, 104, 140, 179, 184, 208, 212, 229, 230, 234, 236, 248, 252–3–4–5, 258–9, 266–7, 269, 274–5–6–7, 281, 283, 293–4–5, 298–9, 300–1, 303–4, 307
U.S.S.R., 58, 63, 67, 79, 81, 92, 99, 102, 104, 126–7, 131, 135, 151, 156–7, 160, 168, 172, 175, 181, 205, 216–7–8, 220–1, 233–4–5–6, 238, 240, 243–4, 246, 248, 251, 253, 256, 258–9, 261, 263, 265, 267–8–9, 270–1, 276–7, 279, 280, 284, 290, 293–4–5, 297–8–9, 300–1, 310, 312

VANSITTART, SIR ROBERT (now Lord), 134, 141, 171, 176, 178
Victoria, Queen of England, 31
Vienna, 15, 117, 187
Viet Minh, 301
Viet-Nam, 301, 312
Vogue, 284
Voroshiloff, 127
Vyshinsky, 280

WAIKIKI, 70
Wakefield, Bishop of, 48
Warwick, Countess of, 47, 49, 65
Warwick, Countess of (*see* Eden, Marjorie)
Warwick and Leamington Division, 46, 65, 91–2, 158, 200, 273, 310–1
Washington, D.C., 210, 226, 240, 242, 281, 293

Wateler Peace Prize, 305
Watercolours by Emily Eden, 18
Wavell, General, 225–6, 229
Wayfarers' Benevolent Association, 123
Welles, Orson, 284
Welles, Sumner, 210
Wellington, Duke of, 17
Western Front, 38
Westminster Bank Ltd., 266
Wheeler-Bennett, John W., 116
Whistler, 29
Wilmot, Chester, 258
Wilson, Maitland, 226
Wilson, Mr., 31
Winant, John G., 229, 230–1–2, 235, 290, 315
Windlestone Hall, Durham, 20, 22–3, 31, 33, 42, 104, 122, 155
Wing, Tom, 45
Women's Franchise Act, 88
World Economic Conference, 107
World Security Council, 255
Woolger, 23, 31
Wraxall, 15
Wyatt, Woodrow, 315

YALTA CONFERENCE, 255, 257–8, 261, 263, 312
York, Archbishop of, 48
The Yorkshire Post, 48, 50, 52, 56, 69, 72, 86, 91, 271
Yugoslavia, 118, 120, 227–8, 261, 263, 312

ZEELAND, VAN, 158